# THE HYKSOS

A New Investigation

# THE HYKSOS

## A NEW INVESTIGATION

BY JOHN VAN SETERS

WIPF & STOCK · Eugene, Oregon

Wipf and Stock Publishers
199 W 8th Ave, Suite 3
Eugene, OR 97401

The Hyksos
A New Investigation
By Van Seters, John
Copyright©1966 by Van Seters, John
ISBN 13: 978-1-60899-533-2
Publication date 4/1/2010
Previously published by Yale University Press, 1966

TO ELIZABETH

# PREFACE

THE PROBLEM of the Hyksos has long been a subject of considerable interest to both the Egyptologists and the historians of the Asiatic Near East. Most studies of this problem betray a certain prejudice in their treatment, either from the side of Egyptian studies or from Palestinian archaeology. This is perhaps inevitable; there are few scholars who can be expert in both areas. While the present writer does not pretend to have mastered all the necessary areas covered, the two-part division of the book indicates that at least a balance between the two areas of interest has been attempted.

The theme of the book is controversial, and with the constant flow of new evidence the present study can scarcely claim to be definitive. This study is intended to encourage open discussion and a fresh approach to the historical data rather than to force them into old, inadequate ways of thinking about the Hyksos. In this respect the book is a protest against an abuse of terminology, particularly as it relates to the archaeological data. The theory of a "Hyksos invasion" is posited, and then certain aspects of the material culture are arbitrarily associated with the invaders —even when there is no evident break in the cultural continuity. The result is the incorrect use of the term "Hyksos" to designate as foreign certain features of the culture which may not be foreign at all. Too many archaeological discussions have become confused on this basis. In making this protest for a more accurate historical method, I am not seeking to belittle the efforts of previous scholars. On the contrary I feel a deep sense of indebtedness to those scholars though I differ with them at a number of points.

The book is the result of a doctoral dissertation done for Yale

vii

University in 1964. Since that time and the final preparation of
this book for publication, a number of books and articles have
appeared which are relevant to this study. It has not been possible
to incorporate all these works into the text, though the most
important new works are acknowledged in the notes. One work
in particular, J. von Beckerath, *Untersuchungen zur politischen
Geschichte der zweiten Zwischenzeit in Ägypten* (Glückstadt,
1964), came to me just before the manuscript went to press.
This is an important work particularly on the problem of the
dynasties of the Second Intermediate Period. But as the emphasis
as a whole lies in a different area than my work, I have not
attempted any major revision. In the area of the Hyksos dynasties,
our conclusions, though reached quite independently, are similar.

I wish to acknowledge my indebtedness to the members of
the Department of Near Eastern Studies at Yale University, for
their continued encouragement in my research and for the
gracious way in which they often made their own resources
available. In particular I wish to thank Mr. Harald Ingholt,
the director of my dissertation, for his many helpful suggestions
and criticisms and Mr. W. K. Simpson, who read through the
manuscript a number of times and has given me much advice
and instruction in the Egyptian sources. He has greatly assisted
me in getting the manuscript to publication.

I am also grateful to Yale University and Dean Perry Miller
for awarding me a post-doctoral fellowship from the Agusta-
Hazard Fellowship Fund for study and field experience in
archaeology in the Near East in 1964-65. I was also able to
visit the Eastern Delta in Egypt and examine for myself certain
areas under discussion in this book. Over the last year I have
also had fruitful discussion by personal contact or through
correspondence with a number of scholars on the problems of
the Hyksos, especially G. Ernest Wright, Ruth Amiran, Briggs
Buchanan, and Labib Habachi. Their helpfulness is deeply
appreciated.

I wish to thank Yale University Press for their full cooperation and Mrs. Jane Isay of the Press for her many helpful suggestions. Mr. Robert Jones, a student of Waterloo Lutheran University, deserves a word of thanks for the two maps in the book.

The book is dedicated to my wife, who greatly assisted in the preparation of the manuscript and in seeing the book through to completion.

JOHN VAN SETERS

*Waterloo Lutheran University*
*February 1966*

# ACKNOWLEDGMENTS

I wish to express my gratitude to the following authors and publishers for their kind permission to use materials from their publications: To G. Ernest Wright for the use of charts 5 and 6 from "The Archaeology of Palestine," in *The Bible and the Ancient Near East,* edited by G. Ernest Wright. Copyright 1961 by The Biblical Colloquium. Reprinted by permission of the author and Doubleday & Co. And also to Wright and the Drew-McCormick Archaeological Expedition for the use of figures 9 and 41 in *Shechem, the Biography of a Biblical City,* McGraw-Hill, publishers. To Ruth Amiran for the use of illustrations from *The Ancient Pottery of Eretz Yisrael.* Copyright by the Bialik Institute and the Israel Exploration Society. To Kathleen M. Kenyon for the use of figure 43 from *Archaeology in the Holy Land,* Ernest Benn, publishers. To W. B. Emery for the use of the drawing on Plate II, and a quotation from pp. 71 f. of his report on Buhen, in *Kush, 8* (1960). To R. Maxwell-Hyslop for the use of drawings from her article on Western Asiatic axes and swords in *Iraq, 8* (1944), and *11* (1947). To O. Tufnell and the Trustees of the late Sir Henry S. Wellcome Trust for the use of scarab drawings from Plates 30 and 32 of *Lachish IV, The Bronze Age.* To the Society of Antiquaries of London for the use of figures 35 and 55 in *Alalakh: An Account of the Excavations at Tell Atchana in the Hatay, 1937-49,* by C. L. Woolley. To the University of Chicago Press for the use of figures 247, 378, and 382 in *Megiddo II, Seasons of 1935-39,* by G. Loud. Copyright 1948 by the University of Chicago Press. To Harvard University Press for use of quotations from *Manetho,* by W. G. Waddell, in Loeb Classical Library published by Harvard University Press.

# CONTENTS

# LIST OF ILLUSTRATIONS

# ABBREVIATIONS

| | |
|---|---|
| *AASOR* | *Annual of the American Schools of Oriental Research.* |
| *Adm* | *Admonitions of Ipuwer.* |
| *AfO* | *Archiv für Orientforschung.* |
| *AHL* | K. M. Kenyon, *Archaeology in the Holy Land,* New York, Praeger, 1960. |
| *AJA* | *American Journal of Archaeology.* |
| *AJSL* | *American Journal of Semitic Languages and Literatures.* |
| *ANEP* | J. B. Pritchard, *The Ancient Near East in Pictures,* Princeton, Princeton University Press, 1955. |
| *ANET* | J. B. Pritchard, ed., *Ancient Near Eastern Texts,* 2nd ed. Princeton, Princeton University Press, 1955. |
| *Ann Serv* | *Annales du service des antiquités de l'Égypte.* |
| *AP* | W. F. Albright, *The Archaeology of Palestine,* Baltimore, Penguin Books, 1961. |
| *BANE* | G. E. Wright, ed., *The Bible and the Ancient Near East* (Essays in honor of W. F. Albright), Garden City, N.Y. Doubleday, 1961. |
| *BASOR* | *Bulletin of the American Schools of Oriental Research.* |
| *BIA* | *Bulletin of the Institute of Archaeology,* London. |
| *Bibl Or* | *Bibliotheca Orientalis.* |
| *BMB* | *Bulletin du Musée de Beyrouth.* |
| *BMQ* | *British Museum Quarterly.* |
| Breasted, *Anc Rec* | J. H. Breasted, *Ancient Records of Egypt,* 5 vols. Chicago, University of Chicago Press, 1906–07. |
| *BSFE* | *Bulletin de la société française d'Égyptologie.* |
| *CAH²* | *The Cambridge Ancient History,* revised edition, issued in separate fascicles, Cambridge, Cambridge University Press, 1961–66. |

*Chr d'Eg*    *La Chronique d'Egypte.*

CRAIBL    *Comptes-Rendus de l'Académie des Inscriptions et Belles-Lettres.*

*Dict géog*    H. Gauthier, *Dictionnaire des noms géographiques*, 7 vols. Cairo, Société royale de géographie d'Egypte, 1925-31.

*Griffith*    S. R. K. Glanville, ed., *Studies presented to F. Ll.*
*Studies*    *Griffith (on his Seventieth Birthday)*, London, Egypt Exploration Society, H. Milford, Oxford University Press, 1932.

HUCA    *Hebrew Union College Annual.*

IEJ    *Israel Exploration Journal.*

IFAOC    L'Institut français d'archéologie orientale, Cairo.

JAOS    *Journal of the American Oriental Society.*

JARCE    *Journal of the American Research Center in Egypt.*

JBL    *Journal of Biblical Literature and Exegesis.*

JCS    *Journal of Cuneiform Studies.*

JEA    *Journal of Egyptian Archaeology.*

JESHO    *Journal of Economic and Social History of the Orient.*

JNES    *Journal of Near Eastern Studies.*

JPOS    *Journal of the Palestine Oriental Society.*

MAM    André Parrot, *Mission archéologique de Mari*, 2 vols. in 4; *1, Le Temple d'Ishtar, 2* (in 3 parts), *Le Palais*, Paris, Geuthner, 1956-59.

MDIK    *Mitteilungen des deutschen Instituts für ägyptische Altertumskunde In Kairo.*

MDOG    *Mitteilungen des deutschen Orientgesellschaft.*

*Nachr*    *Nachrichten von der Kgl. Gesellschaft der Wissen-*
*Göttingen*    *schaften zu Göttingen.*

OIP    Oriental Institute Publications, University of Chicago Press.

PEQ    *Palestine Exploration Society Quarterly.*

| | |
|---|---|
| Porter and Moss, Top Bibl | B. Porter and R. L. B. Moss, *Topographical Bibliography of Ancient Egyptian Hieroglyphic Texts, Reliefs, and Paintings*, 7 vols. Oxford, Clarendon Press, 1927–51. |
| QDAP | *Quarterly of the Department of Antiquities*, Palestine Museum. |
| RAss | *Revue d'Assyriologie et d'archéologie orientale.* |
| RB | *Revue biblique.* |
| Rec de trav | *Recueil de travaux relatifs à la philologie et à l'archéologie égyptiennes et assyriennes.* |
| REg | *Revue d'Egyptologie.* |
| RSO | *Rivista degli studi orientali.* |
| SAOC | The Oriental Institute, Studies of the Ancient Oriental Civilizations, University of Chicago Press. |
| SPAW | Sitzungsberichte der preussischen Akademie der Wissenschaften. |
| Strat comp | C. F. A. Schaeffer, *Stratigraphie comparée et chronologie de l'Asie occidentale*, Oxford, Oxford University Press, 1948. |
| TCL | *Textes cuneiforms*, Musée de Louvre. |
| Urk | *Urkunden des ägyptischen Altertums*, Leipzig, Hinrichs, 1903– . |
| Wb | A. Erman and H. Grapow, *Wörterbuch der ägyptischen Sprache*, 5 vols. and Belegstellen, Leipzig, Hinrichs, 1926–53. |
| ZÄS | *Zeitschrift für ägyptische Sprache und Altertumskunde.* |
| ZDMG | *Zeitschrift der deutschen morgenländischen Gesellschaft.* |
| ZDPV | *Zeitschrift des deutschen Palästina-Vereins.* |

# INTRODUCTION

The Hyksos problem has so often been considered and reconsidered that a new study, such as the present one, calls for some justification. About twenty-five to thirty years ago a number of monographs appeared that dealt with various aspects of the problem. The (subsequently published) doctoral dissertation of P. Labib, *Die Herrschaft der Hyksos in Ägypten und ihr Sturz*,[1] discussed primarily the Egyptian epigraphic and literary sources known at the time. R. M. Engberg, in *The Hyksos Reconsidered*,[2] emphasized the archaeological evidence known from Palestine. H. Stock, in *Studien zur Geschichte und Archäologie der 13. bis 17. Dynastie Ägyptens*,[3] attempted a reconstruction of the dynasties in the Second Intermediate Period, depending heavily on a stylistic analysis of the scarabs. Although these studies contain much of value, they have been made obsolete by recent discoveries.[4]

In more recent years the Hyksos have been discussed in a number of articles or chapters within larger works. Three of these studies deserve special mention. In 1951 T. Säve-Söderbergh

1. *Die Herrschaft der Hyksos in Ägypten und ihr Sturz* (Glückstadt-Hamburg-New York, 1936).

2. *The Hyksos Reconsidered*, SAOC, 18 (Chicago, 1939).

3. *Studien zur Geschichte und Archäologie der 13. bis 17. Dynastie Ägyptens*, Ägyptologische Forschungen, 12 (Glückstadt-Hamburg-New York, 1942).

4. Two more recent monographs, by R. Weill, *XII<sup>e</sup> Dynastie, royauté de Haute-Egypte et domination Hyksos dans le nord*, IFAOC, Bibliotheque d'Etude, 26 (Cairo, 1953), and Z. Mayanni, *Les Hyksos et le monde de la Bible* (Paris, 1956), contain such serious methodological weaknesses and arrive at such unacceptable conclusions that they add virtually nothing to the study of the Hyksos. For a review of Weill see J. A. Wilson, *JNES, 14* (1955), 131–33, and for reviews of Mayanni see T. O. Lambdin, *JBL, 77* (1958), 272–74, and H. Brunner, *AfO, 18* (1958), 434.

published an article, "The Hyksos in Egypt," [5] which suggested
that the Hyksos domination in Egypt represented an internal
coup d'état in which Asiatic immigrants played a leading role,
aided by active cooperation from many Egyptians. His position
was largely supported by A. Alt in "Die Herkunft der Hyksos
in neuer Sicht," [6] who suggested that there was little reliability
in Manetho's picture of a great invasion, and that the Hyksos
ought to be completely dissociated from the Hurrian movement
and connected rather with the Amurrite settlement of Phoenicia-
Palestine as evidenced in the Execration texts. Recently the
position of these two scholars has been challenged by W. Helck
in his work, *Die Beziehungen Ägyptens zu Vorderasien im 3.
und 2. Jahrtausend v. Chr.,*[7] in which he supports the view
of the Hyksos presented by Manetho and their connection with
the Hurrian movement. The debate at the present time is
thus posed between the alternatives: Säve-Söderbergh and Alt on
the one hand, and Helck on the other.[8]

There is, therefore, some justification for a new treatment of
the whole problem if a resolution of these two positions can be
reached. For this purpose, a comprehensive study on the many
aspects of the subject is necessary. In the last few years much new
evidence relevant to the Hyksos period has come to light. This
evidence is both archaeological and epigraphic.

Part One of this study will deal with the archaeological evidence. There is so much additional data since Engberg published his study that his whole description of the culture of

5. *JEA, 37* (1951), 53–71.

6. Berichte über die Verhundlungen der Sächsishen Akdd. der Wissenschaften
zu Leipzig. Phil.-hist. Klasse. *101*, Heft 6 (1954). Reissued in *Kleine Schriften
zur Geschichte des Volkes Israel* (München, 1959), *3*, 72–98.

7. Ägyptologische Abhundlungen, 5 (Wiesbaden, 1962).

8. J. von Beckerath, in *Untersuchungen zur politischen Geschichte der zweiten
Zwischenzeit in Ägypten* (Glückstadt, 1965), is much more in line with the
positions of Säve-Söderbergh and Alt. He is at variance with Helck's basic
conclusions on the origins and character of the Hyksos rule.

Syria-Palestine during the Hyksos period must be revised. A part of any revision must be a new approach to the archaeological data. In the past many archaeologists, including Engberg, abused the term "Hyksos" by using it to describe certain cultural aspects in Palestine, Syria, or Egypt—"Hyksos" fortifications, "Hyksos" pottery, "Hyksos" scarabs, etc.[9] The use of the term in this way implies that "Hyksos" is an ethnic or cultural designation. But "Hyksos" is not an ethnic term; to use it as such begs the whole question of an openminded consideration of the archaeological evidence. The use of the term "Hyksos" to designate a style or type has created great confusion in the study of the archaeology of the period.[10] Consequently, it is best to restrict the use of this term to refer to the period of foreign rule in Egypt and to use archaeological nomenclature when dealing with archaeological data from Syria and Palestine.

Some scholars, such as Helck, reject the use of any archaeological data of the Middle Bronze Age of Syria-Palestine in considering the Hyksos problem.[11] A justification for considering such data, however, should be obvious from the Egyptian language itself. The terminology used for the foreigners of the Second Intermediate Period, i.e. *ḥḳȝ ḫȝswt* (Hyksos) for their leaders and *ʿȝmw* or *sṯtyw* for the foreign population, is the same

9. Engberg, in *The Hyksos Reconsidered*, reads Manetho's ethnic use of this term back into the Hyksos period. R. Dussaud, in his review (*Syria, 21* [1940], 343 f.), strongly criticizes Engberg on this point.

10. It is evident in the works of such scholars as W. F. Albright, *The Archaeology of Palestine* (Baltimore, 1960), pp. 84 ff., and K. M. Kenyon, *Archaeology in the Holy Land* (New York, 1960), pp. 182 ff. (where she has unfortunately confused Mari and Nuzu).

11. Helck, *Beziehungen*, pp. 97 ff. Also H. Otto ("Die Keramik der mittleren Bronzezeit in Palestine," *ZDPV, 61* [1938], 266 ff.) is an example of how a preconceived notion of the Hyksos has prejudiced the investigation. Because the culture of Syria-Palestine represents such a homogeneity since 1900 b.c. and was very likely a part of the Amurrite (*ostkanaanäisch*) settlement of Mesopotamia, he finds no way of associating with it a "foreign" culture, such as the Hyksos. Therefore the Hyksos must be nomadic, and their presence archaeologically unobservable.

as that used of the peoples of Syria-Palestine and their rulers in the Middle Kingdom.[12] Furthermore, when the foreign elements in the Egyptian culture of the Hyksos period are considered together with the archaeological evidence of Syria and Palestine in the Middle Bronze Age, it will become apparent that the two areas are part of a cultural unity in the Levant during the Hyksos period.

The reason for Syria and Palestine occupying such a dominant place in the discussion on archaeology is that there has been as yet no site excavated in Egypt that can be identified with the foreign cultural phase of the Hyksos period. The nearest one can come to such a site in Egypt are the Delta sites of Tell el-Yahudiyeh and Ezbet Rushdi-Khataᶜna. Both sites give some evidence of actual settlements of foreigners, but the data even from these sites is quite limited. In Syria and Palestine, on the other hand, there are a number of well-stratified sites where the whole cultural phase is so well known that it would be best to begin here and tie to it the Egyptian evidence.

The method of approach, therefore, will be to indicate the stratigraphic, chronological, and geographic limits of the cultural phases associated with the Hyksos period. Once this framework has been established, the various archaeological data which make up the Middle Bronze Age culture, contemporary with the Hyksos period, can be discussed in detail. An understanding of this culture is basic to a discussion of the literary evidence which reflects close contact between Egypt and Syria-Palestine from the Middle Kingdom to the end of the Hyksos period.

Part Two of this study will attempt to reconstruct the rise of the Hyksos and their rule in Egypt, using the epigraphic and literary evidence from Egypt. Among recent discoveries in this area, the most important are the Kamose stela, found in 1954, from the end of the Hyksos period and a papyrus, discovered in the Brooklyn museum and edited by W. C. Hayes, which dates

12. On terminology see below, Chapter 13.

from the Thirteenth Dynasty—just before the Hyksos rise to power. The new information has called for a reevaluation of some Egyptian texts that have been known for many years. In this category is the *Admonitions of Ipuwer*, long associated with the First Intermediate Period. The present study will endeavor to show that the work belongs, instead, to the Second Intermediate Period; when taken together with other evidence from about the same period, the *Admonitions* has much to say about the Hyksos problem.

Many aspects of this subject remain highly controversial: the way in which the Hyksos rose to power; the nature of their rule; their ethnic origin; the location of their capital; and the so-called "dynasties" of the Hyksos. Even the attempt to relate the Hyksos period of Egypt with the corresponding culture of Syria-Palestine involves the debate over the chronology of the Middle Bronze Age of Palestine. A study of the Hyksos, therefore, runs the risk of entering into endless debate and overwhelming detail. An attempt will be made to deal with each major problem, individually and on its own merits. Then it will be possible to indicate the significance of the various solutions to a reconstruction of the Hyksos period as a whole. In spite of the risks involved in such a comprehensive approach, there is the challenge to make sense out of this period of history. The following study is the product of this challenge.

PART I


ARCHAEOLOGY OF THE MIDDLE BRONZE AGE

# CHRONOLOGY AND STRATIGRAPHY

The broad archaeological phase to which the Hyksos period of Egypt must be related is the Middle Bronze Age, or Middle Bronze II, using Albright's terminology.[1] This whole phase is a cultural unity although it contains minor phases and developments. Clearly discernible criteria define its beginning and end. The end of the Middle Bronze Age is clear and undisputed. Here the break is not a cultural one, for there is definite continuity in architecture, pottery, and art.[2] The division is characterized by widespread destruction of a number of sites in southern Palestine and by the appearance of new pottery styles in addition to older forms. The destructions can best be understood as the activity of the Eighteenth Dynasty pharaohs and the date for the end of Middle Bronze would be about 1550 B.C.

Preceding the Middle Bronze Age proper is Middle Bronze I, also known as Intermediate Early Bronze-Middle Bronze because it represents an interruption of seminomadic culture between the more advanced periods of urban life in the Early and Middle Bronze Age.[3] The chronology of this intermediate period is very much debated, but the question must be faced since it has a bearing on one's reconstruction of the relations

---

1. This nomenclature by Albright corresponds to the following terms used by Kenyon: MB I (Albright)—Intermediate EB–MB (Kenyon); MB II A (Albright)—MB I (Kenyon); MB II B–C (Albright)—MB II i–v (Kenyon).

2. Kenyon, *AHL*, p. 162; "Syria and Palestine c. 2160–1780 B.C.," *CAH*[2], *1*, ch. 21, pp. 38–61.

3. Ibid., pp. 135 ff.

between Egypt and Syria-Palestine in the whole of the Middle Bronze Age. There are two proposals for dating the period relative to Egyptian chronology: one, by K. Kenyon, is that MB I coincides with the First Intermediate Period of Egypt;[4] the other, by Albright, is that it is contemporaneous with the Twelfth Dynasty of Egypt.[5]

To clarify the issue between these two positions it is necessary, first to describe the essential characteristics of this culture. Kenyon was able to distinguish the MB I phase in her excavations at Jericho.[6] At this site the preceding Early Bronze III city was violently destroyed, and in its place appeared a rather poor seminomadic phase with very crude brick huts as the only architecture. This lack of monumental architecture and planned urban life is characteristic of MB I throughout Palestine.[7] Only in Megiddo is it possible to ascribe a monumental building, a temple, to this phase, and even this is doubtful.[8]

This dramatic break in urban life is accompanied by a clear break in ceramic traditions.[9] A new repertory of pottery comes in, which has only a few elements in common with the previous Early Bronze period. The forms, decorations, and mode of manufacturing the ware, separate MB I from EB III beyond any doubt. These differences are likewise apparent in other artifacts, such as weapons, in which the use of copper takes the place of flint.[10]

---

4. Ibid.

5. Albright, "Abram the Hebrew: A New Archaeological Interpretation," *BASOR, 163* (1961), 36–54; "The Chronology of Middle Bronze I," *BASOR, 168* (1962), 36–42. R. Amiran, "The Pottery of the Middle Bronze Age I in Palestine," *IEJ, 10* (1960), 204–25.

6. Kenyon, *AHL*, pp. 135 ff.

7. Albright, *AP*, p. 82.

8. Kenyon, *AHL*, pp. 155 ff. Cf. G. E. Wright, *The Bible and the Ancient Near East* (Garden City, N.Y., 1961), p. 108 n.

9. Kenyon, *AHL*, p. 136. Cf. Albright, *BASOR, 168* (1962) 38.

10. Albright, "Soundings at Ader, a Bronze Age city of Moab," *BASOR, 53* (1934), 15 f. Wright, *BANE*, p. 86.

Cultural changes are noticeable in burial customs also.[11] Instead of the multiple burials of the Early Bronze Age, there are single burials, or at the most two or three persons, in large shaft graves cut into the rock. Consequently, the graves of MB I were very numerous and many were reused in a later period. The tombs often vary in shape and the kinds of burial goods used. While most of the graves had only one chamber, those at Megiddo often had four well-cut and skilfully arranged chambers.

One can only conclude from all these innovations that MB I represents the settling in Palestine of a new people. I cannot agree with Albright, therefore, that we have to do merely with a "cultural drift associated with the diffusion of the Syro-Meso-potamian culture" [12] into Palestine. Kenyon's interpretation, that we are dealing with an interlude of seminomadic peoples, is to be preferred.[13]

Moreover, the end of MB I is as decisively delineated as the beginning. With the coming of MB II A, the repertory of pottery changed completely.[14] Urban life was reestablished throughout Palestine and steadily progressed without serious interruption to a very high level.[15] The coming of a new sedentary population was not the decisive factor which led to the overthrow of MB I. Actually the rise of MB II A was gradual and sporadic and took place on only a few of the previous MB I sites. Most of the MB I settlements were simply abandoned and the MB II A settlement came in to fill a vacuum.

While the picture of MB I was a rather seminomadic interlude between two periods of highly developed urban life is true of Palestine west of the Jordan, it is not at all the case in Trans-

11. Kenyon, *AHL*, pp. 137 ff.

12. Albright, *AP*, p. 80.

13. Hence her designation, Intermediate Early Bronze-Middle Bronze, *AHL*, p. 135. So also Wright, *BANE*, p. 86 f.

14. Kenyon, *AHL*, pp. 136, 162 f. Cf. Amiran, *IEJ*, *10* (1960), 205.

15. Wright, *BANE*, p. 88 f.

jordan. The difference between the two regions is, in fact, so striking that it has caused a great deal of confusion in the treatment of MB I. During MB I in Transjordan there was a very significant sedentary civilization. Nelson Glueck, who has surveyed hundreds of MB I sites in this region, comes to the conclusion that "there was an extensive and intensive agricultural civilization in the land. Most of the sites are large, strongly walled, and frequently built on an eminence easy of defence. . . . The dwellers of the land were industrious tillers of the soil, who built strong walled villages in which they lived and used much excellent, if on the whole somewhat coarse, hand-made pottery." [16] A number of large fortified settlements,[17] such as Reseifeh, Iskander, Balu'ah, Lejjun, and Ader, have been found, and these run along the main line of communications throughout the length of Transjordan. Nor do these settlements end east of the Dead Sea, for they continue on across the Wadi Arabah and through the Palestinian Negev to the borders of Egypt.[18] To be sure, the settlements in the Negev are not nearly as impressive as those of Transjordan. Nevertheless, they represent an attempt, during MB I, to set up seasonal agricultural communities.

Albright, in discussing the MB I ruins in the Negev, concludes that the purpose of the settlements was to support a caravan trade between Palestine and Egypt.[19] The evidence for this coming from the Negev, itself, is very persuasive indeed, but there is little to suggest that caravan activity came through Palestine.

16. N. Glueck, *Explorations in Eastern Palestine*, Part 3, *AASOR*, *18–19* (1937–39), p. 83.

17. For descriptions of these settlements see Glueck, *Explorations*, Part 1, *AASOR*, *14* (1933–34), pp. 44–47, 53–56, Part 3, *AASOR*, *18–19* (1937–39), pp. 127 ff., 206. See also P. Parr, "Excavations at Khirbet Iskander," *ADAJ*, *4–5* (1960), 128–33; R. Cleveland, "Soundings at Khirbet Ader," *AASOR*, *34–35* (1954–56), 79 ff., and Albright, *BASOR*, *53* (1934), 13–15.

18. For a description and bibliography see Albright, *BASOR*, *163* (1961), 36 ff.

19. Ibid., p. 38.

It is much more likely that the great overland trade route came through Transjordan with its line of fortified way stations. Only the sedentary culture of Transjordan would have been able to establish and support a line of communications across the Negev; it alone would have the incentive to do so. The line of communications between Palestine and Egypt was either by the coastal road or by sea.

The coming of the MB I people into Transjordan does not, as in Palestine, represent an invasion and sudden destruction of the previous EB III civilization. It is instead an immigration and settling, for the most part, on previously uninhabited sites. The rise of a new sedentary population began when the Early Bronze tradition of ceramics was still strong. The first phase of the new immigration is often known as EB IV because it is contemporaneous with the last of the EB peoples of Palestine and Transjordan and learned certain ceramic traditions from them. The mixture of ceramic styles of EB IV and MB I cannot be easily distinguished stratigraphically in Transjordan,[20] and therefore Glueck's designation EB IV-MB I for the whole period in Transjordan is a good one. There can be no doubt that this whole period is a homogeneous cultural development and that it extends throughout MB I to the beginning of MB II A.[21]

The decline of MB I in Transjordan and the Negev is catastrophic. Very few settlements survived into the succeeding MB II period. In fact there is a general absence of sedentary life for several hundred years. Likewise in Palestine, MB I was very likely followed by a gap in settlement, but of a much shorter duration. The resettlement of Palestine by MB II A, at a few sites at least, began only a few years after the MB I period ended.

To sum up, it seems clear that a new sedentary culture, EB IV-MB I, arose in Transjordan at a time when EB III was still

20. See the conclusions of P. Parr, *ADAJ*, 4–5 (1960), 132 f.
21. See Glueck's conclusions in *Explorations*, Part 3, p. 268.

strong in Palestine. The center and most highly developed element of this new culture was in Transjordan throughout the whole MB I phase. Some of the rather nomadic elements that came with the new immigration pressed into Palestine and destroyed the last of EB III there. However Palestine was never seriously settled with urban life in this period, with the possible exception of Megiddo. Most of their settlements, like Jericho, were probably seminomadic. When the MB I culture declined, it did so drastically and simultaneously in Transjordan, the Negev, and Palestine, leaving a short hiatus in settlement in Palestine and a much longer one in Transjordan and in the Negev.[22]

We come now to the question of chronology: how is the MB I period to be fitted into the known historical context of the Near East? Since there are no written documents from Palestine for this period, we are forced to rely upon ceramic typology. It is now generally recognized that the new repertory of pottery forms comes from Syria and represents an extension of the "caliciform" tradition of the North.[23] The connections are particularly evident in the material from the Orontes Valley, in Hama J (early phases), in Qatna tomb 4, and from coastal Syria in Ras Shamra, level II: 1. The Syrian pottery is in turn related to the pottery of the Akkad dynasty in Upper and Lower Mesopotamia.

From Egypt comes a type of large storage jar covered with a pattern combing which is found throughout the Old Kingdom (2500–2200 B.C.). This style of jar, which obviously originated in Syria, is dated to the end of Early Bronze but is also found in

22. The contemporaneity of MB I in Palestine and Transjordan calls for further comment. Albright has long separated the two and regards the EB IV–MB I period in Transjordan as belonging essentially to the Early Bronze Age (*AP*, pp. 77 ff.; *BASOR, 168* [1962], 40 n.). This, however, is quite contrary to the conclusions of Glueck, who sees close connections between Transjordan and the Negev in MB I ("The Seventh Season of Archaeological Exploration in the Negev," *BASOR, 152* [1958], 20 ff.) and equally close connections between Transjordan and Palestine for MB I (*Explorations*, Part 3, pp. 251 ff.).

23. Amiran, *IEJ, 10* (1960), 215 ff.; also Wright, *BANE*, p. 86.

strata contemporary with MB I as in Hama J4 and Megiddo XV.[24] Taking the Mesopotamian and Egyptian evidence together, the MB I period would certainly have to begin before 2200 B.C.

| Period | Tell Beit Mirsim | Megiddo | Tell el-Ajjul | Egypt | Syria | Iraq |
|---|---|---|---|---|---|---|
| 1450 Transition to Late Bronze 1550 | | IX | Palace II City II | Dynasty XVIII | VI-V | Kassites Hittite Invasion |
| MB II C (MB II iv-v) 1650 | D | X | Palace I City I | Second Intermediate Period | | |
| MB II B (MB II i-iii) 1750 | E | XI XII | Courtyard Cemetery | Dynasty XIII | II.3 VII H VIII II.2 T.1 | Temple of Obelisks Byblos Royal Tombs First Dynasty of Babylon Mari Age Khabur Ware Cappadocian Colonies |
| MB II A (MB I) 1900 | F G | XIII | | Dynasty XII | | |
| MB I (EB-MB) 2100 | H I | XIV XV | Copper Age Cemetery | First Intermediate Period | Hama J Alalakh Ras Shamra II.1 Qatna T.4 | Ur III |

Fig. 1 Comparative stratigraphy and chronology of the Middle Bronze Age

Another piece of chronological evidence introduced by Albright is a decorative style on pottery found in Egypt in the Second Intermediate Period.[25] It consists of a pattern of straight and wavy incised lines often accompanied by a series of jabs. Albright compares this decoration with similar styles on MB I ware and uses the evidence from Egypt as a *terminus ad quem* for the

24. Albright, *BASOR, 168* (1962), 40. Also M. W. Prausnitz, "Abydos and Combed Ware," *PEQ* (1954), 91 ff.

25. *The Excavations of Tell Beit Mirsim*, Part 1, *AASOR, 12* (1932), pp. 9 f.; *BASOR, 168* (1962), 38.

MB I period. He reasons that this style of pottery, although dying out in Palestine by about 1800 B.C., was coming into vogue in Egypt, through slow cultural diffusion, by about 1700–1550 B.C.

A number of weaknesses in this piece of evidence, make it quite unacceptable. First, the decorative style of incised wavy and straight lines is very well attested from Syria and Palestine for the MB II B–C period.[26] It is found in Ras Shamra level II: 2. At Hama it is the characteristic decorative motif in H, occurring on craters in very much the same way as it does in the MB II B–C strata of Hazor. It is attested at Kadesh in a MB II context and at Nahariyeh, a site on the north Palestinian coast, with MB II B–C material only. This later dating is entirely in keeping with the fact that in Egypt this decorative motif occurs along with other foreign wares and artifacts which are dated to MB II B–C.[27] Secondly, Albright's notion of time lags lasting hundreds of years for the diffusion of culture from Upper Mesopotamia and Syria does not square with the evidence which points to movements of peoples from the Northeast into Transjordan, Palestine, and the Negev. The idea of active caravan trade from the latter regions into Egypt likewise cannot be squared with Albright's two-to three-hundred-year lag between the Negev and Egypt.

The resulting chronology for MB I, based on ceramic evidence

26. Ras Shamra: C. F. A. Schaeffer, *Ugaritica* (Paris, 1962), *4*, 271, Pl. IV, 17–19, 21–22. Hama: E. Fugmann, *Hama. L'architecture des périodes pré- hellénistiques* (Copenhagen, 1958), pp. 90, 95, 101, 104, 108, 111; Pl. X. Hazor: Y. Yadin, *Hazor* (Jerusalem, 1958), *1*, 100 ff., Pls. XCIII, 9, 10; XCIV, 19, 20; CXII, 14; CXIII, 2–5; CXVII, 11–15; 2, Pl. CX. Kadesh: M. Pezard, *Qadesh* (Paris, 1931), Pls. XXXV–XXXVI. Nahariyeh: I. Ben-Dor, "A Middle Bronze Age Temple at Nahariyeh," *QDAP, 14* (1950), 29, Pls. IX, 7–17; XI, 12–16. Ben-Dor cites parallels from Tell Beit Mirsim E–D (MB II); Albright, *Tell Beit Mirsim*, Part I, Pl. 10:10; Part IA, #28.

27. Albright, ibid., Part I, p. 9, states: "Several of the scarabs found with this Egyptian pottery are identical in type with scarabs from our stratum D." The pottery of Egypt should therefore be contemporary with that of D and not that of I–H.

alone, would suggest the EB IV-MB I began in Transjordan by about 2300 B.C. and in Palestine and the Negev by 2200. Allowing a reasonable length of time for the period, the final terminus would be about 1950 B.C. This fits quite well with the evidence for dating the beginning of MB II A, to be considered below. Thus the main period for MB I in Palestine and Transjordan is about 2200–1950 B.C.[28]

If these dates are taken as correct, then MB I must be associated with the First Intermediate Period in Egypt. With the fall of the Old Kingdom of Egypt there was a large measure of disunity and feudalism. This situation encouraged Asiatics to enter Egypt for trade and to make raids on the settled communities of the Delta.[29] The Asiatics also gained control of the Sinai mines for a time in order to obtain valuable supplies of copper. MB I sherds were found at Serabit el Khadim,[30] and it is a fact that there was a great increase in the use of copper during the MB I period.[31] It seems clear, therefore, that the MB I people had much to gain by an overland route through the Negev during the First Intermediate Period.

For the security of Egypt, the existence of a line of settlements through the Negev to the doorstep of Egypt, with free access into the Delta and with a route to the Sinai mines, was intolerable. Action was first taken by Khety II of the Tenth Dynasty whereby an extensive line of fortifications was established in the Eastern Delta.[32] This was augmented under Amenemhet I at the beginning of the Twelfth Dynasty, about 1990 B.C., with

28. These dates agree closely with Kenyon, *AHL*, pp. 158 f., and are not essentially different from those of Wright, *BANE*, pp. 86 ff.

29. See "The Instructions for King Merikare," *ANET*, pp. 414–18, and "The Prophecy of Neferrohu," *ANET*, pp. 444–46.

30. B. Rothenberg, *God's Wilderness, Discoveries in the Sinai* (London, 1961), pp. 135, 180 n.

31. Wright, *BANE*, p. 86.

32. *ANET*, p. 416b.

a fortification built at the eastern end of the Wadi Tumilat, called the Wall-of-the-Prince.[33] Its location is of interest: the fortress was placed at a point where the caravan route through the Negev enters Egypt.[34] Likewise under this pharaoh a campaign was conducted by a certain general, Nesumontu, against the "settlements of the Asiatics." [35] These I understand to be the settlements of the Negev, possibly as far as Transjordan. In addition, the *Story of Sinuhe* reflects the military activity of Senwosret I against the Asiatics of Palestine and the policy of strictly forbidding their access into Egypt.[36] In matters of foreign trade, the Twelfth Dynasty reestablished the royal monopoly and conducted most of the trade with Syria by ship through the ports of Byblos and Ugarit.[37] Consequently, whether because of direct military attack or through economic depression, the MB I culture rapidly declined after the rise of the Twelfth Dynasty, about 1950 B.C. at the latest. During the twentieth century B.C., the population of Palestine was greatly reduced. Resettlement of the land by the MB II people began between 1950–1900 B.C.

A "high" chronology for MB I has important implications for the history of Egypt's relations with Palestine. It matters a great deal that the MB II period began before the middle of the Twelfth Dynasty—by 1900 B.C.—since those texts which come from the latter half of the Twelfth Dynasty must be related to the MB II period and not to MB I, as Albright has done. When the Egyptian texts are understood in the light of the more advanced urban civilization of MB II, they have much to say about

33. Ibid., p. 446 a.

34. Albright, *BASOR, 163* (1961), 37 f.

35. J. H. Breasted, "When did the Hittites Enter Palestine?," *AJSL, 21* (1904), 153–58.

36. *ANET*, pp. 19b, 21b.

37. W. A. Ward, "Egypt and the East Mediterranean in the Early Second Millennium B.C.," *Orientalia, 30* (1961), 38, mentions the fact that there was an expedition of twenty ships (military or commercial?) to Syria in the time of Amenemhet I.

the rise of the Hyksos, a fact which has long been obscured by dating the rise of MB II too late.

The stratigraphy of Middle Bronze II is best worked out in the correlation of three representative sites: Tell Beit Mirsim, Megiddo, and Tell el-Ajjul.[38] Other archaeological sites of Palestine, discussed later, can be related to these three. At the same time it is necessary to relate the strata of the Palestinian sites to corresponding archaeological material of Syria, in order to indicate the lines of cultural continuity and to clarify problems of chronology.

The Middle Bronze II period represents a surprising homogeneity in culture, from Northern Syria to Southern Palestine. It is generally subdivided into two basic phases, MB II A and MB II B–C. The first phase is not yet fully represented by many sites in Palestine and seems to indicate a gradual resettlement of the land after a somewhat seminomadic period. This phase is found at Tell Beit Mirsim in strata G–F,[39] at Megiddo stratum XIII,[40] and in a few graves of the courtyard cemetery at Tell el-Ajjul.[41] It is also found in considerable quantity at Ras el-Ain [42] and at Shechem.[43]

38. The chart is adapted from those by G. E. Wright in *BANE*, pp. 89, 92. These three sites form the basis, at present, of Palestinian stratigraphy for the Middle Bronze Age. When the excavations of Hazor and Shechem appear in final publication they will furnish a very important supplement to these. See also von Beckerath *Untersuchungen*, p. 122.

39. Albright, *Tell Beit Mirsim*, Part II, pp. 17 ff.

40. G. Loud, *Megiddo II: Seasons of 1935–39* (Chicago, 1948), pp. 6 ff., 84 ff. Wright, following the excavators, also includes strata XV–XIV in MB II A and gives an explanation for MB I pottery appearing in these strata (*BANE*, p. 108 n.). On the other hand, Kenyon explains these levels as MB I or earlier and considers the MB II A material, which came entirely from tombs, as intrusive ("Some Notes on the Early and Middle Bronze Age Strata of Megiddo," *Eretz-Israel*, 5 [1958], 51* ff.). This latter explanation is followed here.

41. W. M. F. Petrie, *Ancient Gaza* (London, 1932), 2, Pls. 28, 30–32 (forms marked X–XI Dyn.). See most recently O. Tufnell, "The Courtyard Cemetery of Tell El-Ajjul, Palestine," *BIA*, 3 (1962), 1–37.

42. J. H. Iliffe, "Pottery from Ras el-Ain," *QDAP*, 5 (1936), 113 ff. J. Ory, "Excavations at Ras el-Ain II," *QDAP*, 6 (1938), 99 ff.

43. L. E. Toombs and G. E. Wright, "The Fourth Campaign at Balatah,"

With the settlement of MB II A in Palestine, new sedentary culture came into the land and brought with it a high level of urban life. The pottery of MB II A clearly indicates that this new population is Syrian and Upper Mesopotamian in origin. The repertory of forms, the production technique, and the painted decoration all attest to this fact (see Fig. 2).[44] The earliest of the MB II A must be associated with tomb I at Qatna and the latest levels of Hama J, which in turn are related to the Khabur culture of Upper Mesopotamia. The dates given by Fugmann for the whole of Hama J are 2400–1900 B.C.[45] On the other hand, there are forms from Megiddo in MB II A which resemble those found in the tombs I and II of the princes of Byblos.[46] These royal tombs are dated to the last pharaohs of the Twelfth Dynasty, about 1840–1790 B.C. These foreign connections would suggest that MB II A must be dated about 1950–1750 B.C. The fact that Egyptian cultural influence is quite rare in Palestine in MB II A, but very pronounced in MB II B–C, would suggest a terminal date by 1750. Only after the Thirteenth Dynasty was there a great deal of free commercial activity between Egypt and Palestine.

Furthermore, since the predominent culture of Mesopotamia and Syria at this time was Amurrite, the data of MB II A would

---

*BASOR, 169* (1963), 6 ff. There is much more MB II A material from the fifth campaign at Shechem (1964), as yet unpublished.

44. Figs. 2, 3, 9, 10, are adapted from the drawings of R. Amiran et. al., *The Ancient Pottery of Eretz Yisrael,* in Hebrew (Jersusalem, 1963), Pls. 27, 33–37, 48.

45. Du Mesnil, du Buisson, *Les Ruines d'el-Mishrifé* (Paris, 1927), pp. 39 ff.; Fugmann, *Hama,* pp. 69 ff.

46. P. Montet, *Byblos et l'Egypte* (2 vols. Paris, 1928–29), 2, pp. 199 ff., Pls. CXVI–CXIX. The chronology of MB II A as it relates to the royal tombs of Byblos has been dealt with most recently by Albright, "The Eighteenth-Century Princes of Byblos and the Chronology of Middle Bronze," *BASOR, 176* (1964), 38–46. In this article he associates two of the royal tombs, III and IV, with princes of Byblos between 1790–1720, thereby lowering the end of MB II A and making the period coextensive with the eighteenth century. The evidence for this reconstruction is very slim indeed and does not carry conviction. Far better criteria than simply the Byblos tombs are the Egyptian monuments and the Execration texts which will be dealt with later.

indicate an extension of Amurrite urbanization into Palestine.[47] This fact may be confirmed by the mention of Hazor [48] in the Mari correspondences. Hazor was an important new city created by this resettlement of peoples in Palestine. It is likely that the Execration texts, which mention the names of numerous Amurrite kings in Palestine, also date from the end of this period or the beginning of the next.[49]

The last phase of the Middle Bronze Age, known as MB II B–C, is the phase of primary concern to us: it is largely contemporary with the Hyksos in Egypt. Yet it cannot be emphasized too strongly that this phase is a direct continuation and development of the preceding phase in every major cultural aspect. The MB II B–C phase is represented at Tell Beit Mirsim in strata E–D, at Megiddo in strata XII–X, and at Tell el-Ajjul in most of the courtyard cemetery, in Palace I and city stratum I.[50] Besides these sites, it is found at almost all major tells in Palestine. This phase may be easily identified by certain important cultural features. For instance, the fortifications of the cities are characterized by great ramparts with sloping glacis of *terre pisée* or of battered-stone construction. We find a high level of urban life with monumental architecture of palaces and temples. Cultural relations with Egypt become apparent in the arts and crafts, and particularly in the appearance of scarabs in Palestine for the first time and in great quantity. The most notable new feature in pottery is the style known as Tell el-Yahudiyeh ware. These features will receive individual consideration later.

First, however, a few preliminary remarks about chronology

47. This period is often called by archaeologists the period of Amurrite urbanization. See Wright, *BANE*, p. 88.

48. On trade between Mari and Hazor see J. R. Kupper, "Northern Mesopotamia and Syria," *CAH* [2], 2, ch. 1, p. 15.

49. See below, Chapter 7.

50. Tell Beit Mirsim: Albright, *AASOR*, 17 (1936–37), 26 ff. Megiddo: Loud, *Megiddo II*, 8 ff., 87 ff. Tell el-Ajjul: Petrie, *Ancient Gaza* (4 vols. London, 1931–34), 2, 2–3. See also Albright, "The Chronology of a South Palestinian City, Tell el-Ajjul," *AJSL*, 55 (1938), 337–59.

and Palestine's relation to Syria in this period. For the present, the discussion will be limited to ceramic typology. The pottery of MB II B–C continues and develops almost every form found in MB II A. This fact, so apparent in ceramic development, is also true of architecture and burial customs. There is no correspondence at various sites between the strata division based on architecture and the division of the two phases based on pottery; some strata, such as Megiddo XII, overlap the two phases.

The division between MB II A and MB II B–C is based primarily on innovations and changes in pottery styles. The painted styles of MB II A (see Fig. 2) are discontinued, and a new style of decoration takes its place. This is the so-called Tell el-Yahudiyeh ware, a punctured, white-filled style which decorates black burnished piriform and cylindrical juglets (see Fig. 9).[51] Another innovation is the imported painted ware from Cyprus which is the beginning of a strong Cypriot influence in Syria and Palestine. There is also much limitation of metallic forms in this period, particularly in the flaring carinated bowls and vases with the pedestal base (see Fig. 3). Prototypes of such pottery in metal have been found in Byblos.[52]

Another point of difference between MB II A and MB II B–C is the change in Palestine's relation with Syria. The strong ties with inland Syria of the earlier phase became much weaker; and the connection with the Syrian coast in the later phase became very strong. The fact that Tell el-Yahudiyeh ware is very common in Palestine and coastal Syria, but is almost completely lacking in the Orontes valley,[53] indicates this in terms of pottery. The same is true of the pointed "dipper" juglets, the piriform

---

51. Albright proposes that Tell el-Yahudiyeh ware starts in TGM G–F, but he offers no examples in his plates (*Tell Beit Mirsim*, Part IA, pp. 78 f.). Likewise Engberg's evidence from Megiddo is from intrusive burials, and his statement that Tell el-Yahudiyeh ware occurs as early as MB I is impossible (*The Hyksos Reconsidered*, p. 29 n.).

52. Montet, *Byblos et l'Egypte*, Pls. LXVII, CXIII, CXIV.

53. R. Amiran, "Tell el-Yahudiyeh Ware in Syria," *IEJ*, 7 (1957), 93–97.

juglets, and the forms with exaggerated carination (see Fig. 3). These are plentiful at Byblos and Ras Shamra but scarce inland. This unity between Palestine and coastal Syria is reflected in

*Fig. 2* Pottery types of Middle Bronze II A

the place-names of the Execration texts. As will be seen below, they probably date from the very end of MB II A or early MB II B–C.

This does not rule out all contact between inland Syria and

Palestine. There are strong connections between the styles of
Hama H and the MB II B–C levels of Hazor.[54] Likewise at
Alalakh, there is sufficient evidence from ceramic styles to relate

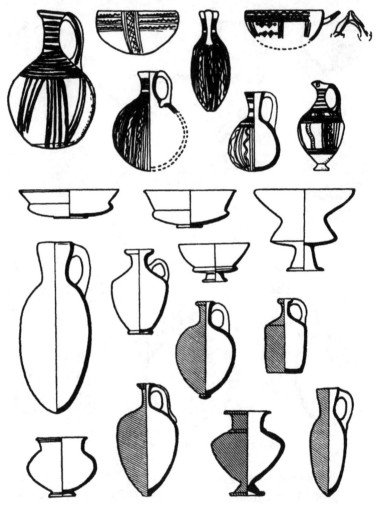

*Fig. 3*   Pottery types of Middle Bronze II B–C: Cypriot ware, carinated bowls, juglets

54. See p. 16 n.

level VII to MB II B–C of Palestine.[55] Woolley's observation of a scarcity of painted styles in this level, although they are common in level VIII and again in levels VI–V,[56] points out another similarity to Palestine. Since Alalakh VII is well documented to the late Old Babylonian period, this connection proves an important chronological synchronism for the MB II B–C period.[57] Although the synchronism does not immediately solve the controversy over Mesopotamian chronology, it carries important implications: level VII appears to be entirely within the framework of the MB II B–C phase—MB II B–C begins before and ends after level VII. This means that MB II B–C is contemporary with the great period of Amurrite rule in Syria and Mesopotamia.

Furthermore, the pottery of Alalakh VII has importance for the stratigraphy of Syria. For instance, Alalakh VII is to be related to Ras Shamra level II:2–3. C. F. A. Schaeffer, in his *Stratigraphie comparée,* dated Alalakh VII between 1900–1700 B.C., using Ras Shamra as a basis of comparison.[58] It is clear, however, from the historical texts of Alalakh, that his dates for both Alalakh and Ras Shamra should be revised. Unfortunately, Ras Shamra provides little in the way of strata for MB II; the material from this period came primarily from test pits and tombs encountered on the tell. Schaeffer's dating is, in fact, strictly typological; his criterion for Syrian, Minoan, and Cypriote ware is the occurrence of these pottery types at Kahun in Egypt.[59] With respect to Kahun, Schaeffer followed Petrie in dating all the foreign sherds

55. Albright, *BASOR, 144* (1956), 26–30; H. Kantor, *JNES, 15* (1956), 158 n.

56. L. Woolley, *Alalakh: An Account of the Excavations at Tell Atchana in the Hatay,* 1937–49 (Oxford, 1955), pp. 313 ff.

57. S. Smith, *Alalakh and Chronology* (London, 1940). B. Landsberger, "Assyrische Königsliste und 'Dunkles Zeitalter'," *JCS, 8* (1954), 31–45, 47–73, 106–33. A. Goetze, "On the Chronology of the Second Millennium B.C.," *JCS, 11* (1957), 53–61, 63–73. J. R. Kupper, "Northern Mesopotamia and Syria," *CAH²,* 2, ch. 1, p. 33.

58. C. F. A. Schaeffer, *Stratigraphie comparée et chronologie de l'Asie occidentale* (Oxford, 1948), pp. 101 ff.

59. Ibid., p. 19.

to the time of Senwosret II, about 1900–1875 B.C., because the town appeared to be associated with this pharaoh's pyramid. All the dateable evidence from the settlement, however, points to a date of occupation at the end of the Twelfth Dynasty and the Second Intermediate Period, at least a hundred years later than Schaeffer's upper limit.[60]

Almost all the material that Schaeffer ascribes to Ras Shamra II:2–3 belongs to MB II B–C. This conclusion was recently confirmed by soundings made by A. Kuschke in the so-called Palace garden at Ras Shamra.[61] He found a structural grave in level II similar to many of Megiddo XII–X, containing typical MB II B–C pottery, including Tell el-Yahudiyeh ware, pointed "dipper" juglets, and a scarab of the *anra* type. Kuschke dates the grave to the Hyksos period. This find, along with other stratigraphic evidence and a number of tomb deposits, shows occupancy of the tell throughout the MB II B–C period.

A reevaluation of the material from Byblos and Ras Shamra in the light of Alalakh and Palestine strongly suggests that these coastal cities had flourishing kingdoms during the Hyksos period. This cultural unity of coastal Syria and Palestine must certainly indicate important social, economic, and political ties as well. Some of these, perhaps, may be illuminated by a study of the individual features of the archaeological data. It is, therefore, to a consideration of these that we now turn.

60. See H. J. Kantor, "The Chronology of Egypt and its Correlation with that of Other Parts of the Near East in the Periods before the Late Bronze Age," in R. W. Ehrich, ed., *Relative Chronologies in Old World Archaeology* (Chicago, 1953), pp. 10 ff. Also Helck, *Beziehungen*, p. 75.

61. A. Kuschke, Ch. III, "Bericht über eine Sondage im Palastgarten von Ugarit-Ras Shamra," *Ugaritica*, 4, 256 ff., 292 ff. Cf. the remarks of Schaeffer, ibid., pp. 301 ff.

CHAPTER 2

# FORTIFICATIONS

The system of fortifications used by the MB II culture of Syria-Palestine is one of the most characteristic aspects of this period. Its most dominant features were the use of the glacis, a steeply sloping scarp of plastered limestone encircling the sides of the ancient mound on which the city was built; the heavy battered stone revetment wall at the base of the glacis; and the large city wall around the summit. Many sites, excavated in Syria and Palestine, were found to have been fortified in this way (see Fig. 4).[1] The first step in the construction of the defenses was

1. For a description of these fortifications, see Y. Yadin, "Hyksos Fortification and the Battering-Ram," *BASOR, 137* (1955), 23–32, and his *The Art of Warfare in Biblical Lands in the Light of Archaeological Study* (New York, 1963), pp. 65 ff. See also Albright, "Palestine in the Earliest Historical Period," *JPOS, 15* (1935), 223 ff.; *AP*, pp. 86 ff. Engberg, *The Hyksos Reconsidered*, pp. 20 ff., 45. Kenyon, *AHL*, pp. 176 ff. T. Säve-Söderbergh, "The Hyksos in Egypt," *JEA, 37* (1951), 60 ff. von Beckerath, *Untersuchungen*, p. 121. In addition to the bibliography on fortifications to be found in these works, one can now add the following references from more recent excavation reports, Shechem: L. E. Toombs and G. E. Wright, "The First Campaign at Tell Balatah (Shechem)," *BASOR, 144* (1956), 9 ff.; "The Second Campaign at Tell Balatah," *BASOR, 148* (1957), 12 ff.; "The Fourth Campaign at Balatah," *BASOR, 169* (1962), 7 ff.; Wright, *Shechem: The Biography of a Biblical City* (New York, 1965), pp. 57–79. Hazor: Yadin, "Excavations at Hazor," *IEJ,* 6 (1956), 123; ibid., 8 (1958), 8 ff.; ibid., 9 (1959), 77 ff. Bethel: J. L. Kelso, "The Fourth Campaign at Bethel," *BASOR, 164* (1961), 5 ff. Tell el-Far⁽ah (North): R. de Vaux, "Excavations at Tell el-Far⁽ah and the Site of Ancient Tirzah," *PEQ* (1956), 129 ff. Jericho: Kenyon, "Excavations at Jericho," *PEQ* (1952), 70 f.; ibid., (1954), 58 ff.; ibid. (1955), 115 f.; ibid. (1956), 79 f. Beth Zur: R. W. Funk, "The 1957 Campaign at Beth-Zur," *BASOR, 150* (1958), 10 ff.

to add a large amount of fill to the outer slopes of the city tell to make its sides higher and steeper. It also had the effect of making the area of the city at the top larger. The fill was put down in layers of various kinds of material, in *terre pisée* fashion. In order to prevent erosion and to bond the whole together, the outer surface was coated with a hard limestone plaster, with tongues of the plaster running back into the fill. The second element in the defense was a battered stone revetment wall at the foot of the slope, usually built of large irregularly shaped boulders. Sometimes there was also a fosse dug around the base of the whole mound; then the excavated materials was used either for fill or as building stone. At the top of the glacis was a strong wall built on a stone base with a carefully laid mud-brick superstructure. The wall usually followed the line of the summit of the tell and was often fortified with towers. Sometimes in subsequent stages in the reconstruction of the plastered scarp it was deemed necessary to rebuild the walls at a point closer to the new edge of the summit, but the style of construction for the wall remained the same. Thus the whole defensive system consisted of a battered stone revetment wall at the base of the tell, a smooth plastered glacis covering the slope of the tell and constructed at an angle of 35° or more, and a heavy stone and brick wall surrounding the city at the top of the tell. There may have been additional features such as a fosse, or certain other modifications depending on the nature of the city mound. Nevertheless, the effect of this type of defense was the same, namely, to make it difficult for the enemy to attack directly the wall of the city.

Besides the Middle Bronze cities which were built on preexisting tells, there were also cities resembling large fortified enclosures, such as Carchemish and Qatna in Syria, Hazor and

Lachish: O. Tufnell, *Lachish 4: The Bronze Age* (Oxford, 1957), pp. 45 ff. Alalakh: L. Woolley, *A Forgotten Kingdom* (Baltimore, 1953), pp. 66 ff.; *Alalakh*, pp. 132 ff. Tel Nagila: R. Amiran and A. Eitan, "A Canaanite-Hyksos City at Tell Nagila," *Archaeology, 18* (1965), 123.

Ashcalon in Palestine, and Tell el-Yahudiyeh and Heliopolis in Egypt. These usually had an acropolis as well, in one corner of the enclosed area. The defenses of these enclosures were built on virgin soil and consisted of large earthen ramparts, built with the terre pisée technique, sloping both on the inside and outside, and

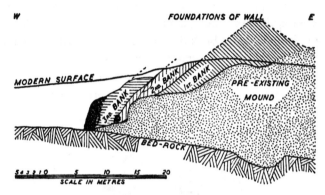

*Fig. 4* Reconstructed section of Middle Bronze II rampart at Jericho

crowned with a brick wall. At Hazor the dirt for the rampart came from digging a large fosse which went around the outside of it. There has been much discussion as to whether the ramparts of Tell el-Yahudiyeh and Heliopolis belong to this latter type of fortification. The alternative explanation—that the embankments were retaining walls for Egyptian terrace platforms[2]—lacks evidence of the latter constructions. Moreover, the similarity with Hazor and Qatna certainly favor the view that they were defensive embankments.

Another important element in the fortification of MB II is the monumental city gate. A good example of a gate from MB II A is the one found in stratum XIII at Megiddo (see Fig. 5).[3] The

2. The view of H. Riche, "Der 'Hohe Sand in Heliopolis'," *ZÄS, 71* (1935), 107–11, and supported by H. Otto, *ZDPV, 61* (1938), 270 ff., and T. Säve-Söderbergh, *JEA, 37* (1951), 60; but rejected by Albright, *Tell Beit Mirsim,* Part II, p. 28 n., and Yadin, *BASOR, 137* (1955), 25 n.

3. Loud, *Megiddo II,* pp. 6 ff.

gate is a single room with a change in axis between the doorways of 90°, probably to make a direct attack difficult. To one side of the gate was a defensive tower which guarded the entrance before the first set of doors. The approach to the gate was stepped with treads over a meter wide and ascended obliquely along the side of the slope. At the top of the approach and before the gate was a wide platform. Along the outer edge of the approach was a wide defensive wall of brick on a stone base. The whole approach and the outer wall was supported by a large retaining wall of battered stone. In addition to the battered-stone wall there was a glacis of limestone which covered the slope below the city.

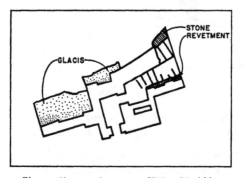

*Fig. 5*   City gate in stratum XIII at Megiddo

Very similar to the gate at Megiddo is the one at Hazor, which belongs to the earliest phase of the Middle Bronze Age city.[4] The gate had a simple passage with a square tower to one side and was set at an angle of 90° to the causeway, the change in axis being made, however, before one entered the gate. The causeway led up to the gate obliquely along the slope and ended in a large platform before the entry at the top. Both the platform and the causeway were supported by a revetment wall of large unhewn boulders similar to Megiddo. The causeway itself was built up artificially by means of the terre pisée technique used in

4. Yadin, *IEJ*, 9 (1959), 85 ff.

the construction of the ramparts. The dating of this gate cannot be much later than the earliest MB II gate at Megiddo.

There is a break in the evolution of the city gate at Megiddo. The subsequent MB II gates lay outside the limits of the excavation, and the gate does not reappear until stratum VIII of the Late Bronze I period. However the later version is clearly a continuation of a type that evolved in the MB II period subsequent to the gate in stratum XIII, a development which may be demonstrated from many other sites in Palestine and Syria (see Fig. 6).[5] The plan consists of a passage flanked on each side by three massive piers, the outer ones forming the jambs of the double doors, and the middle pair probably helping to support the roof. These gates were also joined to one or two towers. In this period the gates were often oriented so as to provide a more direct entrance from the approach; the causeway was no longer stepped, it was gently graded. These latter innovations suggest the use of wheeled vehicles in Palestine. Alone, however, they are not a sufficient basis for proposing that chariotry had now become an important element in tactical warfare in MB II.[6]

A few observations may be made with respect to the dating of the innovations in the defensive system of MB II. First, wherever city walls and gates from the MB II A period have been preserved, as the Megiddo, Tell Beit Mirsim, and perhaps Hazor, they indicate a continuity in the development of the later MB II B–C fortifications. Second, the ideas of a plastered glacis, or rampart, built of terre pisée and of a battered revetment wall are known from the MB II A period at Megiddo and the earliest MB II phase at Hazor.[7] This would put the introduction of these

5. Alalakh: Woolley, *Alalakh*, pp. 145 ff. Shechem: Wright, *BASOR, 148* (1957), 12 ff. Tell Farah: R. de Vaux, "La Troisième campagne de fouilles à Tell el-Farᵉah, près Naplouse," *RB, 58* (1951), 421 ff. Megiddo: Loud, *Megiddo II*, pp. 16 ff.

6. Cf. Yadin, *The Art of Warfare*, pp. 22 f.

7. Yadin, *IEJ, 9* (1959), 84. Loud, *Megiddo II*, pp. 6 ff. I do not understand why Kenyon wants to place the gate of Megiddo XIII and the wall in MB II B–C

defensive innovations before 1750 B.C. One criterion which should
no longer be used in the dating of these defenses is their correlation with the so-called invasion of the Hyksos from the north,

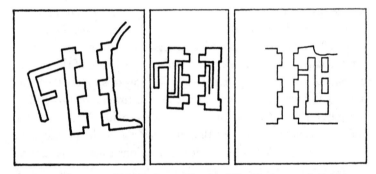

*Fig. 6*   City gates of Middle Bronze II at Megiddo, Shechem, and Alalakh

or the establishment of a Hyksos empire in Syria and Palestine.
Such historical speculation has seriously prejudiced the archaeological evidence.[8] Furthermore, there is no reason, from archaeological data, to suppose that the similar development in fortifications
in Syria preceded those in Palestine or that this style of fortification was originally derived from regions even further north.

(her MB II, ii). Both in area AA and BB the excavators place the wall with
glacis in level XIII. Wright, *BANE*, p. 89 n., has overlooked this glacis completely.
Cf. also Albright, *AP*, p. 88.

8. E. G. Wright, *BASOR*, *169* (1963), 11. Almost every instance of dating
these fortifications has been by means of a correlation with a supposed Hyksos
invasion.

Consequently, the fact that the more sophisticated style of fortifications was used throughout Alalakh VII would confirm the date suggested above for the early stages of this development.

Much discussion has centered around the reason for such fortifications. For a long time it was thought that both the addition of the sloping glacis to the city tell and the construction of the so-called "fortified camps" enclosed with sloping ramparts were to be associated with the introduction of chariotry as a weapon of war,[9] but this notion has been seriously challenged. Yadin has shown that the sloping glacis has nothing to do with chariot warfare.[10] They were built in this manner primarily as a defense against siege warfare. With a ditch and a steep slope, it was almost impossible to bring a siege tower directly against the wall or to maneuver a battering ram. The glacis also kept the attackers exposed to the fire of the defenders on the wall. The same is true of the gate, always oriented so as to prevent any direct assault on it with a battering ram.

The early history of siege warfare and the defenses used against it can be illuminated from both Egyptian and Mesopotamian sources. In the Beni Hasan tombs in Egypt, dating from the Eleventh and early Twelfth Dynasties, there are three representations of the siege of a fortress by means of a battering ram.[11] Even more instructive are the Middle Kingdom fortresses recently excavated in Nubia, of which the best preserved is Buhen (see Fig. 7).[12] W. B. Emery describes the fortifications as follows:

9. See Albright, *AP*, pp. 86 ff.

10. Yadin, *BASOR*, 137 (1955), 23–32.

11. P. E. Newberry, *Beni Hasan* (4 vols. London, 1893), Tomb no. 2, Part 1, Pl. XIV; Tomb no. 15, Part 2, Pl. V; Tomb no. 17, Part 2, Pl. XV. One of these is reproduced in Yadin, *The Art of Warfare*, p. 159.

12. See W. B. Emery, "A Preliminary Report on the Excavations of the Egyptian Exploration Society at Buhen, 1957–60," *Kush*, 7 (1959), 7–14; ibid., 8 (1960), 7–10; ibid., 9 (1961), 81–86. On the other forts in Nubia with the same features, see G. A. Reisner, "The Egyptian Forts from Halfa to Semna,"

This elaborate defense system consisted of a massive brick wall 4.18 m. thick and at least 9 m. high, relieved on its outer face at regular intervals with square bastions with a base measurement of 2.25 × 1.90 m. . . . At the foot of the wall was a brick paved rampart, protected by a loopholed parapet overhanging the scarp of the rock-cut ditch, which was 8.40 m. wide and 6.50 m. deep. The counterscarp on the other side of the ditch was surmounted by a narrow covered way of brickwork beyond which was a glacis rising from the natural ground level. Projecting into the ditch from the scarp were round bastions with double rows of loopholes. . . . The most strongly fortified part of the structure was the great gate built into the wall on the axis of the rectangular town area. . . . We have evidence of great double doors in the gateway through the main wall and of a wooden draw-bridge which was pulled back on rollers.[13]

This fort and similar ones in Nubia are certainly the finest extant examples in the whole Near East of fortifications for this period. Furthermore, they clearly indicate that by the time of the Middle Kingdom, contemporary with MB II A, a great deal was known about constructing effective defenses against siege warfare.

Another important historical source on siege warfare, cited by Yadin, is the Mari correspondence from the time of Shamshi-Adad and his sons.[14] A number of statements in the letters speak of siege warfare. They deal with such matters as building an as-

---

*Kush*, 8 (1960), 11–24; N. F. Wheeler, "Diary of the Excavations of Mirgissa Fort," *Kush*, 9 (1961), 87–179; G. R. Hughes, "Serra East," *Kush*, 11 (1963), 124 ff. See also W. S. Smith, *The Art and Architecture of Ancient Egypt* (Baltimore, 1958), pp. 98 ff.

13. Emery, *Kush*, 8 (1960), 7 f.

14. The references are collected by J. R. Kupper, "Notes lexicographiques." *RAss*, 45 (1951), 125 ff. See also his remarks, *CAH*², 2, ch. 1, p. 7.

sault ramp, methods of blockade, and transportation and use of siege machinery, such as the siege tower (*dimtu*) and the battering ram (*iašibu*). The term for battering ram is also found in a pre-Hammurapi lexical list in which three Sumerian ideograms as well as additional terms for parts of the battering ram are given. It is of interest to note that one of the ideograms, *giš.gud.si.Aš*,

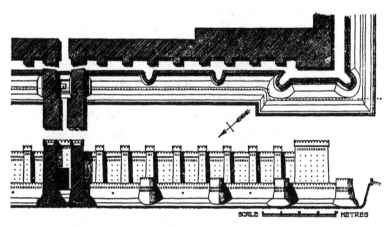

*Fig. 7*   The Middle Kingdom fortification at Buhen

occurs in a late Hittite text containing a legend which describes the siege of Uršu, a town in Northern Syria, by a king of the Old Kingdom. The text mentions the use of the battering ram (*giš.gud.si.Aš*) "in the Hurrian manner," as well as other siege operations, such as mounding up earth to storm a wall. On the basis of the Mari texts, it is clear that the Hurrians did not invent either the battering ram or other methods of siege warfare. They received them as part of a very considerable heritage from the Amurrite world; through the Hurrians of North Syria, the techniques were passed on to the Hittites.[15]

Egypt, in the Middle Kingdom, and the Amurrite world of Syria and Mesopotamia, in the Old Babylonian period, were entirely familiar with the best methods of siege warfare—and defenses against them. There is no need to go further to explain the development of these defenses in Palestine.

One matter, however, must still be considered, the so-called "fortified camps." Albright and others have long proposed that such sites as Qatna and Hazor represent great encampments for horses and chariots; there was no room in the small cities to quarter such armament. While the notion is attractive, it has certain weaknesses: there is no evidence of armies with large numbers of fighting chariots in the Mari Age, by which time the ramparts of Hazor and Qatna were very likely built; one can hardly explain as a fortification for chariotry the enclosure found at El-Lejjun in Transjordan of MB I date.[16] This latter enclosure was 700 meters by 250 meters, surrounded by a wall with towers and strengthened by a revetment. Enclosures of this kind probably owe their existence to their strategic positions on important caravan routes, where they acted as important way stations.[17] The notion of Hazor as a fortified camp in the MB II period has been challenged by Yadin, the most recent excavator of the site. With evidence furnished by test trenches in various parts of the site, he

15. Note the statement by A. Goetze, "Warfare in Asia Minor," *Iraq*, 25 (1963), 128: "It deserves special note that the battering ram is here credited to the Hurrians. It seems that they who had made the open battle obsolete were also instrumental in devising means to reduce fortresses into which conventional armies had been forced to retire." This needs some qualification in the light of the Mari evidence.

16. N. Glueck, *Explorations*, part 1, pp. 44 ff., 95, Pl. 9.

17. See J. Lewy, "Old Assyrian Institutions," *HUCA*, 27 (1956), 1–80.

concludes that the whole of the site was occupied by dwellings during the MB II period.[18] Moreover, a system of fortified camps with only two in Palestine, at the Northern and Southern extremities, Hazor and Ashcalon, would imply a political unity that the country never possessed. The archaeological and literary evidence suggest that Syria and Palestine were made up of city-states with individual states joined together only by loose confederations.[19]

There is no reason whatever to postulate, for the so-called Hyksos defenses, any immigration either of a new people or of a new warrior aristocracy in the latter part of the MB II period. The fortifications are the products of development inspired in part by the Amurrite and the Egyptian worlds and in part by native inventiveness applied to materials and geography. They show in this respect the same skill, flexibility, and eclectic borrowing of neighboring cultures that characterizes many other features of their civilization. In the architecture of city defenses this culture laid a good foundation for achievements of the succeeding periods.

18. Yadin, *IEJ*, *8* (1958), 8.
19. See below, Chapter 11.

CHAPTER 3

# URBAN LIFE

In contrast to the preceding MB I period which is regarded as seminomadic, the MB II period begins a phase of well-organized urban life.[1] The towns are laid out well, with houses organized in blocks and clearly delineated streets running between them. The streets were often paved with small stones and supplied with run-off curbs. Most cities had a fine system of covered drains which continued in use through successive building phases. Kenyon has excavated what seems to be a street that constituted one of the city markets in Jericho. Along the street were one-room shops that were noncommunicating with the rest of the building in which they were set. Evidence of the kind of commodities these merchants had for sale was found in the debris of these shops.

### ARCHITECTURE

The center of town life was undoubtedly the palace, and a building of monumental proportions, best construed as a palace, has been found in many sites. The construction and planning of these buildings is often of high quality. One such example is the palace at Shechem which lasted through four stages, beginning toward the end of MB II A and going through MB II B (ca. 1800–1650 B.C.).[2] In plan, it consists of two or three open courts, together with rooms around each one. Within the palace is evidence of a variety of workrooms. There appears to have been a

1. For a general treatment of this period see Kenyon, *AHL*, pp. 162 ff.
2. L. E. Toombs and G. E. Wright, *BASOR*, *161* (1961), 22 ff. Cf. ibid., *169* (1963), 11 ff.

private sanctuary in one of the courts during one phase of the palace, since a large storage jar full of animal bones was found buried in a niche in the corner. Wright has suggested interpreting the whole structure, in all its phases, as a temple of the Hittite courtyard type,[3] but I prefer to view the building as a palace containing a royal chapel similar to the palace of Zimri-Lim at Mari.[4] The plan of small rooms about a large court, with workshops in some of the rooms, is also similar to the Mari palace.

A large palace dating to MB II C—the height of the Hyksos period—is the palace of Tell el-Ajjul; its outside measurements are about 150′ × 75′.[5] The foundation of the building consists of a high stone socle base made of dressed sandstone, carefully drafted on the outer face. The material for this building was quarried from the foot of the tell where the stone was removed to form a great defensive fosse. The walls above the stone base were of mud brick. The palace was laid out with a large central court surrounded by small casement-like rooms, similar to Shechem. One was a bathroom finished off with white plaster and equipped with bath, drain, and cesspit. The plan and workmanship of this building is comparable to the fine contemporaneous palace of Alalakh.[6] On the other hand, it is far superior to the succeeding, very much smaller, building that Albright suggests as the headquarters of an Egyptian official of the early Eighteenth Dynasty.[7]

Besides the palaces, there were other well-constructed houses which obviously belonged to members of the patrician class.[8] These houses were of two stories: the ground floor was probably

3. Wright, BASOR, 169 (1963), 17 f. Compare the temples in O. R. Gurney, The Hittites (Baltimore, 1961), p. 146.

4. A. Parrot, MAM, Le Palais, part 1, pp. 266 ff.

5. Petrie, Ancient Gaza, 2, 2 f.; Pls. III:1–3, XLV, XLVI. See also Albright, AJSL, 55 (1938), 337–59.

6. Woolley, A Forgotten Kingdom, pp. 69 ff.

7. Albright, AJSL, 55 (1938), 352.

8. See Albright, AP, pp. 91 f.

for animals and domestics; the second floor provided living quarters for the family. Most of the people, however, lived in much meaner dwellings; the general prosperity of the period was enjoyed by relatively few.

The temples of MB II in Syria and Palestine display a marked simplicity in plan, a simplicity which continues unbroken for a very long period of time. A good example is the temple at Shechem, dated in its first two phases, to MB II C (See Fig. 8).[9] The temple, built on a platform of marl fill six meters thick, was a massive rectangular structure consisting of a cult room and a simple entrance hall. The entrance hall, formed by two tower-like projections before the doorway, was 7 meters wide $\times$ 5 meters deep. The doorway, 3.25 meters square, led into the central cult room, 11 meters $\times$ 13.50 meters. The cult room or cella was divided, in the first phase, into three aisles by two rows of three columns each. The column bases were still in situ and a capital of rather Egyptian style was also found. In the second phase the column bases were plastered over, so that the cella may have been open to the sky. The walls of the temple were over five meters thick, indicating that the temple was tall. It is for this reason that G. E. Wright identifies this type of temple with a *migdol,* meaning "tower." The history of the *migdol* temple continues down to the Iron Age.

Very similar to the temple of Shechem is the one found in Alalakh VII.[10] This latter temple was probably a royal chapel, for it was directly connected with the palace. It was a simple rectangular structure consisting of a cella, procella, and an open forecourt, with a service chamber off the court. Like Shechem's temple, the walls of the sanctuary were very thick. Another similar temple is that of Megiddo stratum VIII.[11] It is of interest to

9. Toombs and Wright, *BASOR, 161* (1961), 28; ibid., *169* (1963), 18 ff., 29 ff. Also R. J. Bull, "A Re-examination of the Shechem Temple," *BA, 23* (1960), 110 ff.

10. Woolley, *Alalakh,* pp. 59 ff.

11. Loud, *Megiddo II,* pp. 102 ff. Note Wright's discussion of the date in *BASOR, 148* (1957), 20 n.

note that in all three places, Megiddo, Alalakh, and Shechem, there are very similar temples and city gates.

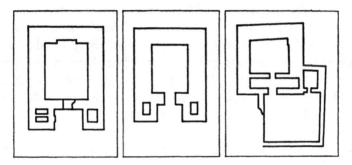

*Fig. 8* The *Migdol* type temples of Middle Bronze II at Megiddo, Shechem, and Alalakh

## RELIGIOUS PRACTICES

Two features found with many temples of this period likewise manifest a long history in Palestine and Syria, namely, the *maṣ-ṣebah* (pl. *maṣṣeboth*) and the *bamah*.[12] Both phenomena have a long history extending from the MB I period to the Iron Age; they are generally regarded as features of "Canaanite" religion. *Maṣṣebah* is a biblical term which refers to independent, standing stones or pillars, set up in a holy place for religious or commemorative purposes. The *maṣṣeboth* do not seem to be uniform in size, shape, and general displacement, nor are they associated with any one type of temple. While the term *maṣṣebah* may refer to an inscribed stela or obelisk, it usually applies, in archaeological discussion, to uninscribed standing stones. The *bamah* is another

12. See A. G. Barrois, *Manuel d'archéologie biblique* (Paris, 1953), 2, 345 ff.; "Pillar," in *The Interpreter's Dictionary of the Bible* (Nashville, 1962), 3, 815 ff. G. H. Davies, "High Place," in *The Interpreter's Dictionary*, 2, 602 ff.

biblical term, usually translated by "high place," which refers to an open-air place of worship. It may or may not be associated with a temple building, but its most dominant feature is a large altar for burnt offering, elevated several steps high.

Examples of holy places with a *bamah* and *masseboth* are fairly common in MB II. In Gezer a "high place" was discovered which had a series of *masseboth* related to it.[13] Megiddo also had a *bamah* which seems to go back in its earliest phases to the Early Bronze Age.[14] The *bamah* consisted of a large oval-shaped altar, built of unhewn stones, with several steps leading up to the top. During MB I it was associated with a number of temples. Its later history is not entirely clear, but there is evidence to suggest that it lasted through MB II as well, although its outline and significance was not very certain to the excavators. In stratum XII (MB II B) there was a field of *masseboth* connected with this holy place, and toward the end of Middle Bronze a temple of the *migdol* type was erected on the spot.

The best example of a temple with a *bamah* of MB II is the one excavated at Nahariyeh on the Mediterranean coast a short distance south of Tyre.[15] The temple was built in the open, far from any settlement; the nearest occupied site was Achzib, two miles away. A holy place was located in this desolate spot because of a fresh water spring by the edge of the sea. The temple itself, at first a simple rectangle, in time was enlarged to include two additional rooms. In the temenos on one side of the temple was a large stone-built *bamah,* and to one side of the *bamah,* before the temple entrance, was a small stone altar and a *massebah.*

At B;blos there were a number of temples dating to the Middle Kingdom and the Second Intermediate Period of Egypt (MB

13. R. A. S. MacAlister, *Gezer* (London, 1912), *3,* 377 ff. See also Barrois, *Manuel d'archéologie,* 2, 355 ff. and Albright, *AP,* p. 104.

14. Loud, *Megiddo II,* pp. 73 ff.

15. I. Ben-Dor, *QDAP, 14* (1950), 1–41. M. Dothan, "The Excavations at Nahariyeh, 1954–55," *IEJ, 6* (1956), 14–25; "Some Aspects of Life in Palestine during the Hyksos Rule," *Antiquity and Survival,* 2 (1957), 121–30.

II).[16] Associated with one of the temples was a large elevated platform, described by the excavator as a truncated pyramid. This was undoubtedly a *bamah* similar to the one at Nahariyeh. A number of *masseboth* or obelisks of varying sizes were placed in the open forecourt of the Temple of Obelisks. One of the obelisks was inscribed by a prince of Byblos in honor of a member of his court. In another small cella nearby was found a row of seven short unhewn blocks placed in front of an altar.

The practice of setting up *masseboth* in holy places, either in groups or individually, continued in Syria and Palestine into the Late Bronze Age. In a temple at Hazor (LB II) a group of *masseboth* were found together with a seated statue of a deity.[17] In Shechem, a large single *massebah* was found associated with the Late Bronze temple.[18] The symbolic meaning of the *masseboth*, however, continues to be problematic.

Some idea of the cult practices of Palestine in MB II may be gained from the finds in the temple at Nahariyeh.[19] It is evident that sacrifices were made and offerings deposited at this site. The lower courses of stone of the *bamah* were saturated with oily matter, and between the stones were placed small pottery bowls each with seven miniature cups (primitive kernoi). Votive offerings of tiny pottery vessels, bowls, jugs, jars, and cups, were found on the *bamah* and on the courtyard floor. Other cult objects found were seven-wick saucer lamps and fragmentary incense stands. There were remnants of hearths in the courtyard, and near them were animal bones and sherds of cooking pots indicative of sacrificial meals. The gifts include many beads of semiprecious stones and jewelry of bronze, silver, and gold in the form of earrings, pendants, and a scarab ring. There is only slight evidence

16. M. Dunand, *Fouilles de Byblos*, Part 2 (Paris, 1958), pp. 646 ff. Also N. Glueck, "Archaeological Research in Palestine, Transjordan, and Syria," *AJA, 42* (1938), 172 f.

17. Yadin, *IEJ, 8* (1958), 11 ff.

18. Bull, *BA, 23* (1960), 114.

19. See above, n. 15.

that weapons were offered. Most interesting are the figurines which obviously represent a female deity. They were of two kinds, either thin silver plaques, or silver or bronze figurines in the round, cast in a mold. Besides the deities were clay or stone models of animals: sheep, bulls, doves, and a small, well-carved lion.

The closest parallels to the material at Nahariyeh are found at Byblos in the offering deposits of the temples, particularly the Temple of Obelisks.[20] The pottery from the temple would indicate a date of MB II. The finds in the Byblian temple include the groups of seven cups, or kernoi, and much miniature votive pottery. The clay and stone figurines in this temple, although much more numerous and varied than those in Nahariyeh, still resemble them in appearance. The Temple of Obelisks also had quantities of figurines of both the flat plaque type and in the round, but they were of a male deity (or deities). The weapons in the Byblian temple were abundant, of bronze and gold, and highly ornamented. On the other hand, only a little jewelry was found; this consisted of pendants and torques. It seems clear that at Byblos a male warrior deity was worshiped, while a gentler female divinity was honored at Nahariyeh. The religious practices, however, are essentially the same.

These cult practices, furthermore, are not limited to Nahariyeh and Byblos. From Megiddo come a number of similar cult objects found in stratum XII–X in the region of the *bamah* and the *maṣṣeboth*.[21] At Ugarit a sounding was made beneath the temple of Baal into a temple of the preceding MB II period, in which a large cache of votive weapons, a bronze figurine of a bull, and a large statue of Baal were found.[22] Also listed among the finds are miniature votive pottery and seven-cup kernoi. The evidence

20. Dunand, *Fouilles*, Part 2, Pls. XC–CXLI.
21. See Loud, *Megiddo II*, Pls. 19:19, 47:9, 233–34.
22. Schaeffer, *Ugaritica*, 2, #37, pp. 85 ff., and #46, pp. 121 ff.

would seem to indicate a homogeneity of religious practices in this period in Syria and Palestine.

## BURIAL CUSTOMS

With the coming of Middle Bronze II there was a marked change in burial customs which would strongly suggest an influx of new peoples into Palestine.[23] In MB I it was the practice to bury the dead in cemeteries outside the city, in shaft tombs with one burial to a grave. In MB II, however, burials were often made in shallow graves within the city area, and multiple burials were very common in larger tombs. Although the people of MB II often reused the shaft tombs of MB I, they seldom bothered to make new ones.

Throughout the MB II period there was great diversity in burial customs. In spite of this variety, however, we find no indication that different ethnic groups were involved: there is no corresponding distribution in time, locality, or accompanying burial goods. At Megiddo, for example, almost every style is evident throughout the course of MB II and into the Late Bronze Age. The diversity may be explained in terms of the internationalism of the Amurrite period: certain regional practices in the construction of tombs were used over wide areas. Thus, the Mesopotamian tendency was to build cist tombs of brick or stone with corbelled roofs or, in Upper Mesopotamia, with large slabs of stone covering the tops.[24] In Syria the general practice was to cut shaft tombs into the soft rock, after the Egyptian manner. Shallow pit graves within the structures of houses are also known from Syria. All these styles came into vogue in Palestine, with no clear geographic or chronological distribution.

The MB II A tombs of Ras el-Ain in central Palestine illustrate

23. See Kenyon, *AHL*, pp. 188 ff.

24. V. G. Childe, *New Light on the Most Ancient East* (New York, 1957), pp. 148 ff., 216.

this new internationalism.[25] They consist of rectangular pits, lined on the long sides with stone walling and covered by stone slabs, much like the large tomb of Til Barsip on the northwestern Euphrates.[26] In the walls of the Palestinian tombs were recesses which served as ossuaries. The tombs were equipped, as usual, with bronze weapons and much pottery whose style has strong connections with Northern Syria and Upper Mesopotamia. This type of tomb is frequently found in the following MB II B-C phase, usually within the confines of the tell and built into the debris of previous building levels, at Megiddo and Ugarit for example.[27]

Similar to the stone-lined tomb was the brick-built tomb with a corbelled roof. An example of this type was found in Jericho in MB II A.[28] Others were found at Tell el-Yahudiyeh in Egypt, in which scarabs and the Tell el-Yahudiyeh ware of the Hyksos period were found.[29] These structured tombs, built within the city, contained multiple burials and were probably intended as family vaults.

Also common to the whole of the MB II period were single burials in simple grave pits. At Tell el-Ajjul the so-called courtyard cemetery, which is made up of such graves, seems to overlap both MB II A and MB II B. At Megiddo such graves are known from both periods, while at Hazor they are common in MB II B-C. Similar examples may be cited from Syria at Hama, Ugarit, and Alalakh.[30]

---

25. Iliffe, *QDAP*, 5 (1936), 113–26. J. Ory, *QDAP*, 6 (1938), 99–120. See also Schaeffer, *Strat Comp*, pp. 178 ff.

26. Ibid., 81 ff.

27. Loud, *Megiddo II*, pp. 15 ff., 87 ff. Schaeffer, *Strat Comp*, pp. 20 ff.

28. Kenyon, *AHL*, p. 169; *PEQ* (1956), 81 f.

29. Petrie, *Hyksos and Israelite Cities* (London, 1906), pp. 10 ff.

30. Tell el-Ajjul: Petrie, *Ancient Gaza*, 2, 5; O. Tufnell, "The Courtyard Cemetery of Tell el-Ajjul, Palestine," *BIA*, 3 (1962), 1–46. Megiddo: Loud, *Megiddo II*, pp. 87 ff. Hazor: Yadin, *Hazor*, 2, 76. Ugarit: Schaeffer, *Ugaritica*, 4, 255 f. Alalakh: Woolley, *Alalakh*, pp. 221 ff.

Shaft tombs were also frequently used in MB II. The most famous are the royal tombs of Byblos, belonging to the end of MB II A and the early MB II B period.[31] In Jericho, Megiddo, Lachish, and Tell Farah, shaft tombs were in use, often reusing tombs cut in the MB I period.[32] In contrast to MB I, however, the burials were almost always multiple, averaging about twenty burials to a tomb. Occasionally there was a single burial in a shaft tomb, but it was probably an honor reserved for princely persons.

The tombs contain the customary funeral deposits of pottery and a few bronze objects.[33] The wealth of the buried person is indicated by the presence of jewelry and even royal gifts, as in the case of the royal tombs of Byblos. In a number of tombs from Jericho, various household objects of wood and textile were preserved, giving the impression that the person buried was to be well-equipped for the afterlife. Of particular interest in this respect is the presence of animal bones in a few tombs. It is clear in many cases that some of these animals, such as sheep and goats, were intended as food. In a few cases, such as a single burial at Jericho and a few tombs at Tell el-Ajjul, there were horses or donkeys buried with the humans.[34] They may signify the special princely status of the persons and may be a distant anticipation of the later Aegean practice of a burial with a chariot and a team of horses.[35] The data are, however, too slight for any historical conclusions.

Very few skulls have been analyzed with respect to racial type. Two very fragmentary skulls from Megiddo have nevertheless suggested to Engberg an immigration into Palestine of a new

31. Montet, *Byblos et l'Egypte,* pp. 143 ff

32. Kenyon, *AHL,* p. 189.

33. Ibid., pp. 190 ff.

34. Kenyon, *Excavations at Jericho* (London, 1960), *1,* 306 ff., 535 f. Petrie, *Ancient Gaza, 1,* 4.

35. See Karageorghis, "Horse Burials on the Island of Cyprus," *Archaeology, 18* (1965), 282–90.

people.[36] These parts of skulls, however, came from tombs in which there was a great deal of mixture with material of a later date. At Ugarit, the examination of skulls was much more controlled; there was no danger of contamination in the tombs from a later period.[37] Six skulls were from the MB II period, and all were of the type known as Mediterranean—the type usually associated with the Semites. Even the skulls of the Late Bronze Age at Ugarit were predominately Mediterranean, but a few were of the "Alpine" type associated primarily with the Aegean population. It is probably to this period and region that the "Alpine" skulls of Megiddo are to be assigned. At any rate, they can hardly be used to prove a Hurrian migration for MB II, as Engberg had suggested.

36. Engberg, *The Hyksos Reconsidered*, p. 41; *Megiddo Tombs* (Chicago, 1938), pp. 64 ff.

37. Schaeffer, *Ugaritica, 4,* 567 ff.

# CHAPTER 4

# CRAFTS AND ARTS

## POTTERY

The pottery of this period has been sufficiently discussed under the heading of stratigraphy so that a general discussion need not be repeated. However, two particular wares call for further attention. The first of these is the Tell el-Yahudiyeh ware, often associated by archaeologists with the Hyksos.[1] To do so is very misleading, since it is one of a number of types which made up the ceramic repertory of the MB II B–C period and was very much in vogue in Palestine and coastal Syria, but not inland.[2] The name, Tell el-Yahudiyeh ware, was coined by Petrie when he found large quantities of it in graves at this Egyptian site.[3] The ware is identified primarily by its mode of decoration as a white-filled punctured design, usually on a dark brown or black, burnished surface. The characteristic shapes for this ware are the piriform or cylindrical juglets, although the white-filled technique is sometimes used for other forms as well (see Fig. 9). Since these forms are entirely characteristic of Palestinian and Syrian pottery in MB II B–C, there can be no question as to its place of origin and distribution.[4]

1. Engberg, *Hyksos Reconsidered*, p. 18.
2. Amiran, *IEJ*, 7 (1957), 93–97.
3. Petrie, *Hyksos and Israelite Cities*, p. 14.
4. A Nubian origin for this pottery was proposed by H. Junker, "Der nubische Ursprung der sogen. Tell el-Jahudiyeh-Vasen," Akademie der Wissenschaften in Wien, Philos.-hist. Klasse, Sitzungsberichte, 198: 3. Abhandlung (Vienna, 1921); but this has since been refuted by subsequent finds. See R. Dussaud, "Obser-

The place of the Tell el-Yahudiyeh ware in the ceramic typology of the Levant and in Egyptian chronology is now fairly
clear. It belongs to MB II B–C, which corresponds to the Second
Intermediate Period. Some scholars have proposed that Tell el-

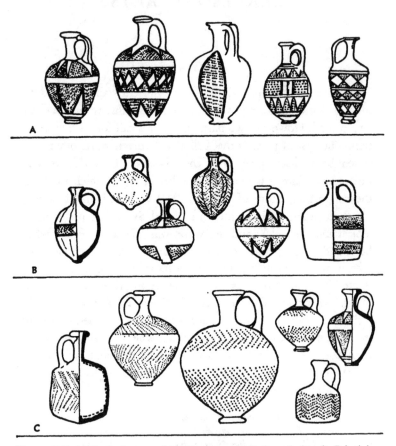

*Fig. 9*  Tell el-Yahudiyeh ware of Middle Bronze II B–C: a. Syrian; b. Palestinian;
c. Cypriot and Egyptian

vations sur la ceramique du II° millenaire avant notre ère," *Syria,* 9 (1928),
147 f.

Yahudiyeh ware occurs in Egypt in the Twelfth Dynasty,[5] but the evidence for this is entirely faulty, and the occurrences are actually to be dated later.[6] It is nevertheless possible to arrive at a closer dating within the Second Intermediate Period by differentiating between two styles.[7] The first may be called Syrian; the form of the juglet, piriform with high round shoulders and disc or ring base, is characteristic of coastal Syria in this period. The pattern is contained within lines and consists of a picked design in triangular or diamond zones (see Fig. 9a). The second style is Palestinian and may best be regarded as a degenerate form of the Syrian style. The juglet shapes may be squat piriform, cylindrical with convex bottom, or baggy. The patterns are usually not contained in lines, but they may be in simple, parallel horizontal zones. The picking is done in chevron or zig-zag patterning (see Fig. 9b).

The distribution of these two styles is significant. The Syrian type is found in coastal Syria throughout the whole period. It also occurs in Palestine, particularly at Megiddo, but usually in an imitated form, where the juglets are more globular and the base is button-shaped. The Syrian types are also found in Egypt at Khataᶜna in the Delta, at Kahun in Middle Egypt, and at Buhen and Kerma in Nubia.[8] The Palestinian style is found in Egypt primarily in the Delta at Khataᶜna and Tell el-Yahudiyeh, with perhaps a few pieces in Middle Egypt, but none in Nubia. This style is also found in Cyprus at Enkomi (see Fig. 9c).

5. Engberg, *Hyksos Reconsidered*, pp. 26 f.

6. Engberg follows the dating of Egyptian archaeologists by typology quite uncritically. On the foreign pottery of these sites see ibid., p. 63 n.

7. For an earlier classification based on the Egyptian and Nubian ware see G. A. Reisner, *Excavations at Kerma IV–V* (2 vols. in 5 parts Cambridge, 1923), 2, pp. 386 ff.

8. See S. Adam, "Report on the Excavations . . . at Ezbet Rushdi," *Ann Serv*, 56 (1959), Pls. XV, XVI (following p. 226). W. M. F. Petrie, *Illahun, Kahun, Gurob* (London, 1891), Pl. 1, nos. 17, 20, 21. D. Randall Maciver and C. L. Woolley, *Buhen* (Philadelphia, 1911), pp. 133 f., Pls. 49–92. Reisner, *Kerma IV–V*, 2, 381 ff.

It is precarious to draw far-reaching historical conclusions on this proposed classification and distribution. Yet it appears safe to say that in the earlier part of MB II B–C Syrian merchants had access to Egypt and Nubia directly. With the rise of the Nubian kingdom in the latter Second Intermediate Period, Nubian trade was no longer in foreign hands. Likewise, in the Delta in the so-called Fifteenth Dynasty (ca. 1675–1575 B.C.), contact with Palestine was greatly strengthened, and Tell el-Yahudiyeh was probably made a Palestinian settlement. Furthermore, the Hyksos seem to have traded directly with Cyprus and probably obtained much of their copper from Enkomi, even at this time an important smelting center.[9]

Another ware which calls for some consideration is the so-called bichrome pottery with patterns of birds, "union jacks," cartwheels, fish, and multiple geometric designs (see Fig. 10). Engberg characterizes this pottery as "Hurrian" and associates it with a late Hyksos phase.[10] However, Albright has clearly shown that this pottery must be dated after MB II B–C, since it occurs only in levels after the destruction associated with the expulsion of the Hyksos.[11] Engberg's evidence from Megiddo X, moreover, is inconclusive. The pottery was found in graves which were probably dug into level X from level IX above it. Furthermore, the pottery cited from Egypt [12] is all dated on the basis of typology, and nothing speaks against an early Eighteenth Dynasty date. In Syria at Alalakh, this style does not occur in level VII but is common in levels VI–V.[13] The ascription of this ware as "Hurrian" is questionable. The ware is far more characteristic of coastal Syria, Palestine, and the Eastern Mediterranean than it

9. Enkomi seems to have also supplied Mari with copper in the Old Babylonian period. See Kupper, *CAH²*, ch. 1, p. 15.

10. Engberg, *Hyksos Reconsidered*, pp. 19, 35 f.

11. *Tell Beit Mirsim*, Part 2, pp. 58 ff.

12. Engberg, *Hyksos Reconsidered*, p. 19 n.

13. Woolley, *Alalakh*, pp. 340 ff.

is of distinctively Hurrian reigons.[14] The bichrome pottery does not belong to MB II, but rather to the transitional period before the Late Bronze Age proper. It has, in fact, no relevance whatever to the Hyksos problem.

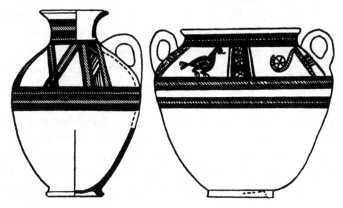

*Fig. 10*   Bichrome ware, transition to Late Bronze I

## METALLURGY

There is every indication that the MB II B–C culture of coastal Syria and Palestine covered a period in which the use of bronze came to the fore. In MB I, copper was the metal primarily used, and bronze was only introduced slowly in the MB II A period. This agrees well with evidence from Egypt, where bronze seems to have been used first in the Middle Kingdom—and then only to a rather limited extent.[15] Byblos was the most important center in the Levant for the production of bronze, and a number of large caches of metal objects have been found there. Schaeffer has suggested that this was due to the fortuitous circumstance that

14. Schaeffer, *Strat comp,* pp. 378 f.

15. A. Lucas, *Ancient Egyptian Materials and Industries* (4th ed. London, 1962), p. 220. See also G. A. Wainwright, "The Occurrence of Tin and Copper near Byblos," *JEA,* 20 (1934), 29–32.

the two necessary metals, tin and copper, occurred together in
their natural state in the immediate vicinity of Byblos.[16]

The caches of metal objects were found either in tombs of
important persons or in offering-deposits in temples. A number
of metal vessels came from the tombs of the princes, dated to the
end of the Twelfth Dynasty.[17] These metal prototypes, archaeologists have felt, inspired the carinated forms in bowls and vases of
the MB II B–C period. There were also a few bronze vessels in
the offering deposits, but in addition there were large quantities
of torques and armlets, bronze figurines, and weapons. The
Temple of Obelisks contained the richest deposits: weapons and
other objects made of gold and silver, often bejeweled, and skill-
fully ornamented with embossed designs.[18] We have previously
noted the close connection between this temple and the one at
Nahariyeh—at least in cultic practices. It is also significant that
an obelisk of this temple honors a Lycian of Southern Anatolia.[19]
On this evidence and from pottery as well, there is strong indication of active commercial contact between Byblos and other
important centers of culture in the Aegean and Eastern Mediterranean. Byblos was also very likely an important supplier of
metals for the Hyksos rulers of Egypt, a fact that may be safely
deduced from the Kamose stela.[20]

This wide range of contact with the East (Mesopotamia) and
the West (the Aegean) may be illustrated from the typology of
metal objects—although such evidence must be used with considerable caution in the creation of historical hypotheses. Torques
and toggle pins, for instance, have been found from Persia and
the Caucasus to Anatolia, the Levant, and as far as the Danube

16. Schaeffer, *Ugaritica*, 2, 67 ff.

17. Montet, *Byblos et l'Egypte*, pp. 189 ff.

18. Dunand, *Fouilles*, 2, Pls. CXVII–CXXII, CXXXI–CXXXVII.

19. Ibid., 878, no. 16980. On this monument see Chapter 5.

20. In lines 13 ff., there is mention of shiploads of silver, turquoise, and
bronze axes "without number" coming from Retjenu to Apophis. See Habachi,
"Preliminary Report on Kamose Stela," *Ann Serv*, 53 (1956), 201.

valley in Europe. Schaeffer has proposed an explanation for the distribution of this metal industry in which Byblos played a primary role.[21] Trade was the most likely means for the wide dissemination of similar types of objects—caravan trade in the east and maritime trade in the west. As yet, however, too little is known about primary and secondary agents in this transmission of culture.

It seems best to limit the present discussion to a consideration of some bronze weapons of Syria-Palestine in the MB II period. Many styles of weapons of this period have a fairly clear typological relationship with the earlier weapons of Mesopotamia. The metallurgists of Syria-Palestine, however, made important improvements in the manufacture of their weapons. One example is the so-called window axe, common in Syria-Palestine in the MB II period (see Fig. 11:5-7).[22] Examples were found among the treasures of the Temple of Obelisks in Byblos, made of gold and embossed with human or animal figures and geometric designs.[23] This type, according to R. Maxwell-Hyslop, is a development of the earlier crescented axe which originated in Mesopotamia and was also known in Palestine and Syria in the Early Bronze Age (see Fig. 11:1-3). It is noteworthy that the developed window axe is also found as an import in the Aegean on the Anatolian coast near Smyrna and at Vapphio in the Greek Peloponnesus.[24]

Another achievement of Syrian metallurgy is in daggers and swords.[25] The Babylonian smiths developed a dagger with a low midrib and a short tang with holes for rivets. This type of weapon was known all over the Near East by the beginning of the Second

21. Schaeffer, *Ugaritica*, 2, 67 ff., 119 ff. See also C. Hawkes, "Gold Ear-rings of the Bronze Age, East and West," *Folklore*, 72 (1961), 438–74.

22. See R. Maxwell-Hyslop, "Western Asiatic Shaft-Hole Axes," *Iraq*, 11 (1947), 90–130.

23. Dunand, *Fouilles*, 2, Pls. CXIX–CXXI, CXXXII–CXXXV.

24. Maxwell-Hyslop, *Iraq*, 11 (1947), 119 f.

25. Maxwell-Hyslop, "Daggers and Swords in Western Asia," *Iraq*, 8 (1944), 1–65, Pls. I–VI.

Millennium. It was improved in two ways in Syria and Palestine. First, as a dagger, the blade was widened and made with numerous ribs, and the tang was made long and narrow and secured at the end of the handle to a limestone or ivory pommel (see

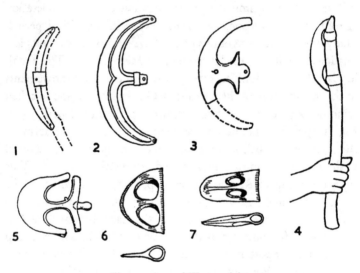

*Fig. 11*   Axes of Western Asia

Fig. 12:1).[26] This weapon is characteristic of MB II in Syria-Palestine and is also known in the Bronze Age in Europe. The second improvement on the earlier Mesopotamian weapon is the development of the sword (see Fig. 12:2).[27] This was done by lengthening the blade and strengthening the midrib. These tech-

26. Type 25: ibid., p. 26.
27. Type 26: ibid., p. 27.

nical advances were due to the skillful use of the closed mold
found in Syria-Palestine in this period.

Another type of sword was developed, distinguishable in the
treatment of the hilt (see Fig. 13).[28] Instead of a long narrow
tang which was inserted into a wooden handle and secured by
rivets, the tang was now cast in such a way that it formed the

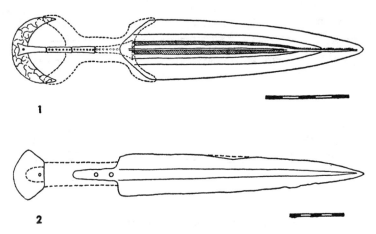

*Fig. 12*   Daggers of Western Asia

full outline of the hilt, and the edge of the tang was flanged so
as to contain a wooden or bone inlay. The inlay was secured by
rivets. In some cases the tang, in fact, became the hilt. This last
type can be seen in the Saqqara dagger with the name of Apophis
on the hilt.[29] This type of sword is found in MB II B–C from
Alalakh to Tell el-Ajjul. A number of transitional examples between the two types of swords may also be seen from Byblos.
Both kinds seem to have inspired the development of swords in
the Aegean—the first type in Crete, the second on the Greek
mainland.[30]

28. Types 31 and 33: ibid., pp. 33 ff.
29. Labib, *Die Herrschaft der Hyksos*, p. 28.
30. N. K. Sandars, "The First Aegean Swords and their Ancestry," *AJA, 65*

Another important weapon of the MB II period is the so-called
scimitar, the Egyptian ḫpš (see Fig. 14).[31] This weapon resembles
a sickle, except that the cutting edge is on the outside—not on
the inside. The scimitar is well known from Mesopotamia, particularly in iconography, in the Old Babylonian period. It is
often seen in the hands of a god or king and is generally inter-

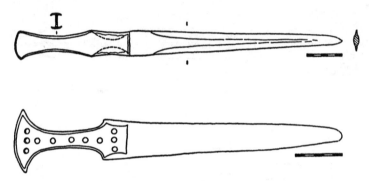

*Fig. 13*  Swords of Western Asia

preted as the symbol of might and victory (much the same as
the mace). This weapon is likewise found in Syria-Palestine,
where it seems to retain its symbolic character. It is entirely
appropriate that a scimitar should be found in a royal tomb of
Byblos and ornamented with the king's name and an Egyptian
uraeus serpent.[32] It is likely that this symbolic weapon was introduced into Egypt during the Hyksos period and became an
important element in the iconography of gods and kings in the

(1961), 17–29. See also F. H. Stubbings, "The Rise of Mycenaean Civilization,"
*CAH²*, 2, ch. 14, pp. 9 ff., who suggests that the parallels from the shaft graves
indicate the Hyksos came to the Greek mainland when they were expelled from
Egypt. This is extremely unlikely, and the archaeological evidence may be accounted for entirely on the basis of trade between Syria, Egypt, and the Aegean
so much in evidence in the MB II period.

31. Type 34: Maxwell-Hyslop, *Iraq, 8* (1944), 41.

32. Montet, *Byblos et l'Egypte,* 174 ff. See also ibid., 178 f., for references
to this weapon in the story of Sinuhe.

New Kingdom. Its connection with the Hyksos may be seen in one of the prenomina of Apophis, namely, *nb-ḫpš-rˁ*.

The Syrian metallurgists of MB II often give evidence of advanced technique. Besides the use of the closed mold, there are also examples of the technique known as metal-polychromy, or niello.[33] A bronze scimitar found in a royal tomb of Byblos has

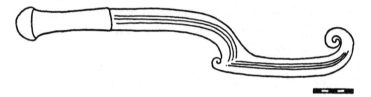

*Fig. 14*   The "Sickle-sword"

a raised midrib on which an Egyptian uraeus and a hieroglyphic inscription are inlaid with gold and silver wire on a blackened background. The motives are Egyptian, but the workmanship is certainly Syrian. The earliest example from Egypt is an early Eighteenth Dynasty dagger of Ahmose.[34] Among the finest examples of niello in the ancient world are those on the daggers and swords of the shaft tombs of Mycenae dated to the sixteenth century. N. K. Sandars has shown that the styles of weapons in these graves are ultimately derived from Syria.[35] He also states, "the 'Royal Tombs' of Byblos . . . with their stock of gold and silver vessels, sceptre and dagger mounts, jewelry and niello work, foreshadow to a startling degree the shaft-graves of Mycenae." [36] Consequently, in the matter of niello technique as in other areas of metallurgy, the Aegean world seems to have learned from the Syrian craftsmen.

33. See H. Frankfort, *Art and Architecture of the Ancient Orient* (Baltimore, 1954), p. 137.

34. W. S. Smith, *The Art and Architecture of Ancient Egypt*, Pl. 84 b. See also axehead, ibid., Pl. 86

35. Sandars, *AJA*, 65 (1961), 18 ff.

36. Ibid., p. 21.

## EGYPTIAN CRAFTS IN SYRIA-PALESTINE

Many of the crafts developed in Syria-Palestine in the MB II
B–C period exhibit a close relationship to Egypt. The most obvious, of course, is the scarab which, however, will be discussed
with the art of the period. Less conspicuous are such items as
furniture, alabaster vases, and faience objects. These give some
indication of the cultural exchange and commercial intercourse
between Egypt and the Levant as it affected the more normal
course of everyday life.

It goes without saying that very little furniture has escaped
deterioration from the MB II B–C period in Palestine. Nevertheless, in some of the tombs of this period at Jericho, a number of
wooden objects have been sufficiently preserved to indicate their
form and manner of construction.[37] These objects consisted primarily of tables, stools, toilet boxes, and wooden platters. The
workmanship was of a high order; the forms and construction
methods were similar to those of Egypt. Furthermore, the toilet
boxes were overlaid with bone inlays much as in the Egyptian
fashion. Such inlays are very common in this period and are
found in graves at other sites. They are the only remaining hint
of furniture—the wood has completely disintegrated.

Egypt had a venerable trade in alabaster vases, and many of
them found their way into Syria and Palestine from the time
of the Old Kingdom on. In the MB II B–C period, however,
they are very numerous everywhere in Palestine. There is also
evidence that during this period a local alabaster industry was
established in Palestine.[38] This industry seems to have centered
in Beth Shan and possibly also in Jericho. The local industry,
while it drew much of its inspiration from Egyptian models,
developed new techniques for carving the inside of the jars
that were quite different from those of Egypt.[39] New Pal-

37. Kenyon, *Jericho, 1*, pp. 527 ff.
38. I. Ben-Dor, "Palestinian Alabaster Vases," *QDAP, 11* (1944), 93–112.
39. Ibid., p. 102. Ben-Dor notes that the Egyptian method was to make a

estinian forms were introduced along with those of Egyptian origin. The industry does not seem to have outlasted the MB II B–C period.

During the MB II B–C period, glazed stone and faience objects, vessels, jewelry, and animal figurines, are common throughout Syria and Palestine.[40] Like the alabaster, it is probable that some of the faience jars were made locally. Palestinian shapes are sometimes found. Furthermore, scarabs of local manufacture were usually made of glazed stone rather than from gems. Nevertheless, most of the faience objects are characteristic of types and designs known from Egypt, particularly Kerma in Nubia.[41] There was undoubtedly an active trade of this luxury ware between Egypt and the Levant in the period.[42] It is likewise clear from these crafts that Egyptian culture was accessible to its Asiatic neighbors and provided a great stimulus to the MB II civilization of Syria-Palestine.

## ART

### Scarabs

One of the most dominant characteristics of the MB II B–C period is the great quantities of scarabs that begin to appear in strata in Palestine and, to a lesser extent, in coastal Syria.[43] They are a valuable index of contact between Asia and Egypt in the Second Intermediate Period. A discussion of these objects is, however, greatly handicapped by the large degree of uncertainty among scholars about their development.[44] It is clear that the

---

straight bore into the vessel, whereas the Palestinian method was to carve out the inside of the vessel following the outer contours of the pot.

40. Albright, *Tell Beit Mirsim*, Part 1, pp. 29 ff. See O. Tufnell, *Lachish IV*, p. 83 and Pl. 26:12–17 (12 is Palestinian; the rest are Egyptian).

41. Reisner, *Kerma IV–V*, 2, 134 ff.

42. Kantor, in *Relative Chronologies*, p. 13.

43. For a general treatment see H. Stock, *Studien*. Also O. Tufnell, *Lachish IV*, pp. 92–126.

44. On the use and development of the scarab see P. E. Newberry, *Scarabs* (London, 1906), pp. 12 ff.

scarab, or sacred beetle, developed from the combination of a stamp seal with a scarab amulet. There is evidence of development in the early Middle Kingdom, although at that time the scarab was still quite rare.[45] Their widespread use as charms cannot be dated much earlier than the end of the Twelfth Dynasty. Large cemeteries at Dendereh, Hu, and Beni Hasan with hundreds of graves of the Eleventh and early Twelfth Dynasties do not contain a single scarab.[46] Another indication of a late date for the rise of scarabs is the fact that there are numerous scarabs containing titles of important officials.[47] This seems to reflect the centralization of administration carried out by Senwosret III.[48]

This conclusion with regard to the dating of scarabs is essential for a consideration of the royal scarabs of the Twelfth Dynasty. Scarabs with the names of Twelfth Dynasty pharaohs on them were not always contemporary with these kings; they were made mostly in the Second Intermediate Period, solely for amuletic purposes. The only exceptions may have been in the case of the last two or three pharaohs of the Twelfth Dynasty, but even this is doubtful.[49] The scarabs of the Twelfth Dynasty pharaohs found in Palestine, therefore, do not reflect contact between the two regions in the Middle Kingdom but only in the Second Intermediate Period.

Our present concern is primarily with the artistic motives em-

45. H. E. Winlock, *Excavations at Dier el-Bahri, 1911–1931* (New York, 1942), Pl. 30.

46. Newberry, *Scarabs,* pp. 66 ff. Consequently the cemetery investigated by Brunton at Hu and dated to the Twelfth Dynasty on the basis of typology must be late in this period or the Second Intermediate Period.

47. See W. M. F. Petrie, *Scarabs and Cylinders with Names* (London, 1917), Pls. XIV–XVII. G. B. Fraser, *A Catalogue of Scarabs* (London, 1900), pp. 11 ff. Newberry, *Scarabs,* pp. 125 ff., Pls. XI–XVII.

48. On this administrative development see below, Chapter 7.

49. See Stock, *Studien,* pp. 17 f. Cf. R. Weill, *XII° Dynastie, royauté de Haute-Egypte et domination Hyksos dans le nord.* Weill's attempt to date all royal scarabs to the time of the king named on the scarab has led him to absurd conclusions.

ployed on scarabs of this period. Very characteristic are the patterns made of spirals, guilloches, concentric circles, rope, and other geometric designs (see Fig. 15). The source of inspiration for these designs is generally considered to be the Middle Minoan

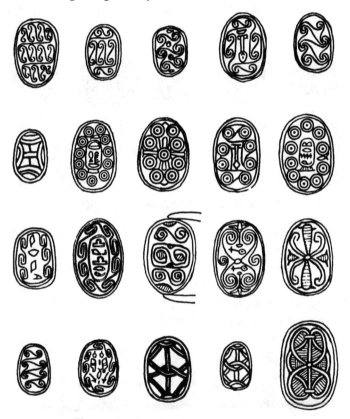

*Fig. 15* Scarabs with geometric patterns

culture of the Aegean; use by the Egyptians may be explained by their contact with Minoan culture through the intermediary Syrian ports such as Byblos.[50] These motives were frequently

50. H. J. Kantor, "The Aegean and the Orient in the Second Millennium B.C.," *AJA, 51* (1947), 17 ff.

used as decorative designs in the Old Babylonian period, as can
be seen by their use in the Palace of Zimri-Lim in Mari.[51]

Another feature characteristic of scarabs of this period is the use
of hieroglyphs as good-luck signs. The signs were usually associated with royalty, "life," "health," or "prosperity," used in
symmetric patterns or as fillers with names or figures (see Fig. 16).

*Fig. 16* Scarabs with royal and goodluck signs

This use of "lucky" hieroglyphs is probably Egyptian in origin,
but it was certainly taken over by Asiatics. The Asiatics also
developed the so-called *anra* scarabs (see Fig. 17), which made
use of three hieroglyphs with the value ‹ , *n*, and *r*. Margaret
Murray has attempted to interpret these in terms of a wish
formula for the protection of one's name.[52]

*Fig. 17* Scarabs with *anra* signs

A large number of scarabs of this period have human or animal
figures. There is a mixture in these of Egyptian and Asiatic

51. Parrot, *MAM, Le Palais*, part 2, pp. 1 ff.
52. M. A. Murray, "Some Canaanite Scarabs," *PEQ* (1949), 95.

elements; they are a typical product of the MB II B–C period in Syria-Palestine. It is also possible to see a development from purely Asiatic themes to Egyptian ones.[53] For instance, there are a number of scarabs in which human figures are associated with a palm tree or a lotus blossom. One person may be holding a branch or flower, or two people may be grouped antithetically about the plant, in a kneeling or standing position. These motives have a long history in Syrian and Mesopotamian iconography. However, on the scarabs the person often becomes a falcon-headed deity, and the palm branch or flower, an uraeus serpent (see Fig. 18).

*Fig. 18* Scarabs with human figures

Although most figures seem to be dressed in a short skirt, O. Tufnell has examined a number of scarabs in which the figures are wrapped in an elaborate robe, leaving only one shoulder and one arm free (see Fig. 19).[54] The robe may be represented as made of striped material, or it may be plain with a heavy border. This type of robe is entirely foreign to Egypt, but it is quite characteristic of Syria, as may be seen from the glyptic. The striped variety is also known from the illustrations of Asiatics in the Beni Hasan tomb of Khnemhotep II from the time of Senwosret II (1897–1877 B.C.). It is likely that these figures on the seals are intended to represent royalty in the Second Intermediate Period in Palestine.

A large number of scarabs of this period have figures of animals on them (see Fig. 20). They are of a high quality of workman-

---

53. Ibid., pp. 92 ff., Pls. IX–XI.

54. O. Tufnell, "'Hyksos' Scarabs from Canaan," *Anatolian Studies*, 6 (1956), 67–73.

ship; the outlines are clearly cut, and the bodies are filled in with hatching. Their style is not Egyptian, but Palestinian, in origin. It may be surprising, therefore, to find the crocodile displayed on so many of them. However, the Egyptian crocodile god, Sobek, was

*Fig. 19*   Scarab with a Syrian Prince

honored in the region of Khataᶜna (Avaris) since the Thirteenth Dynasty,[55] and the diffusion of this motif may have stemmed from this area. Other animals which are common on scarabs are lions and heraldic beasts. The sphinx, obviously inspired by Egyptian models, was well known from royal objects given to Syrian princes by the pharaohs of the Middle Kingdom. Lions and griffins are common in Syrian glyptic iconography,[56] so that their place on scarabs is not surprising. Another favorite theme on scarabs is the hunt. This may be represented by a deer or a gazelle on the run, or it may be illustrated by wild game being attacked by a lion, often including a hunter with a weapon. This theme occurs in a similar manner on the dagger of Apophis found at Saqqara.[57]

*Fig. 20*   Scarabs with animals

55. On the identity of this region with Avaris, see Chapter 9.
56. H. Frankfort, *Cylinder Seals* (London, 1939), pp. 268 ff.
57. See below, Chapter 10.

## Cylinder Seals

A word must be said about Syrian cylinder seals, for they are an important expression of the art of this period.[58] The publication of the seals and seal impressions of Alalakh has gone far to clarify a number of problems with respect to the Syrian style of cylinder seals. It now appears that this style runs parallel in its development to Alalakh VII, although it begins in VIII—a few years before Hammurapi—throughout most of the MB II period.[59] This style is clearly based on the Mesopotamian traditions of cutting and of glyptic iconography. In fact, in excellence of execution, concern for detail, and molding of figures, as well as in iconography, North Syria and Mari stand together and give evidence of a high quality in Amurrite seal carving.[60] Nevertheless, Syrian seal cutters seem to have experimented more with new elements derived from other sources. They introduced Egyptian motives, such as hieroglyphs or falcon-headed deities, or Aegean themes, such as the guilloche, acrobatic figures fighting and bull-leaping, or animals in "flying gallop." [61] This style undoubtedly had its primary center in North Syria, probably the kingdom of Yamkhad. However, other examples of this glyptic style have been found in Syria-Palestine at Ugarit, Byblos, and Megiddo. In Palestine, a more local style also rendered the figures in mere outline, a technique common to scarabs.[62]

58. See Frankfort, *Cylinder Seals*, pp. 252 ff. See also B. Parker, "Cylinder Seals from Palestine," *Iraq, 11* (1949), 1–42, especially Pls. II–III. On the recent debate regarding Syrian style, see H. Kantor, "Syro-Palestinian Ivories," *JNES, 15* (1956), 153 ff.; E. Porada, "Syrian Seal Impressions on Tablets Dated in the Time of Hammurabi and Samsu-iluna," *JNES, 16* (1957), 192 f.; B. Buchanan, "On the Seal Impressions on Some Old Babylonian Tablets," *JCS, 11* (1957), 47 ff., 74 ff.; W. Nagel and E. Strommenger, "Alalaḫ und Siegelkunst," *JCS, 12* (1958), 109–23.

59. Buchanan, *JCS, 11* (1957), 50.

60. See P. Amiet, "Notes sur le répertoire iconographique de Mari à l'époque du Palais," *Syria, 37* (1960), 215–32.

61. On the Aegean elements see Kantor, *AJA, 51* (1947), 62 f.

62. See Parker, *Iraq, 11* (1949), Pl. III. Dunand, *Fouilles, 2*, Pl. CXXIV, no. 2497.

The importance of Syrian glyptic in showing the development of Syrian art has been emphasized by Helene Kantor:

> The glyptic from Alalakh VII can now be added to the other evidence which supports the view that Canaanite art, as a clearly recognizable and coherent school of craftsmanship, came into being in the final stage of the Middle Bronze period, the phase contemporary with the Second Intermediate Period of Egypt.[63]

If we accept this statement by Kantor—and the other evidence we have examined thus far indicates that we should—we are left with the problem of accounting for a very strange fact: the rapid decline of this excellent style of Syrian glyptic. It has long been supposed, on the basis of Frankfort's work, that the Syrian style lasted almost to the end of the Late Bronze Age. On the basis of seals from Alalakh, however, the style does not outlive level VII or MB II B–C, as Buchanan recently pointed out.[64] After level VII there is a rapid degeneration. The motives are vaguely retained, but the workmanship is quite inferior. The true Syrian style, when it occurs in later archaeological contexts, must be regarded as the late reuse of earlier seals—a practice very common with royal seals in level IV period.[65]

The inferior style which becomes apparent in levels VI–V and continues almost to the end of Alalakh is generally classified as Mitannian. This designation gives the clue to the causes of the decline of Syrian glyptic. The center of this art was Northern Syria around Aleppo or Alalakh. At the time when the Kingdom of Yamkhad was overthrown by the Hittites (the end of Alalakh VII), Northern Syria was caught in the Hurrian–Indo-Aryan movement which resulted eventually in the rise of the Mitanni kingdom. The accompanying cultural upheaval in Northern Syria is evident in the glyptic style. There is an effort to retain a con-

63. Kantor, *JNES, 15* (1956), 160 n.
64. Buchanan, *JCS, 11* (1957), 50 ff.
65. Ibid.

tinuity with the past, a fact also apparent by the reuse of old seals, but the obviously accomplished style of the earlier period is gone.

This decline in glyptic art is evident, likewise, in coastal Syria and Palestine in the Late Bronze Age, since the dissemination of glyptic style was from Northern Syria, now under Mitannian (or Hurrian) control. In other areas of art, however, coastal Syria and Palestine maintained a continuity with the previous period; Kantor's statement is amply justified. The development in ivory carving and the brilliant metal work attest to the great artistic inheritance from the MB II B–C period of which Syrian glyptic gave evidence. In the later context of Syria-Palestinian art, moreover, the Mitannian seals are foreign and inferior to other areas of art. Consequently it is the so-called Canaanite culture which became heir to the Amurrite civilization of Syria-Palestine in the MB II period,[66] while Northern Syria and Upper Mesopotamia came under the shadow of the Mitannian culture. To be sure, Hurrians and Indo-Aryans did find their way into Palestine by the time of Thutmose III and had some political importance

66. A brief statement on terminology is necessary. It is difficult to arrive at an acceptable designation for the population of Phoenicia-Palestine in the MB II period. It is clear, by their names, that they belong to the Northwest Semitic family of peoples, for which the designation "Amurrite" is now most commonly used. The term "Canaanite," favored by Albright (in *BANE*, pp. 335 f.), is anachronistic before the Late Bronze Age. Furthermore, the earliest occurrence, in the *Biography of Idrimi* (lines 19 f.), indicates a rather restricted area, probably only a part of the Syrian coast. Later the term "Canaanite" came to include a large part of Palestine also, probably due to the fact that the coastal dialect spread southward through active trade relations and cultural contact. These developments of the Late Bronze Age, particularly the dialectical differences of "Canaanite" from "Amurrite" (A. Goetze, "Is Ugaritic a Canaanite Dialect?" *Language, 17* [1941], 134–37), should not be allowed to obscure the obvious cultural and ethnic continuity between the later "Canaanites" and the Amurrites of the Old Babylonian period. This is clearly evident at Ugarit, whose language stands linguistically closer to Amurrite but culturally closer to Phoenicia-Palestine. Perhaps the best term to use in order to describe the whole cultural continuum in Phoenicia-Palestine in the Middle and Late Bronze Ages is the double term "Amurrite-Canaanite." Nevertheless, I regard "Canaanite" as essentially a subcategory, both in time and in locality, of the whole Amurrite civilization.

in the Amarna Age. But the real migration was spent before it
reached Palestine. Their effect on its culture was much more
limited than it had been in Northern Syria at the end of MB II.[67]

## Ivories

The MB II B–C period marks the beginning in Syria-Palestine
of a long tradition of bone and ivory carving. Many of the bone
inlays are of simple geometric patterns and stylized birds; they
have little value as showing the art of the period. At Tell Beit
Mirsim, however, there are two pieces of a bone inlay in which
the outlines of a pair of graceful deer are represented in "flying
gallop." [68] Kantor has discussed the "flying gallop," which is quite
un-Egyptian according to the canons of the Old and Middle
Kingdoms, and points to Crete as the source of its inspiration.[69]
The style became common in the Levant and Egypt in the Late
Bronze Age, but its beginning in Syria-Palestine is definitely
dated to the MB II B–C period.

From a tomb at El-Jisr in Palestine comes a collection of ivory
fragments which were part of a complex inlay.[70] Although the
state of the inlay was too fragmentary to reconstruct the scene, the
composition obviously contained human figures, animals such as
lions, horses, oxen, and birds. The human figures show a mixture
of influence. The costume of the men is Egyptian, but the women
are dressed in Asiatic style. Although the ivories of this period are
few in number, they indicate the same mixing of artistic traditions
in their compositions.

## Metal Work

Kantor's designation of the art of this period as a *Mischkunst* [71]
also applies to the ornamentation of metalwork.[72] In this connec-

67. The Hurrian problem is dealt with below, Chapter 13.
68. Albright, *Tell Beit Mirsim*, Part 2, p. 51 n., Pl. 34.
69. Kantor, *AJA*, *51* (1947), 62 f.
70. J. Ory, *QDAP*, *12* (1946), 42. See also Kantor, *JNES*, *15* (1956), 153.
71. Kantor *JNES*, *15* (1956).
72. Frankfort, *Art and Architecture*, pp. 137 ff.

tion we should remember the niello work on a scimitar found in a royal tomb in Byblos. There the motives in rendering an uraeus serpent and the rather crude hieroglyphs which formed the name of the local prince were entirely Egyptian. From the Temple of Obelisks, on the other hand, comes a different method of ornamentation, that of embossed and engraved work on sheet gold. A fine example of this is a dagger with a beautifully embossed hilt and sheath.[73] On one side of the hilt is a figure done in Egyptian style with short skirt and a crown resembling the "White Crown" of Egypt. On the other side of the hilt are two antelope standing on their hind legs, back-to-back, but with their heads turned and facing each other. This is certainly an Asiatic motif and is common on Syrian glyptic. Above the two antelope is a third in a more natural pose, grazing. The design on the sheath is also a mixture. There are Egyptian motives, such as the boy with the baboon, the wild dog, and the fish; the two men are also dressed in Egyptian style. But the theme of the lion, antelope, and hunter, as well as the man on a donkey carrying a scimitar, are Asiatic. On some of the other embossed work found in the Temple of Obelisks, executed in a rather granular fashion, are motives familiar from Mesopotamian iconography, for instance, the confrontation scene of a king before a seated deity and the "bull men." [74]

Also important for a consideration of art in the Hyksos period is the dagger found in a tomb at Saqqara with the name of Apophis on it. The style of the hieroglyphs and the raised figures on a black background is similar to the niello work on the scimitar in the royal tomb of Byblos. The sword type is Asiatic, and Frankfort describes the design as "of Syrian workmanship." [75] A hunting scene with a man in an energetic pose attacking a lion is on part of the hilt. He is dressed in a short Egyptian skirt but

73. Dunand, *Fouilles*, 2, Pl. CXVIII. See also Frankfort, *Art and Architecture*.
74. Dunand, *Fouilles*, 2, Pl. CXXXII.
75. Frankfort, *Art and Architecture*, pp. 138 f.

has Asiatic armlets, a torque, and bands with discs crisscrossing his chest. The two animals, a lion and a gazelle, are also portrayed in "flying gallop." In many ways this piece sums up the technical achievements, the artistic eclecticism, and the political and economic interdependence common to Syria-Palestine and Hyksos Egypt in the MB II B–C period.

# CHAPTER 5

# EGYPT'S RELATIONS WITH ASIA IN MIDDLE BRONZE II A

The cultural homogeneity and general prosperity of MB II in Syria-Palestine is freely acknowledged by Palestinian archaeologists. An interpretation of this period in terms of the general history of the Near East has, however, been largely neglected. A number of Egyptian monuments and texts of the Middle Kingdom and cuneiform texts of Mari shed some light on the place of MB II A in the Amurrite civilization of Syria-Mesopotamia and the relations between MB II A and Egypt, its most influential neighbor. We must begin with these historical sources, for they hold the key to understanding the second phase, MB II B–C, the phase largely contemporary with the Second Intermediate Period.

In the course of excavations in Syria and Palestine, a number of small Egyptian statuettes and other objects of the Middle Kingdom of a royal or official character have come to light.[1] The more important of these may be listed chronologically. At Ugarit, a bead, undoubtedly part of a necklace, was found inscribed with the name of Senwosret I and dedicated to Hathor. From the middle period of Amenemhet II and Senwosret II comes a sphinx of an Egyptian princess from Qatna and statuettes of an Egyptian queen and a vizier from Ugarit. There are, as

1. These monuments are all listed and discussed by W. A. Ward, "Egypt and the East Mediterranean in the Early Second Millennium B.C.," *Orientalia, 30* (1961), 22–45, 120–55. Also Helck, *Beziehungen*, pp. 69–71. C. F. A. Schaeffer, *Ugaritica, 4,* 212 ff. G. Posener, "Syria and Palestine c. 2160–1780 B.C.," *CAH²,* *1,* ch. 21, pp. 8–21.

yet, no royal monuments from the time of Senwosret III, but there is, from this period, an important private statue of Djehuty-hotep from Megiddo. Two sphinxes of Amenemhet III come from the Baal temple of Ugarit, and another of this king comes from Neirab near Aleppo. A sphinx of Amenemhet IV was found at Beirut. In the royal tombs of Byblos were found pendants, pectorals, stone vessels, and other small objects identified with the cartouches of Amenemhet III and IV as the gifts of these pharaohs to contemporary Byblian princes.

A number of additional private monuments which may be ascribed to the MB II A period have been found in Syria and Palestine and even as far as Anatolia and Crete. Their style is Middle Kingdom, but this attribution would fit equally well for the Second Intermediate Period. With this uncertainty in dating, any statement of their significance must be made with the greatest caution. It is fairly safe to assert that the royal or official monuments were gifts made to leading Syrian princes or their temples; yet, on the other hand, the intention of these objects remains a matter of debate. Some scholars have taken them to be indications of an Egyptian empire in Asia. By themselves they cannot bear the weight of such an interpretation. One need only compare the evidence from Nubia,[2] where large and numerous military installations and accompanying stelae make it quite clear that Egypt conquered and held the Nile valley at least to the second cataract and probably dominated Nubia as far as Kerma below the third cataract. Such clear evidence of political domination has not been found in Asia.

The inscribed objects, however, even the private ones, cannot be interpreted as indicating the presence of Egyptian merchants in Syria on personal business, at least not in the Middle Kingdom.[3] H. Kees states that Egyptian trade abroad was a royal monopoly.[4] He points out that foreign expeditions from Egypt

2. Säve-Söderbergh, *Ägypten und Nubien* (Lund, 1941), pp. 63–116.
3. See Ward, *Orientalia, 30* (1961), 134.
4. H. Kees, *Ancient Egypt, A Cultural Topography* (Chicago, 1961), p. 139.

were always accompanied by a "god's treasurer," and that the navy and seagoing ships were under the command of the pharaoh. Nothing exists in Egyptian sources, whether biographical inscriptions or account records, to suggest in any way the type of commercial activity characteristic of Old Babylonia, with its private banking houses and seagoing merchants.[5] On the contrary, all the records reflect a connection with the royal administration.[6]

The presence of these Egyptian monuments in Syria and Palestine may be explained quite adequately on the basis of clues from the Middle Kingdom literature, of which the most important is the *Story of Sinuhe*.[7] This story offers two reasons for Egyptians being in Asia. The first is exile, which is the case for Sinuhe himself. It is, of course, obvious that if Syria and Palestine were under the direct political control of Egypt, such open exile would be impossible. W. A. Ward has proposed that an exile was also the fate of Djehuty-hotep, whose statue was found at Megiddo.[8] He was the last hereditary nomarch of his nome and, like many of his contemporaries, lived to witness the administrative reform of Senwosret III, whereby the government was thoroughly centralized and the power of the old nobility ended. Thus he may have had a good motive for exile. Nevertheless, contrary to Ward, there is no reason to think that Djehuty-hotep was not buried in his tomb at El Bersheh, and the notion of an exile remains doubtful.[9]

5. See A. L. Oppenheim, "Sea-faring Merchants of Ur," *JAOS*, 74 (1954), 6–17. W. F. Leemans, *The Old Babylonian Merchant* (Leiden, 1950); *Foreign Trade in the Old Babylonian Period* (Leiden, 1960).

6. Examples of official accounts in the late Middle Kingdom are the Illahun Papyri and P. Boulaq 18.

7. See A. H. Gardiner, *Notes on the Story of Sinuhe* (Paris, 1916). G. Posener, *Littérature et politique dans l'Egypte de la XII* dynastie* (Paris, 1956), pp. 108 ff; *CAH²*, *1*, ch. 21, pp. 25 ff.

8. Ward, *Orientalia*, *30* (1961), 40 f. Cf. J. A. Wilson, "The Egyptian Middle Kingdom at Megiddo," *AJSL*, *58* (1941), 231.

9. Ward has misread the passage he cites (P. E. Newberry, *El Bersheh* [London, 1898], *1*, 8), which states that the *father* of Djehuty-hotep was not buried at El Bersheh.

The other reason given in *Sinuhe* for Egyptians being in Asia is that they were official envoys of the Residence.[10] There is, indeed, much in Middle Kingdom literature and inscriptions about royal envoys.[11] A great deal is known about diplomacy in the early second millennium from the Mari archives,[12] and the evidence would suggest that Egypt also sent diplomatic missions abroad. Egypt's primary interest in Asia was in raw products as well as the trade, through Syrian ports, of luxury goods from the Aegean and the East.[13] Egyptian diplomacy was directed toward exploiting and safeguarding these interests. In this respect both the vizier, Senusert-ankh, whose statuette was found at Ugarit, and Djehuty-hotep may have acted as envoys to the courts of important commercial cities. It is hardly likely that they were resident governors of these places; nothing in their titles would indicate this.[14]

Egyptian diplomacy took two forms. The first was the proffering of gifts to local rulers or their temples. The *Story of Sinuhe* indicates that such gifts were expressions of friendship on the part of the pharaoh to Asian rulers.[15] The Tod treasure, which was very likely from Byblos, shows that these diplomatic gestures went in both directions.[16] Such an explanation seems

10. *Sinuhe*, lines B 95 f., 173–77, 200 f., 238 f.

11. *Satire on Trades*, VII:7 ff., in *ANET*, p. 433b; A. Rowe, "Three New Stelae from the South-Eastern Desert," *Ann Serv*, *39* (1939), 189 f. See also Posener, *Littérature et politique*, p. 109.

12. J. M. Munn-Rankin, "Diplomacy in Western Asia in the Early Second Millennium B.C.," *Iraq*, *18* (1956), 68–110.

13. Kees, *Ancient Egypt*, pp. 135 ff. Helck, *Beziehungen*, pp. 72–78.

14. Senusert-ankh was given the "Gold of Honor" and Djehuty-hotep bore the title, among others, of "Door of Every Foreign Country," both of which might suggest some foreign service on behalf of the king. However, Albright's suggestion (*BASOR*, *168* [1962], 39) that Djehuty-hotep was a resident commissioner in an Egyptian fortress in Megiddo must be considered as doubtful. There is no archaeological evidence, whatever, of such a fortress.

15. *Sinuhe*, lines B 175 f., 244 f.

16. R. Bisson de la Roque, G. Contenau, and F. Chapouthier, *Le trésor de Tod*, IFAOC, Documents de Fouilles, 11 (Cairo, 1953).

quite adequate, and there is no need to seek a more speculative one.

Another method of diplomacy was propaganda, and in this the Middle Kingdom excelled.[17] One might mention the passages in *Sinuhe* which heap praise on Senwosret I as the one who can effectively subdue the seminomadic "bowman." These warlike tribal groups were as much a threat to peaceful Asiatic caravan activity as they were to the Egyptian frontier, and any action against them was probably welcomed by the more settled peoples of Syria-Palestine. It is likely that the reputation of Senwosret I was based on actual military activity carried on by Nesumontu, in the coregency of Amenemhet I and Senwosret I.[18]

Egypt's interest was, for the most part, restricted to Phoenicia, the hinterland of Lebanon, and Palestine. This area forms a close unity throughout most of the MB II period. Contact was made beyond this region with the two Amurrite kingdoms in the interior of Syria, Aleppo, and Qatna, as proven by the royal gifts from the pharaohs. The reason for such contact must be seen in the fact that Aleppo and Qatna were vital centers for the caravan trade between Mari and Egypt, via the coastal ports of Syria. In this respect the Mari documents are instructive as to Syria's position in the economy of the Amurrite world at the end of the Middle Kingdom.[19] Syria was an important exporter of many of its natural and agricultural products to Mesopotamia; it was a waystation for copper from Cyprus and luxury goods from Crete. In return it received such valuable commodities as tin and lapis lazuli. Mari dealt directly with Aleppo and Qatna, which, in turn, had strong connections with the coastal ports of Ugarit and Byblos. Palestine also had some contact with Mari through its principal city, Hazor. Generally, however, coastal Syria is

17. See Posener, *Littérature et politique*, passim.

18. Breasted, *Anc Rec, 1*, 227 f.

19. J. R. Kupper, "Northern Mesopotamia and Syria," *CAH²*, 2, ch. 1, pp. 14 ff., 20 ff.

rarely mentioned in the Mari documents, and Egypt, as may be expected, it not mentioned at all.

Very important for the understanding of MB II are the Execration texts from Egypt. These are of two kinds: inscribed on bowls, known as the Berlin texts; [20] and inscribed on figurines, known as the Brussels text.[21] Their dating is an initial difficulty in considering these texts. An early date for the texts is defended by Albright,[22] who dates the Berlin texts to 1925–1875 B.C. and the Brussels texts to ca. 1825 B.C. His first reason for dating them early is based on his identification of the Asiatics (*'Aamu*) of the texts with the seminomadic society of MB I in Palestine. His dating for this period is, however, too low, as I have mentioned above; MB I had certainly ended by the time of the texts. The second reason for Albright's early date is based on the orthographic reproduction of Semitic names in the texts into Egyptian.[23] He shows a development from the earliest Berlin texts, through the Brussels texts, to the stage represented in the slave lists of a Brooklyn papyrus published by Hayes, dated ca. 1740 B.C. Albright allows 150-200 years for this development, but there is no reason for doing so. The orthography of the place-names for instance, remains the same. The development is only to be seen in the personal names. The period of greatly increased contact with Asiatics took place in the time of Amenemhet IV, when Asiatics began to enter Egypt in large numbers. It is in this period and the early Thirteenth Dynasty that scribes had an opportunity to become familiar with Semitic names and render them bet-

---

20. K. Sethe, *Die Ächtung feindlicher Fürsten, Völker, und Dinge auf altägyptischen Tongefässscherben des mittleren Reiches* (Berlin, Akad, Abhandlungen, 5, 1926).

21. G. Posener, *Princes et pays d'Asie et de Nubie* (Brussels, 1940). See also the new set of texts found at Mirgissa in Nubia and announced by J. Vercoutter, "Deux mois de fouilles à Mirgissa en Nubie Soudanaise," *BSFE, 37–38* (1963), 28 ff.

22. W. F. Albright, "Northwest Semitic Names," *JAOS, 74* (1954), 224.

23. Ibid., pp. 224 f.

ter phonetically. Considering the closeness in orthography between the Posener texts and the names in the Brooklyn papyrus mentioned above, it is hardly possible to separate them by almost 100 years.[24] It is also fairly certain that both texts must be dated no earlier than Senwosret III (ca. 1880–1840 B.C.), and that there is only about a generation between them.[25] If orthography is a real factor, then both texts should be placed after the end of the Twelfth Dynasty, between 1790–1750, since the Brussels texts belong much less than a generation before Neferhotep (1740–1730 B.C.).

If this low date for the texts is at all likely, what situation do the Execration texts reflect? Helck has recently suggested associating the texts with Egypt's commercial activity in Asia since they indicate that the placement of the cities lay along principal caravan routes: "The Execration texts were written and broken in an accompanying magical ceremony in order to keep the caravan routes open."[26] The fact that nothing is said about trade or for-

24. Albright, ibid., indicates that the Semitic sound $R(L)$ was regularly transcribed into Egyptian in the early MK as 3, but in the NK by Egyptian $R$. In the Sethe texts, $R(L)$ appears in just 10 per cent of legible Semitic names, in the Posener texts about 31 per cent of the Semitic personal names and in the Hayes list about 44 per cent. In representing Y, W, and certain syllabic combinations, the Posener texts are also much closer to the Hayes list. Albright ("Dunand's New Byblian Volume: A Lycian at the Byblian Court," *BASOR, 155* [1959], 34), dealing with an obelisk found at Byblos, notes the orthography as being close to that of the Execration texts. However, it dates from ca. 1700, and not ca. 2000, as Albright suggests; but see his latest remarks in *BASOR, 176* (1964), 38–46.

25. W. F. Edgerton, "The Egyptian Phonetic Writing, from its Invention to the Close of the Nineteenth Dynasty," *JAOS, 60* (1940), 492 n. Posener, *Princes et pays*, pp. 31 ff. M. Noth, "Die syrisch-palästinische Bevölkerung des zweiten Jahrtausends v. Chr. im Lichte neuer Quellen," *ZDPV, 65* (1942), 20 ff. Of importance for dating are the new Mirgissa texts. According to the preliminary report (Vercoutter, *BSFE, 37–38* [1963]), both the Berlin type and the Brussels type were found in close proximity, together with a large quantity of votive objects. Are the votive objects like those in the Temple of Obelisks in Byblos? Final publication of these texts will do much to settle the question of dating all the texts.

26. Helck, *Beziehungen*, p. 63.

eign missions does little to support this proposal. The remarks against the Asiatics are bound up with those against the Nubia and, to a lesser extent, Libya, as well as conspirators within Egypt itself; the Asiatics cannot be treated as entirely different from the others. It is true that there is mention in the Mari texts of nomadic groups and their chieftains, a constant threat to the caravan trade and the settled communities.[27] The Asiatics mentioned in the Execration texts, however, are the inhabitants of cities ruled by kings, and there is no reason to regard them as nomads. By the time of Senwosret III, which corresponds to MB II A, there were city-states in Palestine. This can be seen from the fact that Djehuty-hotep was an important envoy to the court at Megiddo, and Khu-Sebek, a general of Senwosret III, carried out a campaign against the city of Shechem.[28]

It is much more likely that the Execration texts reflect a situation early in the Eighteenth century, when Palestine was the seat of many strong states whose kings and princes were in league with each other. The names of the kings in the Execration texts allows us to identify clearly the rising power in Syria-Palestine as an Amurrite urban society; confirmation of this fact may be found in the Mari texts and other sources of the period.[29] The general distribution of place-names, likewise, corresponds with the basic geographic unity of the MB II culture, Phoenicia-Palestine. These city-states of Palestine presented an increasing threat to Egyptian security, especially in a time of dynastic weakness in Egypt itself. This threat must be placed after the time of Amenemhet III and IV, an era in which there seems to have been the most active cooperation and diplomatic relations between Asia and Egypt.[30]

27. See Kupper, *CAH²*, 2, ch. 1, pp. 26 ff.

28. See *ANET*, p. 230.

29. See Kupper, *CAH²*, 2, ch. 1, pp. 23 f. I. J. Gelb, "The Early History of the West Semitic Peoples," *JCS, 15* (1961), 41.

30. This interpretation of the Execration texts is also followed by A. Alt, "Die Herkunft der Hyksos," pp. 91 ff. See also Posener, *CAH²*, *1*, ch. 21, pp. 26–29.

It is in light of the Execration texts that one must view the stela of Neferhotep in Byblos.[31] On the stela, in relief, is pictured Yantin, the prince of Byblos, doing homage to pharaoh. During the Thirteenth Dynasty, under Neferhotep and his brother Sebek-hotep, there was a brief renewal of Egyptian strength. The archaeological evidence of this period, ca. 1740–1725 B.C., representing the early phases of MB II B, shows that some of the city-states of the Palestine coastal plain suffered severe defeat at this time.[32] This would suggest that the Egyptians made punitive raids into coastal Palestine (but not inland) and did considerable damage in order to reestablish their authority. As a result, Yantin of Byblos pledged allegiance to pharaoh as a loyal vassal. This interlude of Egyptian authority was quite brief, soon to be followed by a period in which foreign domination of Egypt, supported by these kings of Syria-Palestine, was to gain the upper hand in Egypt itself.[33]

31. P. Montet, "Notes et documents pour servir à l'histoire des relations entre l'ancienne Egypte et la Syrie," *Kêmi, 1* (1928), 90 ff. Ward, *Orientalia, 30* (1961), 145.

32. This evidence was kindly drawn to my attention by G. E. Wright in a private communication dated Nov. 3, 1965. His observations are based on the detailed studies of MB II B and MB II C pottery by D. P. Cole and J. D. Seger, as yet unpublished.

33. The history of Byblos and its relations with Egypt has recently been investigated by Albright, "The Eighteenth-Century Princes of Byblos and the Chronology of Middle-Bronze," *BASOR, 176* (1964), 38–46; "Further Light on the History of Middle-Bronze Byblos," *BASOR, 179* (1965), 38–43. A number of his suggestions, however, are quite debatable. For instance, Albright's proposal that the Egyptian influence in MB II B is the result of "many upper-class refugees from Egypt [who] found refuge in Byblos from the Hyksos invaders" (*BASOR, 179* [1965], 41) is unlikely. The whole of Palestine, coastal Syria, and the foreigners of Egypt were Egyptianized. This suggestion follows from his notion of two Hyksos invasions and a great Asiatic empire of the Hyksos. Cf. von Beckerath, *Untersuchungen,* pp. 107 ff., where this notion is sufficiently refuted.

CHAPTER 6

# CONCLUSIONS TO PART I

The archaeological data of MB II are varied and complex. Yet they yield a fairly clear picture:

The MB II period must be considered as a cultural unity, with the same basic civilization lasting throughout. This applies particularly to the Syrian coast and Palestine, where there is the strongest homogeneity of culture. This unity is reflected in all aspects of the culture, and we find a clear continuity in development with no indication of any intrusion in the MB II B–C phase, such as the coming of new peoples. The fortifications, often explained as evidence of a new element in the population, can best be understood as a development of the early MB II culture.

The MB II period is characterized by a very extensive urban society in Palestine which is far advanced in every way over the seminomadic MB I culture. There is no continuity between the two periods; the break would indicate a new colonization of Palestine with an urban society from Syria in the MB II phase.

Palestine is an extension of the same basic culture that dominated Syria from the end of the third millennium B.C. and which, in turn, had the strongest ties with Mesopotamia. This is the great Amurrite civilization centered in such important kingdoms as Babylon, Mari, and Aleppo. The Levant continues to develop its basic Mesopotamian heritage in the MB II period, but with increasing influence from Egypt and the Aegean.

Palestine's relations with Egypt begin in MB II A, as attested by the royal and private monuments from Egypt found in Syria-

Palestine. These do not reflect political domination but Egypt's strong commercial interests in the Levant, which she endeavored to control by means of diplomacy. It may be that a show of force was occasionally used, but there is no evidence of imperial domination. Egyptian influence on the culture of MB II A is limited to the important commercial centers of Syria, primarily Byblos and Ugarit.

The MB II B–C phases in Palestine, on the other hand, show evidence of a great cultural borrowing from Egypt which is not previously apparent. The arts and crafts are developed along Egyptian lines more in this period than in any other, before or after. This development must mean that Palestine had greater opportunity to become acquainted with Egyptian culture after the decline of the Twelfth Dynasty. In MB II B–C, the Second Intermediate Period of Egypt, Asiatics had access to Egypt which was previously prohibited to them. Trade between Palestine and Egypt, carried on by Asiatic merchants, must have flourished in MB II B–C.

In MB II there is the development, along the Syrian coast, of strong contacts with Cyprus and the Aegean, especially in the latter part of the phase. Cypriot ware is found in abundance even in Palestine, and the Kamares ware of Crete is evident in Byblos and Ugarit. The artisans of the Syrian coast transmitted Levantine and Mesopotamian technology, especially in metallurgy, as far as the Aegean and Europe.

The cultural basis of Syria-Palestine in MB II in the pattern of city-state society was established for many centuries that followed. The traditions of monumental architecture remained constant, while the artistic eclecticism continued to the Hellenistic period. In religion, if one may judge from temple architecture, objects of the cult and continuity of holy places, the basic elements of "Amurrite-Canaanite" worship, were in evidence from the MB II period on. The first great phase of maritime activity by the coastal cities, particularly with respect to the Aegean, must be placed in the MB II period, and the contacts thus established played an important part in the subsequent history of the Levant.

Aspects of the MB II B–C cultural phase have been found in Egypt, particularly in the Delta, and may be interpreted as an establishment of certain colonies of this culture in Lower Egypt during the time of the Hyksos domination. The evidence would also indicate commercial activity by foreigners throughout Egypt and as far as Kerma in Nubia.

# PART II

# THE HYKSOS IN EGYPT

# CHAPTER 7

# ASIATICS IN EGYPT IN THE LATE MIDDLE KINGDOM

A discussion of the Hyksos in Egypt must begin with some consideration of the Asiatics in Egypt in the late Middle Kingdom, for it has a direct bearing on the manner in which the Hyksos rose to power. Here we must bear in mind the previous remarks about Egypt's relations with Syria-Palestine in this period. The status of Asiatics in Egypt seems to be a direct reflection of Egypt's foreign relations. The attitude of good will shown in the royal gifts of Amenemhet III and IV to Asiatic princes is reciprocated in the cooperation of Asiatics in the Sinai expeditions. On the other hand, the increasing number of Asiatic slaves in Egypt in the Thirteenth Dynasty may suggest the end of good relations and a period of hostility leading to the rise of the Hyksos.

## ASIATICS AND THE SINAI EXPEDITIONS

An important source of information on the status of Asiatics in Egypt in the Middle Kingdom are the *Inscriptions of Sinai*.[1] From these it is clear that in the time of Amenemhet III, in particular,[2] Asiatics were regularly used to conduct overland caravans

1. A. H. Gardiner, T. E. Peet, J. Černý, *Inscriptions of Sinai*, Part 2 (London, 1955).

2. Ibid., p. 19 J. Černý, "Semites in Egyptian Mining Expeditions to Sinai," *Archiv Orientalni, 7* (1935), 384–89; and Gardiner, "Once Again on the Proto-Sinaitic Inscriptions." *JEA, 48* (1962), 45–48. Except for no. 81, dated to Senwosret III, and no. 120, dated to Amenemhet IV, every mention of Asiatics is to the time of Amenemhet III.

from the Eastern Delta to the Sinai mines for the purpose of transporting valuable turquoise and also perhaps copper. Some of these Asiatics, 'Aamu, are spoken of as coming from *ḥꜣmy,* a place also mentioned in the Brussels Execration texts and probably in Southern Palestine. Most of the 'Aamu, however, were probably resident in Egypt employed for trade and mining expeditions.

Furthermore, the range in status of the Asiatics varies considerably. While most of the ordinary caravaneers were classed along with the slaves, *ḥmw,* a few had positions of authority and honor.[3] These latter were thoroughly Egyptianized, though their ethnic origin may still be recognized by the epithet 'Aam. The cultural contact between Asiatics and Egyptians must certainly have been more than occasional, since it was also in this period that these Semitic Asiatics attempted to write their language in Egyptian hieroglyphs, thereby creating the so-called "Proto-Sinaitic" script.[4]

Mention is likewise made, in the Sinai inscriptions of Amenemhet III, of a certain Khebded, "brother of the prince of Retjenu," and along with him are a number of the "men of Retjenu."[5] Retjenu is a geographical term used in the Middle Kingdom to designate Southern Syria and Palestine, though it is unlikely that it included the Sinai.[6] The term "brother of the prince" is a politi-

3. Helck, *Beziehungen,* p. 82. In no. 123B there is a "chief lector priest, priest and scribe, the Asiatic Werkherephemut," who is probably the leading religious figure connected with the temple of Hathor in the time of Amenemhet IV. Nos. 93, 95, and 98 mention as the leader of a number of expeditions Ameny-Soshenen, "deputy of the chief steward," who was born of an Asiatic mother.

4. This, however, is a matter of some controversy. Cf. Albright, "The early Alphabetic Inscriptions from Sinai and their Decipherment," *BASOR, 110* (1948), 6–22. See, most recently, Gardiner, *JEA, 48* (1962), 45–48; J. Leibovitch, "Deux nouvelles inscriptions protosinaïtiques," *Le Muséon, 74* (1961), 461–66; "The Date of the Proto-Sinaitic Inscriptions," *Le Muséon, 76* (1963), 201–03; Albright, ibid., pp. 203–05.

5. *Inscriptions of Sinai,* nos. 85, 87, 92, 112, and possibly also in 103 and 405. The association of this person with expeditions to Sinai seems to extend for over twenty years.

6. Gardiner, *Ancient Egyptian Onomastica* (Oxford, 1947), *1,* 142\*–49\*.

cal title used in the New Kingdom to designate certain Semitic rulers of Syria-Palestine.[7] Considering the vigorous diplomacy carried on by Amenemhet III, it seems entirely likely that he engaged the assistance of some Asiatic princes and their retainers for his expeditions, such as the Sinai expeditions. Thus Khebded's services may have been acquired in order to take charge of the caravan activity. It is more likely, however, that the Egyptians used him and his companions as desert police. This would fit the pictures of him on the stelae, where he and his retainers are shown as equipped with weapons.[8] There is also a possible parallel in the band of Asiatics with their leader pictured in the Beni Hasan tomb of Khnemhotep II, from the time of Senwosret II. This band may have served as a small trading caravan "bringing stibium from Shut" and as a police group on the northeastern frontier.[9]

It is often assumed that the "brother of the prince," Khebded, came from Sinai itself and resided there between expeditions.[10] This is highly unlikely, because Retjenu probably did not include the Sinai, and the area did not support any permanent settlement at this time. It is much more probable that Khebded came from Palestine and may even have resided in the Eastern Delta. It was from this area that the expeditions left for Sinai, and from this area the workers and other personnel were recruited.[11] A similar situation may be cited with respect to the South of Egypt. In *P. Boulaq 18* of the Thirteenth Dynasty is mention of *mdȝyw* and their chieftains (*wrw*) residing within Egypt and receiving their payment for their mercenary duty from an administrative

7. See Leibovitch, "Le problème des Hyksos et celui de l'exode," *IEJ, 3* (1953), 101 f.

8. *Inscriptions of Sinai*, nos. 112, 115, 405.

9. Helck, *Beziehungen*, p. 44.

10. Gardiner, *Onomastica, 1,* 143*.

11. Kees, "Ein Handelsplatz des MR im Nordostdelta," *MDIK, 18* (1962), 1–11.

official in Thebes.[12] The same procedure is altogether likely in the Northeast.

## ASIATICS IN EGYPT

Egypt's relations with Asia in the Middle Kingdom must also be considered in the light of the large Asiatic slave population in Egypt. Our chief sources of information on these Asiatic slaves are the Brooklyn Papyrus from Upper Egypt published by Hayes [13] and the Illahun Papyri published by Griffith.[14] There are also a number of references to Asiatic slaves on various stelae of private persons. Posener has recently collected all the relevant material in his new review of the problem.[15] His general observations may be summarized as follows: The references to Asiatic slaves seem to date almost entirely from the time of Amenemhet III to the middle of the Thirteenth Dynasty, and they are much more numerous in the Thirteenth Dynasty than in the Twelfth. They are associated with temples in a few cases but belong primarily to private persons, most of whom have some importance in the administration. Some of the Asiatics attain to positions of responsibility and honor, and a few intermarry with Egyptians. Most of the Asiatics are assimilated to the Egyptian culture in every respect, except for the ethnic designation of 'Aam. Even their names are Egyptian, except for a few (particularly in the Brooklyn Papyrus), who are apparently first-generation immigrants.

The way in which these slaves were acquired, especially by private persons, poses a problem. Hayes notes that the preponderance

12. Borchardt, "Ein Rechengsbuch des königlichen Hofes aus dem Ende des Mittleren Reiches," *ZÄS, 28* (1890), 94 ff.

13. W. C. Hayes, *A Papyrus of the Late Middle Kingdom in the Brooklyn Museum* (Brooklyn, 1955).

14. F. Ll. Griffith, *Hieratic Papyri from Kahun and Gurob* (2 vols. London, 1898).

15. Posener, "Les Asiatiques en Egypte sous les XII et XIII dynasties," *Syria, 34* (1957), 145-63.

of female slaves would suggest that they were prisoners of war.[16] There is only one recorded campaign, a raid in the time of Senwosret III, and just one prisoner is mentioned. Nevertheless, in the Thirteenth Dynasty, around the time of Neferhotep, there is some archaeological evidence to suggest serious hostilities in Palestine. The Execration texts also point in this direction. Consequently, it is altogether likely that the Asiatic slaves in Egypt, after the time of Amenemhet III, represent prisoners taken in Asia itself.

Another suggestion is Helck's opinion that the slaves were acquired through a slave trade.[17] This hypothesis, however, cannot be confirmed by any extant records. Furthermore, a distinction in status between the Asiatics in Egypt during the reign of Amenemhet III and those of the mid-Thirteenth Dynasty seems necessary. The fact that important persons in the time of Amenemhet III felt free to designate themselves as ʿAam or as born of an ʿAamt [18] means that one can hardly consider them as slaves in the ordinary sense as in the Brooklyn Papyrus. One must therefore reckon with a deterioration in the status of Asiatics between the time of Amenemhet III and that of Neferhotep.

Another possibility presented by Posener is that these Asiatics represent seminomadic groups who chose a livelihood in Egypt in exchange for their freedom.[19] In this respect one may compare the ʿAamu with the social phenomenon in the ancient Near East known as the Ḥapiru.[20] In the Nuzi texts one reads of the Ḥapiru, who enter into voluntary servitude for the sake of obtaining a livelihood. This suggestion, while attractive, is entirely speculative.

As early as the time of Amenemhet III a number of ʿAamu

16. Hayes, *Papyrus*, p. 99.
17. Helck, *Beziehungen*, p. 79.
18. See above, p. 88 n.
19. Posener, *Syria*, *34* (1957), 158; cf. *CAH²*, *1*, ch. 21, pp. 12 f.
20. See M. Greenberg, *The Ḫab/piru*, AOS, (New Haven, 1955). J. Bottéro, *Le problème des Ḫabiru*, 4e Rencontre Assyriologique Internationale (Paris, 1954).

seem to have settled in the Eastern Delta, in the Arabian nome, as part of the "corps of Soped, Lord of the East," [21] and were used as caravaneers for expeditions to the Sinai. It was undoubtedly from the Eastern Delta that Amenemhet III drew large bands of workmen for his projects in the Fayyum.[22] The development of the Eastern Delta in the Middle Kingdom and the subsequent connection of Asiatics with it merits further discussion. An important political and economic entity, it constituted the stronghold for the Hyksos domination of Egypt.[23]

## THE EASTERN DELTA IN THE MIDDLE KINGDOM

The sources for a history of this area are few and inconclusive, and for this reason the Eastern Delta, prior to the Hyksos period, has been largely ignored. Yet the whole question of its political importance before the so-called Fifteenth Dynasty is crucial to any view of the Hyksos rise to power.

At the beginning of the Twelfth Dynasty, Amenemhet I paid considerable attention to this region.[24] He strengthened the frontier in the vicinity of Wadi Tumilat, and he left a number of monuments in the region to emphasize his uniting of the two lands. He probably built a *ka* house in honor of Khety, the father of Merikare, who likewise had done much to strengthen the frontier.[25] A continuity of action against invading nomads was thereby established.

21. These Asiatics were either under an administrative official, "the superintendent of works of the Northern department," or they were part of the labor force of a religious institution under the "priest of the corps of Sopdu, Lord of the East." See *P. Kahun*, XII, XIII.

22. See Griffith's remarks in Petrie, *Illahun, Kahun and Gurob*, p. 50. Contrary to Petrie, the settlement of this pyramid town seems to be later than the pyramid of Senwosret II and dates primarily from the time of Amenemhet III. See H. Kantor in *Relative Chronologies*, pp. 10 ff.

23. It is identified as Avaris by Labib Habachi, "Khataʿna-Qantir: Importance," *Ann Serv*, *52* (1954), 558 f.

24. Posener, *Littérature et politique*, pp. 24 ff.

25. H. Kees, *MDIK*, *18* (1962), 2 f.

In spite of this early importance, monuments of the Middle Kingdom in the Delta are rather scarce [26] until the time of Senwosret III, when there was an apparent resurgence of interest in the region. Many of the buildings of Amenemhet I were restored, and the area around Khataᶜna took on considerable importance.[27] According to an inscription on the remains of a temple, the name of Khataᶜna in the Middle Kingdom appears to have been *r w3ty*, "mouth of the two ways." [28] The "two ways" would undoubtedly refer to the two routes to Asia, one leading toward the Way-of-Horus in the northeast and the road to Palestine, the other toward the mines of Sinai.[29] Khataᶜna would constitute an important terminus for trade and mining expeditions.

There are at least two good reasons for a renewal of interest in the Eastern Delta in the time of Senwosret III. First of all, with the rise of the Middle Bronze II A in Palestine, Senwosret III again felt the need to strengthen the frontier and establish his reputation there as one who subdues the "foreign bowmen." [30] The second reason for a rise in importance of the Eastern Delta has to do with his administrative reform.[31] Under this pharaoh the country was divided into three major geographic departments, the Northern *wᶜrt*, which included the nome of Memphis and the whole of the Delta, the Southern *wᶜrt*, which consisted roughly of Middle Egypt, and the *wᶜrt* of the "Head of the South," which comprised the Thebaid and the six adjoining nomes. In the case of the *wᶜrt* of the "Head of the South," Thebes functioned as a secondary administrative capital under Itj-towy. The Southern

26. They consist primarily of royal statues some of whom were usurped by later rulers. Their original location is often rather uncertain. See Porter and Moss, *Top Bibl*, 4.

27. See above, pp. 89 n., 92 n.

28. Adam, *Ann Serv*, *56* (1959), 223.

29. Helck, *Beziehungen*, p. 44.

30. See particularly the *Hymn of Senwosret* III, *P. Kahun*, I–III.

31. See Hayes, "Notes on the Government of Egypt in the Late Middle Kingdom," *JNES*, *12* (1953), 31–33. Cf. Von Beckerath, *Untersuchungen*, pp. 93 ff.

*wᶜrt* probably had no administrative center independent of the Residence. For the Northern *wᶜrt,* however, there are various indications that it also had a secondary capital. In the legal documents of the Illahun Papyri, there appear to be references to offices of the Northern *wᶜrt* in the Arabian nome, the domain of Sopdu, Lord of the East.[32] However, there are also references to the offices of the Southern *wᶜrt,* and these are almost certainly in the Fayyum region and probably at Itj-towy. Another indication that the Northern *wᶜrt* had a capital in the Eastern Delta is that there are very close associations with Lower Egypt and the Delta in the titles of important officials in the Sinai expeditions.[33] Taking the archaeological evidence together with this,[34] it seems safe to assert that Senwosret III created an important center of government in the North, a balance and perhaps even a rival of Thebes.

Amenemhet III continued to emphasize the importance of Khataᶜna and the neighboring region by renewing the buildings of his predecessor.[35] His interest, however, was primarily economic. Khataᶜna was a base for his expeditions to Sinai and Asia. It is also from the time of Amenemhet III that evidence of strong connections between the Eastern Delta and the Fayyum appears. The principal deity of the Arabian nome, Sopdu, was worshiped at Lahun, and the principal deity of the Fayyum, Sebek, was worshiped increasingly in the Eastern Delta. Such a situation must have resulted from a frequent transfer of personnel between the two areas.[36] Moreover, it is entirely likely that Amenemhet III used a number of Asiatic workmen from the Eastern Delta for his building projects in the Fayyum.[37]

32. *P. Kahun,* XII, XIII.

33. *Inscriptions of Sinai,* 2, p. 16.

34. Adam, *Ann Serv,* 56 (1959), 207–26.

35. Porter and Moss, *Top Bibl,* 4, 9.

36. F. Ll. Griffith, *Hieratic Papyri from Kahun and Gurob* (2 vols. London, 1898), *1,* 19 ff.

37. Petrie, *Kahun, Gurob, and Hawara* (London, 1890), pp. 40 ff. See also above, p. 92 n.

From the time of Amenemhet III onward, Khataᶜna seems to increase in importance. The last ruler of the Twelfth Dynasty, Queen Sobeknefru, left three fine statues there.[38] In the Thirteenth Dynasty, a curious dvelopment took place in the monarchy, whereby dynastic rule was replaced by some kind of "election" to the office of pharaoh for an indefinite period of time.[39] Moreover, although the capital remained at Itj-towy and the pharaohs ostensibly ruled the whole land, yet there seems to have been a distinct association by many of them either with the Eastern Delta region or with Thebes.[40] Merneferre Ay, for instance, who had the longest recorded reign of the Thirteenth Dynasty and who almost certainly ruled the whole of Egypt, was very likely buried in the Eastern Delta. The pyramidion of his tomb was found in the region.[41] If Khataᶜna was made the administrative capital of the Northern *wᶜrt*, it would explain the honor it was paid and would also explain how the "election," which sometimes included military commanders,[42] would have alternated between the two military and administrative centers of Thebes and the Eastern Delta. Moreover, since the Asiatics quickly established themselves in positions of importance in the Eastern Delta, it is not surprising, on the basis of the above hypothesis, to find Asiatics "elected" to the kingship of Egypt.[43]

The above reconstruction is largely speculative. Nevertheless, the evidence seems to indicate that the Eastern nome, and Khata ᶜna in particular, steadily grew in political importance in the late Twelfth and Thirteenth Dynasties. In the light of Senowsret III's

38. Habachi, *Ann Serv*, 52 (1954), 458–70.

39. An idea proposed originally by H. Junker is supported by Hayes, *A Late Middle Kingdom Papyrus*, p. 148; *CAH²*, 2, ch. 2, p. 5.

40. This is probably the explanation of what Stock calls "eine Thebanische und eine Tanitische-Memphitische Herrscherreihe," in *Studien*, pp. 51–53.

41. Habachi, *Ann Serv*, 52 (1954), 471–79.

42. Note no. 6.21 in the Turin Canon, who is called "the general." See Stock, *Studien*.

43. See Hayes, *CAH²*, 2, ch. 2, p. 7.

administrative reform—still effective in the Thirteenth Dynasty—
this new political significance of Khataᶜna could only be as a
secondary capital for the bureaus of the Northern *wᶜrt*. Once it
had achieved this status, it was only a step to independence from
the main Residence, as was also the case with Thebes. In a time
of internal stress both the Northern *wᶜrt* around Khataᶜna and
the "Head of the South" around Thebes could maintain their
administrative integrity as independent political entities. This
development, will be a matter for consideration in the next
chapter.

CHAPTER 8

# THE RISE OF THE HYKSOS

## THE 400-YEAR STELA

This important monument has generally been associated with the rise of the Hyksos in the Delta. It was found at Tanis in 1863 by Mariette, who left it at the site, and rediscovered there by P. Montet in 1932.[1] A scene in the upper portion of the stela shows a god, identified by an inscription above him as Seth. Before him is Ramesses II, and behind the King is a person in the posture of adoration who, according to Montet's reconstruction of the text, is the vizier Seti. The text below the group contains twelve lines. The last is partially broken away. Montet suggests that there were at least two more lines in the original. The first part of the text gives the titulary of Ramesses II and his command to make the stela in order to honor "the father of his fathers" (Seth) and his own father Seti I. The second part of the text mentions a past event, dated to the four-hundredth year of Seth as King of Upper and Lower Egypt. Though the text is broken, it clearly indicates that a certain vizier named Seti honored the god Seth in a special way on this important anniversary. It also gives the full titulary of the vizier Seti and of his father Pa-ramesses, also a vizier.

The exact significance of the stela is still a matter of debate among scholars. The first problem is to date the anniversary itself. E. Meyer placed it in the reign of Ramesses to set up the stela for

1. For Montet's discussion of the stela with a complete publication of the scene and text see "La Stéle de l'an 400 rétrouvée," *Kêmi, 4* (1933), 191–215. A translation of the text is also given by Wilson in *ANET*, pp. 252–53.

this occasion.[2] Sethe rejected this view and identifies the vizier Seti as King Seti I, mentioned in the first part of the text.[3] This would date the anniversary in the time of Haremhab, before the rise of the Nineteenth Dynasty, ca. 1320 B.C.[4] Sethe's date takes us back to ca. 1725,[5] which he interprets as the date of the founding of Avaris by the Hyksos.

A number of scholars have recently questioned whether the 400-year stela has any connection with the Hyksos whatever.[6] We must first consider the character of Seth and his early association with the Delta region. Throughout the Early Dynastic period and the Old Kingdom, Seth and Horus are represented as the two patron deities of the monarchy and as the gods who give victory to the king.[7] In the pyramid texts, the king is regarded as incorporating the two gods, Horus and Seth, or as being aided by them in his trip to the other world. These same texts, however, present allusions to myths in which Horus and Seth are bitter rivals. The oldest form of these is the so-called "Contendings of Horus and Seth," a kind of historical saga explaining the unity of Egypt in terms of reconciliation, in the person of the king, of two opposing

2. Meyer, *Geschichte des Altertums*, *1*, pt. 2, (2nd ed. Stuttgart and Berlin, 1909), 292 ff. See also J. von Beckerath, *Tanis und Theben* (Glückstadt-Hamburg-New York, 1951), pp. 38–41, for a summary of the debate up to the present time.

3. K. Sethe, "Der Denkstein mit dem Datum des Jahres 400 der Ära von Tanis," *ZÄS, 65* (1930), 85–89.

4. This is based on the date proposed by M. B. Rowton, "Comparative Chronology at the Time of Dynasty XIX," *JNES, 19* (1960), 15–22. Cf. the discussion by R. A. Parker, "The Lunar Dates of Thutmose and Ramesses II," *JNES, 16* (1957), 39–43, for an alternative, and most recently W. C. Hayes, "Chronology," *CAH²*, *1*, ch. 6, pp. 18–20.

5. The celebration was very likely toward the end of Haremhab's rather lengthy reign, i.e. ca. 1325. One may question whether the figure 400 is to be taken literally.

6. So von Beckerath, *Tanis und Theben*, pp. 40 f., and Helck, *Beziehungen*, p. 102.

7. See von Beckerath, *Tanis und Theben*, pp. 34 f. J. G. Griffiths, *The Conflict of Horus and Seth* (Liverpool, 1960), pp. 22–27. R. O. Faulkner, "The God Setekh in the Pyramid Texts," *Ancient Egypt* (1925), 5–10.

entities, "the portion of Horus"—Lower Egypt, and "the portion of Seth"—Upper Egypt.[8] In a later myth, the Osiris myth, Seth is represented in a cosmic aspect as the murderer of Osiris. By the end of the Sixth Dynasty, the latter myth tended to absorb the earlier one, and Seth was entirely discredited.[9] From the end of the Sixth Dynasty to the end of the Middle Kingdom Horus alone appears as the true patron of the monarchy, and thus the earlier cult of Seth suffered an almost complete eclipse.

Because of his cult place, Ombos near Thebes, Seth is associated with Upper Egypt. In this connection he bears the epithet Ombite (*Nubty*) in the oldest period as well as in the New Kingdom. However, H. Junker has tried to see in the title of an official of the Fourth Dynasty a connection between Seth and a place called ⌷𝍀⊗, *sṯrt*, which he identifies as Sethröe of the Greek sources.[10] Černý supports this identification and sees the same name in the Peribsen inscription of the Second Dynasty which has 𝍀⊗ *sṯt*, a name used later to designate Asia.[11] The connection between these two names and Sethröe has been disputed by Gardiner and Kees.[12] The latter admits only that Seth may have an early connection with Asia, but he does not explain how, in this early form, the name is written with the determinative of a town. Černý suggests that the name was originally associated with a frontier town on the route to Asia and that later the name was applied to the region beyond the frontier. If Seth can be associated with a place in the region of the northeastern frontier, then there may be an instructive analogy between Seth and Soped.[13] Seth would be the

8. Griffiths, *Horus and Seth*, pp. 73 f.

9. Ibid., pp. 26 f.

10. H. Junker, "Phrnfr," *ZÄS, 75* (1939), 77 ff.

11. J. Černý, "La Fin de la seconde dynastie ou la période sethienne," *Ann Serv, 44* (1944), 295 ff.

12. Gardiner, *Onomastica, 2*, 176*. Kees, *Ancient Egypt*, pp. 197 f. So also Helck, *Beziehungen*, p. 106 n. Griffiths, *Horus and Seth*, p. 144.

13. On this god see Gardiner, Peet, Černý, *The Inscriptions of Sinai*, Part 2, pp. 42 f.

god of the Fourteenth nome and its chief place, while Soped would be the god of the Twentieth, or Arabian, nome. Each would be associated with one of the two main routes to Asia, and each would become the god of the region beyond his frontiers: Seth of Asia and Soped of Sinai. These two gods appear side by side, in a relief from the temple of Sahure, leading captives from Asia as early as the Fifth Dynasty.[14] Although Seth is usually associated with Ombos in the pyramid texts, in two instances he is also associated with 🪶☉, *Henty*.[15] While the location of this town is not known, it is probably to be placed in the Delta. His early connection with the Delta has also been deduced from his presence in the *Ennead* of Heliopolis.[16]

Nevertheless Seth's possible early connection with Asia and the northeastern frontier does not constitute evidence, as Montet asserts,[17] for any association of Seth with Avaris in the Old and Middle Kingdom. Consequently Montet's proposal that the names *Seth peḥti* and *Nubty* in cartouches in the text of the 400-year stela refer to a king who set up an independent rule in Avaris with the patronage of the local Seth cult [18] is highly dubious. It is more likely that the names in cartouches represent Seth himself; the stela commemorated both the establishment of his cult in Avaris and his commencement as the patron of the monarchy in Egypt. We are still faced with the problem of how Seth became associated with Avaris and the connection between this event and the 400-year stela.

It is just possible that there is sufficient evidence to reconstruct the situation. An obelisk of a certain Neḥesy was found in Tanis with a number of similar obelisks of the Ramesside period.[19] This

14. L. Borchardt, *Das Grabdenkmal des Königs Sahure II* (Leipzig, 1913), Pl. 5.

15. See Faulkner, *Ancient Egypt* (1925), 5, #734, 1904.

16. Faulkner, *Ancient Egypt* (1925), 7.

17. Montet, *Le Drame d'Avaris*, pp. 54 ff. Cf. Kees, *Topography*, pp. 197 f.

18. Montet, *Le Drame*, pp. 55 f.

19. See J. Leclant and J. Yoyotte, "Les Obelisques de Tanis," *Kêmi, 14* (1957),

Neḥesy is undoubtedly the same as that listed in the Turin Canon as 8:1, coming some time after the strong kings of the Thirteenth Dynasty. On one fragment of the obelisk were traces of a dedication by the "eldest royal son, Neḥesy, beloved of Seth, Lord of *r-ꜣḫt*," and on another fragment the inscription, "beloved of *ḥršf* (Arsaphes)." There is a degree of uncertainty about the location of the place name *r-ꜣḫt*, which means "gateway of the cultivated fields." Montet has suggested that the designation "Seth *r-ꜣḫt*" is the origin of the name of the Fourteenth nome Sethröe.[20] The gateway referred to would then be the region of Ṣile, where the cultivated area meets the desert. Confirmation of this location may be seen in the epithet, "beloved of *ḥršf*." In the Delta, this god was undoubtedly worshiped at Heracleopolis Parva, which was the capital of the Fourteenth nome, at least for a time, and lay perhaps in the neighborhood of Ṣile, being midway between Tanis and Pelusium.[21] A cult place for *Ḥršf* could also be expected in the northeastern frontier as early as the Tenth Dynasty, for the god was a favorite of these pharaohs, and this dynasty first secured the frontiers against the Asiatics.

The likelihood, then, is that, prior to Neḥesy, there were cults of Seth and *Ḥršf* in the northeastern frontier region. Neḥesy, as the "eldest royal son," [22] may have served as a commander of troops in the garrison of this region and adopted these two cults in spite of their apparent royal disfavor in the Twelfth and Thirteenth Dynasties. When Neḥesy became King, he made Seth

50–54. The provenance of this obelisk in Tanis has no significance since it was not found in situ.

20. Montet, *Géographie de l'Egypte ancienne*, pp. 199. His association of *r-ꜣḫt* in the vicinity of Tanis, however, has nothing in its favor. On the Sethröite nome, see below.

21. Gardiner, *Onomastica*, 2, 176*, and Montet, *Géographie*, p. 199, place it further north at Tell Belim; but the location remains uncertain.

22. This title may have been honorific, since there were hardly dynasties and regular succession at this time. Was Neḥesy ("Nubian") a southerner? It may have been a safety precaution to appoint a southerner in the Northern military command, but—if so—it does not seem to have worked.

"Lord of Avaris" [23] as well as of *r-3ht* and gave to Avaris a new religious and political basis. The adoption of Seth in opposition to the preceding royal sentiments can only indicate a break with the past. The fact that the obelisk of Nehesy was found together with similar ones of the Ramesside period may indicate that he was particularly honored by the Nineteenth Dynasty and that they dated the reign of Seth from the reign of this king.

Nehesy's choice of the Seth cult may have a number of causes. Seth was an ancient patron of the monarchy, and the sanction of this deity would give a justification to Nehesy's rule. Moreover, if Seth was associated with the northeast and with Asia he may already have become an important deity for the Asiatics who had settled in this region and whose support Nehesy probably needed to maintain his rule. Some confirmation of this Asiatic support may be seen in an obelisk which was found at Byblos in which the ruler Abishemu (II) uses the epithet "beloved of *Hrsf.*" [24] This monument comes from a building phase very nearly con-

23. The first reference to "Seth, Lord of Avaris," is in an inscription on a monument of Nehesy found at Tell Moqdam: Porter and Moss, *Top Bibl, 4,* 37–38. For additional monuments of Nehesy, mostly scarabs, see Leclant, *Kêmi, 14* (1957), 53, n.

24. See P. Montet, "Notes et documents . . . , XI Herichef à Byblos," *Kêmi, 16* (1962), 89 f. Albright's discussion of this monument, in *BASOR, 155* (1959), 31–34, is seriously weakened by an apparent misdating of the monument to the First Intermediate Period. In this, however, he is contradicted by Montet, *Kêmi, 16* (1962), and by the published archaeological accounts. N. Glueck, in the preliminary report in *AJA, 42* (1938), 172 f., describes how the whole temple was dismantled and rebuilt. He then states: "As a result, five construction stages could be distinguished, the first belonging to the Middle Empire and the last to the period of Ramesses II. The obelisks came from the first four stages. The one with the name of King Abishemu on it is from the third stage. It is certain that this king of Byblos is not the one who was interred in tomb II of the time of Amenemhet IV." The clear indication seems to be that the obelisk must date to the Second Intermediate Period. See Albright's retraction, in *BASOR, 176* (1964), 41 f. If the obelisk does belong to Abishemu II and not Abishemu I, the contemporary of Amenemhet III, as Helck (*Beziehungen,* p. 646) suggests, then a date about 1700 B.C. would fit very well with Albright's proposed dynastic scheme, *BASOR, 179* (1965), 42.

temporary with Neḥesy, and the epithet "beloved of *Ḥršf*" would probably be used by a foreign prince only when such a title was in vogue with the leading power in Egypt. It is likely that the two kings were contemporaries and that the Byblian king was in commercial and diplomatic contact with Neḥesy. Moreover, if Neḥesy was a commander of the frontier garrison before he became King, he could have made important contact with the princes of Palestine and received their support for his rule. These princes would certainly have favored opening up the frontier and freedom of direct trade with the inland ports. Neḥesy's court would also have been made up of a considerable number of Asiatics, and in this way they might have inherited the control of Lower Egypt from him. The choice of Seth by the Hyksos would have been conditioned partly by previous familiarity with the god and assimilation to their own major deity, but primarily by the expediency of political continuity with the previous Egyptian régime of Neḥesy.

This reconstruction is most hypothetical. Nevertheless, it is clear that Neḥesy—an Egyptian ruler between the strong kings of the Thirteenth Dynasty and the main group of the Hyksos—represents a discontinuity with the previous kings and a continuity with the foreigners both within and without Egypt. Further support for this reconstruction will be given by a study of the *Admonitions of Ipuwer* which seems to indicate, likewise, that the independent rule in Lower Egypt was largely the result of an internal coup d'état carried out by the Egyptians and Asiatics together.

### THE ADMONITIONS OF IPUWER

Since the time of A. H. Gardiner's study of the *Admonitions of Ipuwer* in 1909,[25] there has been a general consensus among

25. Gardiner, *The Admonitions of an Egyptian Sage* (Leipzig, 1909). The following discussion on the *Admonitions* is reproduced from an article by the author, "A Date for the 'Admonitions' in the Second Intermediate Period," *JEA*, 50 (1964), 13–23.

scholars that the work was written in, or at least reflects, the First Intermediate Period in Egypt.[26] However, the general observations made by Gardiner himself relating to the problem of dating certainly do not lead to a firm conclusion on the matter.[27] He records that only a single copy is extant, Papyrus Leiden 344 recto, found at Memphis. The papyrus itself is not earlier than the Nineteenth Dynasty, although there are sufficiently strong indications that the scribe used a manuscript, the history of whose transmission may go back to the beginning of the Eighteenth Dynasty. This conclusion is based on the presence of archaisms in palaeography and orthography. The language, on the other hand, is characteristic of literary documents of the Middle Kingdom. In particular, Gardiner cites points of contact with the *Dispute over Suicide, The Instructions of Amenemhet I,* and a text on a writing-board in the British Museum, which he dates to the time of Senwosret II (*Lament of Kha-Kheperre-sonbe*).[28]

The content of the *Admonitions* doubtless reflects a troubled period in Egypt's history; the logical alternatives for its date are the First and Second Intermediate Periods. Gardiner prefers the First Intermediate Period, since he found very little indication of late Egyptian idioms and therefore wanted "to push back the date of the composition as far as possible." However, he concedes that this evidence cannot exclude a date as late as the beginning of the Eighteenth Dynasty.[29] Once the choice was made for the First Intermediate Period, reasons were found to date the *Admonitions* to the very beginning of the period or even to the last

26. See for example Wilson, *The Culture of Egypt* (Chicago, 1961), pp. 107 f. Hayes, *The Scepter of Egypt* (New York, 1953–59), *1*, 35 f. Steindorff and Seele, *When Egypt Ruled the East* (2nd ed. Chicago, 1957), pp. 18 f. Gardiner, *Egypt of the Pharaohs* (Oxford, 1961), pp. 109 f. W. S. Smith, *CAH²*, *1*, ch. 14, pp. 58 f. Stock, *Die erste Zwischenzeit Ägyptens* (Rome, 1949), pp. 22 ff.

27. Gardiner, *Admonitions*, pp. 1–5.

28. Ibid., pp. 97, 110 f. However the same name appears several times in Papyrus Kahun XIV, which dates to the end of the reign of Amenemhet III. See the remarks of Griffith, *Hieratic Papyri*, p. 42.

29. Gardiner, *Admonitions*, pp. 3, 18.

years of Pepi II in the Old Kingdom. J. Spiegel uses the *Admonitions* to present a fairly elaborate hypothetical reconstruction of the historical situation at the end of the Old Kingdom.[30]

This latest approach really runs counter to the evidence of orthography and language. The events are described in such a way as to appear quite contemporaneous with the author himself, and one would certainly expect the text to reflect at least the language of the Old Kingdom.[31] On the other hand, it is difficult to see how the many intimate connections with the Middle Kingdom can all be considered merely as anticipations.[32] There is, in fact, a more acceptable alternative which does full justice to the matter of orthography and language, a date late in the Thirteenth Dynasty. Such a date would indeed still show a strong connection with Middle Kingdom literature and give evidence of new spellings, though not yet the late Egyptian idiom.

Furthermore, the *Admonitions* reflects certain social, cultural, and political developments that may be dated by archaeological and literary material of known date. By the use of such historically controlled data, it is possible to test the alternatives of the First or Second Intermediate Period. This method has been largely neglected in previous considerations.

### Ethnic Terms

Section 14:11–14 gives an important clue to the date in which the *Admonitions* was written:

30. J. Spiegel, *Sociale und weltanschauliche Reformbewegungen in alten Ägypten* (Heidelberg, 1950), pp. 7–59. However, this hypothetical reconstruction of history will not stand up to recent studies on the chronology of the First Intermediate Period. See particularly H. Goedicke, "Zur Chronologie der sogenanten 'Ersten Zwischenzeit,'" *ZDMG*, *112* (1963), 239–54.

31. Gardiner, *Admonitions*, p. 111, tries to overcome this problem by supposing that, while the text portrays a real national calamity in the early First Intermediate Period, the *Admonitions* as a "historical romance" was written in the Twelfth Dynasty. It must be seriously doubted, however, whether this literary classification is appropriate to the work.

32. So G. Posener, *Littérature et politique*, p. 16.

Every man fights for his sister and he protects his own person. Is it the Nubians (*nḥsyw*)? Then we shall make our own protection. Fighting police will hold off the bowman (*pḏtyw*). Is it the Libyans (*ṯmḥw*)? Then we shall act again. The Madjayu (*mḏ3yw*) fortunately are with Egypt.[33]

In this passage Egypt is in conflict with its southern neighbors, the *nḥsyw*. Here, however, they are viewed as quite distinct from another Nubian people, the *mḏ3yw*, who are on the side of Egypt and closely associated, by parallelism, with the "fighting police." A distinction between these two ethnic terms is already known in the Old Kingdom in which *nḥsyw* means the settled river peoples and *mḏ3yw* designates the bedouin of the steppe country.[34] However, it is common to find, as in the biography of Weni from the end of the Old Kingdom, the term *nḥsyw* used to include all the Nubians from both *w3w3t*, the river area, and *mḏ3*, the steppe country. In the Middle Kingdom the distinction between *nḥsyw* and *mḏ3yw* changes somewhat. The *nḥsyw* remains the general designation for the Nubians exclusive of the *mḏ3yw*. The latter, however, were regimented in the Middle Kingdom as professional soldiers and desert police, so that the term *mḏ3yw* comes almost exclusively to mean mercenaries, and this is the meaning which is clearly intended in this passage. The same distinction between *nḥsyw* and *mḏ3yw* becomes apparent at the end of the Hyksos period, when the soldiers of liberation under Kamose include numerous *mḏ3yw*, who remain loyal even though Nubia was hostile to Egyptian rule and under an independent *nḥsy prince*.[35]

The passage quoted above reflects a situation following the

33. The translations are primarily those by Gardiner *Admonitions*, and Wilson, *ANET*, 441–44. However, in a few instances I have adopted other renderings.

34. For a study of *nḥsyw* and *mḏ3yw*, see Posener, Nḥsyw et Mḏ3yw," *ZÄS*, *83* (1957), 38–43.

35. Gardiner, "The Defeat of the Hyksos by Kamose: The Carnarvon Tablet No. I," *JEA*, *3* (1916), 95–110.

Middle Kingdom and not too different from what was presented to us in the Kamose inscriptions. The history of the development of this *mḏꜣyw* mercenary force is also substantiated from archaeology by the so-called "pan graves" in Egypt from the Middle Kingdom period and later. These graves are native to Nubia and have, with good reason, been associated with the *mḏꜣyw*.[36]

The terminology used in the *Admonitions* for Asiatics is more difficult to control.[37] For instance, the term |‿ 𓏏 𓆓 𓈖 𓏥𓏦 *sttyw*,[38] used in 14:11–15:2, is problematic. Although common in the Middle Kingdom, it is rare in the earlier period and occurs only once in an inscription of the Eleventh Dynasty.[39] In this earliest occurrence, *sttyw* is written with the sign 𓏏𓆑 as a generic adjective of the name *stt*, which, however, in the Old Kingdom usually stood for the island of Sehel at the First Cataract and only in a few instances for Asia.[40] On the other hand, in the Middle Kingdom references to Asiatics, *sttyw* is written with 𓏏, and this seems to suggest the meaning, "archers," a derivation from *stt*, "to shoot."[41] The term for Asia, *stt*, in the Middle Kingdom is also usually written with 𓏏, probably by analogy with *sttyw*, and because there was no longer any great phonetic distinction between 𓏏 and 𓏏𓆑. In the New Kingdom there is a tendency to spell *sttyw* and *stt* archaically with 𓏏𓆑. It seems reasonable to conclude that in choice of terminology and in orthography the *Admonitions* here reflects the usage of the Twelfth and Thirteenth Dynasties.

Another term used in the *Admonitions*, though not strictly

36. Hayes, *CAH²*, 2, ch. 2, pp. 35 f. For a different interpretation of this passage see T. Säve-Söderbergh, *Ägypten und Nubien*, p. 38. Cf. G. Posener, "Pour une localisation du pays Koush au Moyen Empire," *Kush*, 6 (1958), 39–68.

37. See W. Max Müller, *Asien und Europen nach altägyptischen Denkmalern*, (1893). This work is manifestly out of date.

38. *Wb*, *4*, 326 f. Gauthier, *Dict géog*, *5*, 92.

39. Breasted, *Anc Rec*, *1*, 423H.

40. Roeder, "Sothis und Satis," *ZÄS*, *45* (1908), 24 f.

41. *Wb*, *4*, 326.

ethnic, is *pdtyw*,[42] which has the general meaning, "foreign bowmen." It is frequently associated with Asiatics in Middle Kingdom literature, and this may account for the development of the term *sttyw* in the sense of "archer" as well as Asiatic. The term *pdtyw* is used in *The Instructions for Merikare* in a description of the *ʿзmw*, and in *The Story of Sinuhe* in close association with *sttyw*.[43] In the *Hymn of Senwosret III*, however, the *pdtyw* seem to include "bowmen" of both Nubia and Asia.[44] While most of the references in the *Admonitions* deal with the *pdtyw* from the north, in 14:13, quoted above, they also refer to hostile Nubians. The period when *pdtyw* were threatening both the northern and southern frontiers was the Second Intermediate Period.

A third term for Asiatics in the *Admonitions* is *ḥзstyw*.[45] This is also a generic form of *ḥзst*, "foreign country," and simply means "foreigners" without any particular country intended. However, from the Middle Kingdom onward, the principal "foreigners" and their rulers, the *ḥkз ḥзs(w)t*, were Asiatics and the term when unqualified came to designate Asiatics in particular. It is apparent in the *Admonitions* that *ḥзstyw* means Asiatics and thus reflects a development of this term appropriate to the Second Intermediate Period.

## Foreign Relations

A passage reflecting Egypt's foreign relations in this period is 3:6–10. Following Montet,[46] it may be rendered:

> No one sails north to Byblos today. How shall we replace for our mummies the cedar (*ʿš*) wood, the importation of which makes possible the making of coffins of the priests.

42. *Adm*, 2:2; 3:1; 14:13; 15:1. *Wb*, *1*, 570. *Dict géog*, 2, 158 f.
43. *Sinuhe*, B 53, 60, 121, 260, 276.
44. *P. Kahun I*, passim.
45. *Adm*, 1:9; 4:5; 10:2; 15:2. *Wb*, *3*, 234 f. *Dict géog*, 4, 160.
46. "Notes et documents . . . , IV. Byblos et le Keftioy," *Kêmi*, *13* (1954), 71–73.

The kings (*wrw*) as far away as Crete (*Keftiu*) are em-
balmed in pitch which is taken from these same cedars.

Trade with Byblos was certainly very ancient, and this Syrian
port supplied Egypt with valuable lumber from early dynastic
times onwards. However, as Winlock points out,[47] at the beginning of the Second Intermediate Period there was a scarcity
of wood from Syria for the construction of rectangular coffins
in Upper Egypt. A change in burial customs took place as a
result of this, with the introduction of anthropoid coffins made
from hollowed-out logs of local sycamore.

The passage also indicates that the Egyptian practice of using
resins and wood pitch for embalming [48] was imitated by foreigners. There is archaeological evidence that such embalming methods spread to Syria and Palestine by the end of the Middle
Kingdom.[49] It is possible, as a result of the active trade between
Syria and Crete in the MM II and MM III periods, that this
practice also reached the Aegean.[50] In contrast to the many cultural contacts between Crete and Egypt in the Middle Kingdom,
on the other hand, it is increasingly apparent to archaeologists
that there is very little evidence for any contact whatever between
these two countries in the Old Kingdom.[51] The word *Keftiu* is
not found in the Old Kingdom and is even rare in the Middle
Kingdom.[52] It is unlikely, therefore, that the degree of Egyptian
cultural influence on Crete implied by this passage was possible

47. H. E. Winlock, *The Rise and Fall of the Middle Kingdom in Thebes* (New
York, 1947), p. 101.

48. A. Lucas, *Ancient Egyptian Materials*, pp. 265 f., 319 ff.

49. Eg. J. Ory, "A Middle Bronze Age Tomb at El-Jisr," *QDAP, 12* (1946),
32 f.

50. H. J. Kantor, *AJA, 51* (1947), 18.

51. Kantor, in *Relative Chronologies*, pp. 10 ff. H. Kees, *Ancient Egypt*, p.140.
W. A. Ward, "Egypt and the East Mediterranean from Predynastic Times to
the End of the Old Kingdom," *JESHO, 6* (1963), 55.

52. J. Vercoutter, *L'Egypte et le monde égéen préhellénique* (Cairo, 1956),
pp. 38 f.

first in the period of weakness following the Old Kingdom.[53] Furthermore, the term *wr* to designate foreign rulers is found from the Thirteenth Dynasty onward.[54] It is therefore safe to conclude that the passage reflects Egypt's foreign relations and cultural influence beyond its borders in the early Second Intermediate Period.

### Social and Administrative Development

The *Admonitions* reflects the social development of the Middle Kingdom, and not the Old Kingdom or the First Intermediate Period. This is particularly evident from the references in the text to slavery. The terminology for slavery in Egypt has recently been studied by Abd el Mohsen Bakir.[55] Also valuable are the remarks presented by Hayes in connection with his publication of a late Middle Kingdom papyrus in the Brooklyn Museum.[56] A comparison between the terminology of the *Admonitions* and the Brooklyn Papyrus is most illuminating.

The institution of slavery, apart from a type of serfdom associated primarily with royal land estates, is not attested for the Old Kingdom.[57] Slavery is, at the earliest, a product of the Middle Kingdom; in this period there is clear evidence for privately owned household slaves, male and female, who were considered as transferable, moveable property.[58] A particularly common term to designate slaves in the Middle Kingdom, but in this sense very rare earlier, is the word *ḥm* (or *ḥmt*).[59] It is used as an epithet with the names of slaves of Egyptian origin in the slave lists of the Brooklyn Papyrus and here denotes household

53. W. S. Smith, *CAH²*, *1*, ch. 14, pp. 38–39.

54. G. Posener, *Princes et pays,* E 50, 51, 62; also in *P. Boulaq 18.*

55. Bakir, "Slavery in Pharonic Egypt," *Ann Serv Suppl, 18* (1952).

56. Hayes, *A Papyrus of the Late Middle Kingdom in the Brooklyn Museum* (Brooklyn, 1955).

57. Bakir, "Slavery," pp. 22 f.

58. Hayes, *Papyrus,* pp. 90 ff.

59. Bakir, "Slavery," pp. 29 ff.

or menial slaves.[60] It is important to observe that this very term is used in the *Admonitions* seven times [61] with the same meaning as in the Brooklyn Papyrus. Moreover, the predominance of female slaves in the Middle Kingdom is also reflected in the *Admonitions*.[62]

In the Old Kingdom the term *b3k* is the general designation for servant, although it often has reference to high government officials.[63] In the Middle Kingdom, however, it has the added meaning of slave, and it is used in the Brooklyn Papyrus as the equivalent of *ḥm*.[64] Likewise in the *Admonitions*, *b3k* is always used in parallelism with *ḥm* and has the obvious meaning of slave.[65] Another term for domestic slave is *ḏt*, and this too was "chiefly used in the Middle Kingdom." It was not known with this precise sense in the Old Kingdom.[66] The words for serf in the Old Kingdom were *mryt* and *isww*. Only *myrt* was used in later periods; this term—and not *isww*—occurs in the *Admonitions*.[67] Consequently the terminology of slavery points to a social development which dates to the late Middle Kingdom.

Another area, not unrelated to slavery, points strongly to this same conclusion: the administration of justice. Here again the Brooklyn Papyrus is pertinent. While a large part of the papyrus has to do with lists of slaves held in private ownership in the Thirteenth Dynasty, part of it dates from the late Twelfth Dynasty, and this main text of the recto is concerned with the administration of justice.[68] It consists of directives from the central government to the "Great Prison" at Thebes concerning crimes

60. Hayes, *Papyrus*, pp. 90 ff.

61. *Adm*, 2:5, 14; 3:2; 4:13, 14; 5:9; 8:12.

62. Hayes, *Papyrus*, p. 91 n.

63. Bakir, "Slavery," p. 17.

64. Hayes, *Papyrus*, p. 125.

65. *Adm*, 2:3–5; 4:12–14. There is no distinction here between *b3k* and *ḥm*, as Bakir supposes, see "Slavery," p. 18.

66. Bakir, "Slavery," p. 37.

67. *Adm*, 9:5. See Bakir, "Slavery," pp. 14, 22 ff.

68. Hayes, *Papyrus*, pp. 64 ff.

against the government. It invokes laws of the criminal code against certain persons and follows their cases through to completion. The terminology is so similar to that of *Adm* 6:5–12 that the *Admonitions* may be clarified by the Brooklyn Papyrus.[69]

There is frequent reference in the *Admonitions* to the *ḥnrt*,[70] an institution which, according to the Brooklyn Papyrus, functioned as both prison and court of law. Concerning the *ḥnrt wr*, "Great Prison," which is probably mentioned in *Adm* 6:5, Hayes states: "Its existence appears to be unrecorded before the Middle Kingdom and the period of its greatest importance—the period during which it is mentioned most frequently and most prominently in Egyptian texts—was without much doubt the XIIth to XVIIth Dynasties."[71] As a center for the administration of justice, the *ḥnrt* possessed a group of ordinances called, in *Adm* 6:9–10, "the laws of the prison" (*hpw nyw ḥnrt*). These probably constituted a criminal code to which certain laws mentioned in the directives in the Brooklyn Papyrus belonged.[72]

The *ḥnrt* also kept census lists of slaves, because many people became slaves as a result of criminal activity, and this status of servitude was subsequently inherited by their descendants.[73] Records such as the Brooklyn Papyrus contained such lists, and a record of the crimes which in previous generations were responsible for the servitude of some of the slaves is listed. These were important for establishing a slave's status. Therefore, when one reads in *Adm* 6:7–8, "Public offices are opened and the census lists are taken away. Serfs become lords of serfs," it seems most appropriate to think of the Second Intermediate Period, when

69. Ibid., pp. 36 ff. This terminology is also common to the Illahun papyri, and *P. Boulaq 18* of about the same date.

70. *Adm*, 6:5, 10, 12. See Gardiner, *Admonitions*, pp. 46 f.

71. Hayes, *Papyrus*, p. 40.

72. Ibid., p. 52.

73. Ibid., p. 132.

records similar to the Brooklyn Papyrus were being destroyed with the subsequent disruption of the social order.[74]

In the same context as the remarks about the *ḥnrt*, "prison," one reads in 6:8–9, "The scribes of the mat, their writings are destroyed. The corn of Egypt is common property." The intrusion of a remark regarding agriculture in this context is clear when we note, as Hayes points out,[75] that officials of the *ḥnrt* often bear titles linking them with the Department of Agriculture as well. Thus a certain Simontu was not only a Scribe of the Great Prison, but also a Scribe of the Mat. This combination resulted from the fact the *ḥnrt* constituted a significant labor force, used for public works, whose rations were supplied by public granaries.

The *ḥnrt* and its bureaus were the outcome of the administrative development of the Middle Kingdom and can hardly reflect an earlier period. Gardiner's whole argument for the First Intermediate Period in this respect rests on the references to the title "overseer of the town" (*Adm* 10:7) and to "Great Mansions," *ḥwt wryt* (*Adm* 6:12), both of which originated in the Old Kingdom. This argument carries no weight, since the significance of both continued through the Middle Kingdom.[76]

Another clue for the dating of the *Admonitions* may be found in the reference to the royal Residence, *ẖnw*. In *Adm* 7:4 we read, "The Residence (*ẖnw*) will be overthrown in a minute," and in 10:6–12 there are several more passages lamenting the recent loss of the former glories of the Residence (*ẖnw*). In these passages, the author is speaking of the present or the very immediate past when the Residence of the king was a reality. Posener[77] has shown that this could only apply to the very beginning of the

74. Note that many of these records were kept in the central office of the northern district in the Eastern Delta. See *P. Kahun* XII, XIII passim.

75. Hayes, *Papyrus*, pp. 39 f.

76. Ibid., p. 74.

77. Posener, *Littérature et politique*, p. 7.

First Intermediate Period, since the texts of the Tenth and Eleventh Dynasties did not speak of their capital as the Residence (*ḥnw*). When they make reference to the Residence, it is to Memphis, the former capital of the Old Kingdom. For this reason scholars have recently been inclined to assign the *Admonitions* to the period between the end of the Sixth Dynasty and the Eighth Dynasty.

The Second Intermediate Period, the alternative possibility, occurs at the end of the Thirteenth Dynasty. Hayes has recently shown that the Residence (*ḥnw*) was a common designation in the Middle Kingdom for Itj-towy, the capital, and that this remained the capital of the pharaohs until it was replaced by Avaris, capital of the Hyksos.[78] According to this alternative, the *Admonitions* would portray the rise of the Hyksos of the Fifteenth Dynasty and be very nearly contemporary with it. Consequently there are only two rather limited possibilities based on the references to the Residence: the end of the Sixth Dynasty and the end of the Thirteenth Dynasty. When all the other factors are taken into consideration, the latter date seems preferable.

### Literature

The genre of literature to which the *Admonitions* belongs also constitutes a problem for supporters of an early date. It cannot be associated with anything from the Old Kingdom; its affinities are certainly with texts of the Middle Kingdom. In its genre it is said to anticipate them, but, in fact, by its evident association with a variety of forms, *Gattungen,* it certainly follows the literary conventions of the Middle Kingdom. The truth of this is all the more apparent when we recognize in the Middle Kingdom a conscious effort in the creation of such new forms. The chief characteristic of this literature, as Posener points out,[79] is

---

78. Hayes, *JNES, 12* (1953), 33–38. See also W. K. Simpson, "Studies in the Twelfth Dynasty: I. The Residence of Itj-towy," *JARCE, 2* (1963), 53–59.

79. Posener, *Littérature et politique,* passim. See also S. Herrmann, *Unter-*

its function as propaganda for the state. However, while the *Prophecy of Neferty* hails the rising star of the Twelfth Dynasty, and while the *Satire on Trades* praises the officialdom of the new Residence, the *Admonitions* is a lament for the decline of both. In fact, the reprimand of the king makes sense only if Ipuwer is referring to well-established dogmas (not just anticipating them); the view of the king as a "herdsman" to his people expressed in the passage of *Adm* 11:11 f. is a dogma of the Middle Kingdom.[80] The power of the king to maintain justice in the state and to keep the neighboring peoples, especially the Asiatic nomads, in check was also a dogma.[81] The view of the king's relation to his people was so entirely different in the Old Kingdom that Ipuwer's appeal to the unnamed king would have fallen on deaf ears. There is, in fact, nothing in the *Admonitions* which reflects the Old Kingdom view of royalty. It is propaganda; it could not have been understood before the Twelfth Dynasty.

One date seems to fit all the requirements: late Thirteenth Dynasty. The orthography and the linguistic evidence have always pointed toward this later date, and our present knowledge of the social and political history of this period confirms this opinion. The political situation reflected by this text remains to be reconstructed.

### Political Situation

The *Admonitions* makes frequent allusion to those Egyptian-Asiatic relations which were the result of developments in the Middle Kingdom. It first refers to the Asiatics who have settled in the Delta area and taken over all its affairs. This may be seen in the statement, "The foreigners (*ḫꜣstyw*) are now skilled in

---

suchungen zur *Überlieferungsgestalt mittelägyptischer Literaturwerke* (Berlin, 1957), pp. 8–37.

80. "Hymn to Senwosret III," *P. Kahun* III:14. See also Wilson, *Burden of Egypt*, p. 132.

81. Ibid. *P Kahun* I–III, passim.

the work of the Delta" (4:8). The *Admonitions* also refers to the fact that many Asiatics have become assimilated to Egyptian culture and have displaced Egyptians in places of authority. This is suggested by the statements, "Foreigners (*ḫ3styw*) have become people (*rmṯ*, Egyptians) everywhere" (1:9), and "there are no Egyptians anywhere" (3:2). At first these statements seem to be quite ambiguous. Yet it is clear that the writers of *Merikare* and the *Story of Sinuhe* considered the Asiatics, ʿ*Aamu,* entirely distinct from the civilized Egyptians in appearance and behavior. The statements about foreigners becoming Egyptians can only refer to the Middle Kingdom Asiatic assimilation to Egyptian culture, when Asiatics in government and religious institutions rose to positions of honor and authority. The statement, "There are no Egyptians anywhere" must mean "anywhere important." The fact that some of the pharaohs of the Thirteenth Dynasty bear Semitic names was noted above; it is entirely possible that there were others with purely Egyptian names whom we cannot identify as foreigners.

Some Asiatics probably "became Egyptians" when the important census lists of slaves were destroyed, as is mentioned in *Adm* 6:7. Most of the slaves in these lists were Asiatics, many with Egyptian names, and their ownership titles were deposited in the "Department of the North," in the Eastern Delta. When this area became independent, the destruction of these records may have served to free the slaves, and the result may have been the social upheaval and reversal of fortune described in the *Admonitions.*

Furthermore, the *Admonitions* represents the frontier in the northeast as open to Asia, and bedouin in numbers are found throughout Egypt: "The Desert is throughout the land . . . a foreign tribe from abroad has come to Egypt" (3:1), and "the entire Delta will no longer be hidden; the confidence of the Northland is a beaten path" (4:6). It is true that this description resembles the situation in the First Intermediate Period attested by *Merikare* and the *Prophecy of Neferty*. However, the bedouin problem in the earlier period was the result of a lack of adequate frontier protection. It was remedied by Khety II, Amenemhet I, and the later pharaohs of the Middle Kingdom. The *Admonitions*, on the other hand, speaks of these same frontier fortresses as the "confidence of the Northland" and laments that the "Delta is no longer hidden" but, in fact, has become a "beaten path" by foreigners.[82] The strict precautions that the Middle Kingdom pharaohs took in admitting foreigners into both the North and the South are no longer enforced. In the North, at least, the frontier is out of their hands.

The state of Egypt's frontier defenses and its relations with its neighbors in the North and South is set forth in *Adm* 14:11–15:2;

> Every man fights for his sister and he protects his own person. Is it the Nubians (*nḥsyw*)? Then we shall make our own protection. Fighting police will hold off the bowmen (*pḏtyw*). Is it the Libyans (*ṯmḥw*)? Then we shall act again. The Madjayu (*mḏ3yw*) fortunately are with Egypt. How could any man slay his own brother? The military classes which we marshal for ourselves have become bowmen (*pḏtyw*) beginning to destroy that from which they took their being and to show the Asiatics (*sṭtyw*) the state of the land. And moreover all foreign lands (*ḫ3swt*) are afraid of him.

This passage seems to present striking similarity to the situation presented by the Execration texts in which Egypt's three neighbors and traditional enemies are said to be threatening her frontiers. The description of hostilities is by no means stereotyped; it mentions the *mḏ3yw* as loyal mercenaries in distinction to the *nḥsyw*, a word that became the general term for Nubians in the Middle Kingdom. In the Execration texts the *mḏ3yw* as a group are conspicuously absent from the various Nubian peoples

82. See H. Kantor, in *Relative Chronologies*, p. 13.

(*nhsyw*) said to be rebelling. Only a single *mdзy* with an Egyptian name is recorded as treacherous.[83] The *mdзyw* continued to serve as mercenaries for Upper Egypt throughout the Second Intermediate Period and were used by Kamose in the wars of liberation against the Hyksos.[84]

The greatest threat from foreigners, as indicated by the *Admonitions,* came from the region of the Delta, where Egypt had very likely used foreign mercenaries. Here, however, there was serious defection in which the Asiatics of the region seized control, probably receiving help from abroad to hold the area for themselves. Nevertheless, the expression "to show the *sttyw* [the residents of Asia] the state of the land" does not necessarily imply an invasion; it may suggest fifth-column activity, or it may simply mean that the borders provided complete freedom of access. The passage indicates that a new authority in the Delta took the place of the Twelfth Dynasty pharaohs in their authority over Asia. The statement, "all foreign lands are afraid of him," which in the *Admonitions* refers to a new independent power in the Delta, must be compared with the common epithet of the Twelfth Dynasty pharaohs, *nb sndw hзswt,* "possessor of the respect of foreign lands." [85]

As noted above, the differences between the two Execration texts indicates an increasing threat to Egypt from Asia. The *Admonitions* would thus represent a later stage of the same development in which the "rebellion" on the part of the Asiatics resulted in an independent rule in the Delta dominated by these foreigners. The motivation for such a rebellion would not be freedom from a foreign yoke in Asia or military conquest in Egypt, but probably a breaking of the commercial monopoly in trade between Asia and Egypt of the Residence. Once this freedom of trade was established, Syria and Palestine entered

83. K. Sethe, *Die Ächtung feindlicher Fürsten,* 9.5, pp. 36 f.
84. Gardiner, *JEA, 3* (1916), 95–110.
85. A. Rowe, *Ann Serv, 39* (1939), 189 f.

upon one of the most prosperous periods of their entire histories, namely, the Middle Bronze II B–C period.

The *Admonitions* also gives a vivid picture of the internal political situation which must be placed toward the end of the Thirteenth Dynasty:

> Lower Egypt weeps. The storehouse of the king is the common property of everyone and the entire palace is without its revenues. To it (should) belong wheat, barley, etc.

> Why really, Elephantine and the Thinite nome, the shrine (?) of Upper Egypt does not pay taxes owing to civil strife. . . . What is a treasury without its revenues? [86]

These two passages seem to reflect the breakup of the government of Egypt into three parts, coinciding with the three administrative districts established by Senwosret III which continued through most of the Thirteenth Dynasty. The first quotation indicates that the Department of the North, centering in the Eastern Delta where the royal storehouses for agriculture and foreign trade were situated, was lost to the Residence. The Delta region was firmly in the hands of Asiatics, and it may be that there was an independent, Asiatic-supported régime in the North when the *Admonitions* was written. The Asiatics who formed the basis of the new power in the Delta were essentially the same Asiatics who had settled the region since the Twelfth Dynasty. There is no indication in the *Admonitions* that there was any foreign invasion, although the Delta may have received assistance from the rulers of Syria and Palestine.

In the second passage it appears that the "Department of the Head of the South" had also defected, cutting off the lucrative trade from Nubia. With these two districts gone, the region of Middle Egypt, with its center in the Residence, would be left in

86. *Adm*, 10:3–4; 3:10–13. The geographical limits seem to indicate the area known formerly as the "Department of the Head of the South." See Hayes, *JNES, 12* (1953), 31–33.

a most difficult position. This, in fact, is the situation reflected in *Admonitions* 10:6–12. This section is full of lacunae but it is clear that Ipuwer laments the loss of the former splendor of the Residence. He urges the King repeatedly to "destroy the enemies of the Residence," who have brought about the reversal of fortune in the land and monarchy.

Just as in the Execration texts, the enemies of the state are not all foreign. In 7:2–4 one reads:

> A few lawless men have ventured to despoil the land of Kingship. Men have ventured to rebel against the Uraeus.
> . . . The secret of the land, whose limits were unknown, is divulged. The Residence will be overthrown in a minute.

This may have reference to the manipulation of kingship, probably the case with the so-called "election" system of the Thirteenth Dynasty. The only semblance of one-family rule was the Sebekhotep group, Thebans who represent the last strong pharaohs before the Hyksos period. Since they almost certainly controlled the whole land and extended their influence into Asia, it is probable that the *Admonitions* reflects a time after these pharaohs, when Egypt again enters a dark period. At some time in this period, rival monarchies were established in the North and South; consequently it is about this time that Neḥesy set up a rival rule in Avaris.

There is, at any rate, no basis in the *Admonitions* for any invasion as the cause of the downfall. The indications seem quite clear: the later Hyksos rule of Egypt developed from a rival power in the Delta which drew its support from the Asiatic immigrants in the land. The Asiatic rival, according to the *Admonitions,* had numerous Egyptians as its confederates.[87]

87. Albright, in *BASOR, 179* (1965), 40 f., accepts my date for the *Admonitions* in the Second Intermediate Period, but he would put it toward the beginning of the Thirteenth dynasty. This is entirely possible. But his objection to my later date is based upon his notion of a Hyksos invasion which I cannot accept and his underestimating the seriousness of the situation presented by the *Admonitions.* Nevertheless I admit that there is considerable room for debate.

## MANETHO

A rather debatable source for the rise of the Hyksos is the historian Manetho. The most lengthy account reputed to come from him is found in Josephus. He states:

> Tutimaeus. In his reign, for what cause I know not, a blast of God smote us, and unexpectedly, from the regions of the East, invaders of obscure race marched in confidence of victory against our land. By main force they easily seized it without striking a blow; and having overpowered the rulers of the land, they then burned our cities ruthlessly, razed to the ground the temples of the gods, and treated all the natives with a cruel hostility, massacring some and leading into slavery the wives and children of others. Finally, they appointed as king one of their number whose name was Salitis. He had his seat at Memphis, levying tribute from Upper and Lower Egypt, and always leaving garrisons behind in the most advantageous positions. Above all, he fortified the district to the east, foreseeing that the Assyrians as they grew stronger, would one day covet and attack his kingdom.
>
> In the Saite [Sethroite] nome he founded a city very favourably situated on the east of the Bubastite branch of the Nile, and called Avaris after an ancient religious tradition. This place he rebuilt and fortified with massive walls, planting there a garrison of as many as 240,000 heavy-armed men to guard his frontier. Here he would come in summertime, partly to train them carefully in manoeuvers and so to strike terror into foreign tribes. . . . Their race as a whole was called Hyksos, that is "King-Shepherds." [88]

There has been general scepticism about the reliability of Manetho as a source for the Hyksos period, but Helck has come

88. The translation is taken from W. G. Waddell, *Manetho* (London, 1940), pp. 79–83.

out strongly in support of the Hellenistic historian's testimony.[89]
For Helck the basic question is whether or not there is any evidence for Hyksos in Egypt before the so-called Fifteenth Dynasty, the dynasty represented in Josephus as conquering the
whole land of Egypt. Some scholars have believed that certain
foreign kings, $ḥḳ3$ $ḫ3swt$, such as $ʿnt-ḥr$, $Iʿḳb-ḥr$, and $Smḫn$ could
have been pre-Fifteenth Dynasty rulers residing in Avaris before
the second—and more important—rulers of the Hyksos gained
control of Egypt.[90] As evidence for this they point to the reading
$ʿntiʾ$ in the Turin papyrus IX:29 as indicating the reign of $ʿnt-ḥr$
before the six rulers of the Fifteenth Dynasty. This reading has
since been discredited, and Helck states that these Hyksos, known
primarily from scarabs, could all be secondary rulers in the
Hyksos period.

Helck acknowledges the fact that there were Semitic kings
on the throne of Egypt in the Thirteenth Dynasty. But they were
"elected" just as the other Egyptian kings, and did not gain their
position by any coup d'état. This overthrow of the state only
came with the invaders of the Fifteenth Dynasty, and Helck can
see no connection between them and "the Semitic nomads who
settled in the Delta," not even with the minor Hyksos kings with
Semitic names. He emphasizes, in this connection, that the Hyksos are spoken of as foreign kings and as Asiatics, while nothing
is said of the immigrants. He also states that there is no record
of a small, independent rule of Avaris before the Hyksos period.

Helck also takes strong exception to the conclusions of Säve-
Söderbergh in the matter of archaeology.[91] He agrees with Säve-
Söderbergh that foreign elements in Egyptian culture such as
the Tell el-Yahudiyeh ware came into Egypt before the Hyksos
period and do not indicate a group of invaders; they must be
associated with the immigrant Semites as early as the Twelfth

89. Helck, *Beziehungen*, pp. 92–97.
90. Stock, *Studien*, pp. 64 ff. T. Säve-Söderbergh, *JEA*, 37 (1951), 55.
91. Säve-Söderbergh, *JEA*, 37 (1951), 53–71.

Dynasty. Instead of supporting Säve-Söderbergh's conclusion that there was no invasion, however, Helck maintains that the archaeological evidence simply cannot be used to identify the invading Hyksos. Like the Kassites in Babylonia, they came in as conquerors and were completely assimilated into the culture they found. Helck's conclusion is that, on methodological grounds, one must begin with the testimony of Manetho. It at least has the literary support of the Eighteenth Dynasty inscription of Speos Artemidos, and there is nothing from either Egyptian or Syria-Palestine sources to contradict it.

Although Helck's case for Manetho appears strong, it is not entirely convincing. He does not take seriously Alt's criticism of Manetho.[92] Alt shows that Manetho's tradition was influenced by invasions of Egypt subsequent to the Hyksos. Similar handling of the history of the Middle Kingdom by Manetho reveals that by the time of the Hellenistic period, Senwosret III is viewed as a great conqueror of Asia as far as the Black Sea, even though he only made a short raid into Palestine.[93] Certainly the mention of the Assyrians in connection with the Hyksos is a serious conflation of traditions; it casts suspicion on the whole account.

It may be asked whether Josephus really represents the best Manethoan tradition, a question Helck does not consider.[94] It seems that the account by Josephus is very liberally embellished. The other accounts give a much simpler picture and yet they are in close agreement with each other. Thus, according to Africanus, Eusebius, and the Scholia of Plato we have the following account:

> The Fifteenth [Seventeenth] Dynasty were Shepherds and brothers: they were foreign kings from Phoenicia, who seized Memphis. The first of these kings, Saites, reigned for 19 years.

---

92. A. Alt, "Die Herkunft der Hyksos," pp. 72–98.

93. Waddell, *Manetho*, pp. 67 ff. (according to the epitomes of Africanus and Eusebius).

94. See likewise Helck, *Untersuchungen zu Manetho und den ägyptischen Königslisten* (Berlin, 1956), 36–38.

These kings founded in the Sethroite nome a town, from which as a base they subdued Egypt.[95]

It is important to note the differences between this version and that given by Josephus. Josephus says that the Hyksos were "of obscure race" and "from regions of the East." The other versions simply give their origin as Phoenicia—a region long in close contact with Egypt. Josephus speaks of an unexpected invasion that took over the whole land at once, without a blow. The other versions speak only of seizing Memphis, which may have been the climax of a long process. Josephus implies that the Hyksos ruled Egypt from Memphis (the Middle Kingdom Residence?) and that Avaris was a secondary frontier post. The other versions state that the Hyksos gained control of Egypt from a base in the Northeastern Delta. The tradition of the epitomes is the more correct here. It is unlikely that the Hyksos used any other capital besides Avaris, and they probably held Avaris before they subdued the rest of Egypt. The fact that the frontier was fortified against intruders in the Middle Kingdom is further evidence against the Josephus version. The Hyksos probably kept an open border. It is obvious that Josephus had access to more than one version of Manetho, but he chose a more embellished account simply for reasons of propaganda.[96]

If we accept the accounts of Eusebius, Africanus, and the Scholia of Plato as more accurately representing Manetho, then there is no basis for believing that there was an invasion. The shorter versions which seem to reflect an ancient chronicle are to be preferred on methodological grounds. The reference to Phoenicia may be taken to refer to Retjenu, which was that part of Asia in closest association with Egypt from the Middle Kingdom to the Hyksos period. The "Shepherds" would refer to the *ḥḳꜣw ḫꜣswt*, which were common enough in the Middle Kingdom. The

95. Waddell, *Manetho*, pp. 91–99.
96. Waddell, *Manetho*, xv f.

"brothers" on the other hand, refer to the "brothers of the princes of Retjenu." [97] We have already noted that one of these cooperated with Amenemhet III on his Sinai expeditions. The fact that they are also common in Syria-Palestine in the New Kingdom would indicate a continuity in political structure throughout the MB II period and into Late Bronze in Syria-Palestine and which included the Hyksos of Egypt. Consequently, even on the basis of Manetho it is difficult to see how Helck can categorically deny any connection between the Hyksos and the Semitic groups in close contact with Egypt in the Twelfth and Thirteenth Dynasties.

When Helck contends, against Säve-Söderbergh, that there is no evidence for the Semitic immigrants of the Delta having any part in the Hyksos movement, he has, of course, not considered the *Admonitions* as evidence for this period. This source largely substantiates Säve-Söderbergh's position; it indicates that the Asiatics were a fifth-column movement, active along with Egyptians themselves. It also indicates that they gained control of Lower Egypt before they seized the Residence. There is nothing in the *Admonitions* to suggest the kind of invasion found in Josephus, although it is not hard to reconcile the other accounts of Manetho to the picture given in the *Admonitions*.

According to Helck, the terminology associated with the Hyksos, "foreign kings" and "Asiatics," indicates foreigners and not immigrants of the Delta, and this statement likewise is open to question. The term in the *Admonitions* which refers to Asiatics in Egypt is *ḫ3styw*, "foreigners," and this is used in a period before the fall of the Residence, Itj-towy (before the Fifteenth Dynasty). It is also certain that *ḫ3styw* refers to the Asiatic immigrants, and it is entirely possible that an independent Asiatic ruler of the Delta who had the support of these foreigners and political alliances in Asia would be regarded as a *ḥḳ3 ḫ3swt*, "Hyksos."

97. J. Leibovitch, *IEJ, 3* (1953), 101 f.

Helck also lays himself open to a rejoinder from archaeology when he seeks to dissociate the archaeological evidence formerly identified with the Hyksos culture from the Hyksos of the so-called Fifteenth Dynasty. It is certainly impossible for a foreign people with no previous contact with Egypt to become so completely assimilated into Egypt without leaving a single trace of their own culture. In citing the Kassites as a parallel, Helck fails to realize that they were in contact with Old Babylonian culture for at least 150 years. A more instructive parallel which Helck overlooks is the Amurrite "invasion" of the Ur III Empire. In this case, the Amurrites were an important part of the régime they eventually displaced, and it was as much a fifth-column activity from within as it was invasion from without. The end result was cultural compromise, and there is indication that the Hyksos culture represented this same kind of mixture. At any rate, the only peoples who could have taken control of Egypt and maintained the high standard of Twelfth Dynasty art and civilization were the Egyptianized Semites of Syria and Palestine. It would be very strange if the Hurrians, who left such a mark in the regions of Mesopotamia, Northern Syria, and Asia Minor, left no traces in MB II in Palestine or in Egypt in the Second Intermediate Period.[98]

In the end there are no considerations, methodological or otherwise, to support Helck's confidence in the Josephus version of Manetho and its notion of a Hyksos invasion. The other renderings of Manetho seem to preserve a more authentic tradition, and they strongly confirm the view held by Säve-Söderbergh. Consequently, apart from the testimony of some dubious propaganda, there is nothing to indicate that the Hyksos invaded Egypt in the manner envisaged by Josephus.

98. For a discussion of the Hurrian problem see below, Chapter 13. See also von Beckerath, *Untersuchungen*, pp. 123–26.

CHAPTER 9

# THE LOCATION OF AVARIS

The location of Avaris, capital of the Hyksos, is still a matter of considerable debate among scholars. The arguments for locating it in either one of two different sites seem to be so strong that even Gardiner has admitted a stalemate.[1] Yet the matter must be considered as more than an academic quibble. The location of Avaris has important implications for an understanding of the Hyksos rule. Unfortunately, while many scholars have debated the virtues of the evidence for a particular location, few have stopped to consider the historical implications of their identification.

There is general agreement that the Hyksos city of Avaris was situated on the same site as the later city of Pi-Ramesses.[2] The argument for this rests primarily on the continuity of the worship of Seth at Avaris and Pi-Ramesses as attested by the 400-year Stela from the time of Ramesses II. Furthermore, there is a similarity in the description of the general neighborhood and of geographical features, such as rivers and nomes, which define the locations of both cities. The reason for bringing Pi-Ramesses into the discussion is that the archaeological evidence about Avaris alone is not sufficient to identify the location. Consequently it is only by finding the capital Pi-Ramesses that Avaris can be located.

The problem has a long history, and many sites have been pro-

1. A. H. Gardiner, *Egypt of the Pharaohs* (Oxford, 1961), p. 258.
2. An exception is R. Weill, "The Problem of the Site of Avaris," *JEA, 21* (1935), 10–25. However, he offers no suggestion for the site of Avaris.

posed for the two capitals.[3] At the present time, however, the
discussion has fairly well settled on the two sites, Tanis and Khata
ʿna-Qantir.[4] Two kinds of evidence may be used to evaluate the
respective claims of these two sites, archaeological and literary;
both should receive independent critical evaluation.

## ARCHAEOLOGICAL EVIDENCE

### Tanis

Basic to the whole discussion of the archaeology of Tanis is the
problem of whether or not any of its architectural features can be
assigned to the Ramesside period. Here the discussion must begin
with the large enclosure walls.[5] In his earlier report of these walls,
J. L. Fougerousse [6] states that the inner enclosure was built by
the Twenty-first Dynasty, as attested by the imprinted cartouche
of Psusennes on the bricks. This wall, he argues, followed the line
of the outer wall and used part of it on the northern and western
sides; the outer wall, then, must be anterior to it and date from
the Ramesside period. However, Montet's later excavation proved

3. For a survey of various proposals with the literature up to 1950, see
H. H. Rowley, *From Joseph to Joshua: Biblical Traditions in the Light of
Archaeology* (London, 1950), pp. 25 ff.

4. The chief exponents of Tanis are: P. Montet, "Tanis, Avaris et Pi-Ramses,"
*RB, 39* (1930), 1–28; *Les Enigmes de Tanis* (Paris. 1952). A. H. Gardiner,
"Tanis and Pi-Ramesses: A Retraction," *JEA, 19* (1933), 122–28; *Onomastica, 2,*
171\*–75\*. For a review of both scholars see R. Weill, *JEA, 21* (1935), H.
Kees, "Tanis: ein Kritischer Überblick zur Geschichte der Stadt," *Nachr.
Göttingen, 1944*, 145–82, and J. von Beckerath, *Tanis und Theben*. The ex-
ponents of the region about Qantir are M. Hamza, "Excavations of the Depart-
ment of Antiquities at Qantir (Faqus District)," *Ann Serv, 30* (1930), 31–68.
W. C. Hayes, *Glazed Tiles from a Palace of Ramesses II at Kantir,* The Metropolitan Museum of Art Papers, 3 (N.Y., 1937); *Scepter of Egypt, 2,* 329. L.
Habachi, *Ann Serv, 52* (1954), 444–562. J. Couroyer, "La Résidence ramasside
du Delta et la Ramses biblique," *RB, 53* (1946), 75–98.

5. See the plan in Montet, *Les Enigmes,* pp. 8–9.

6. J. L. Fougerousse, "Etudes sur la construction de Tanis," *Kêmi, 5* (1935),
19–48.

this conclusion about the outer wall false.[7] As the latest plan shows, the outer wall replaced part of the smaller enclosure, and the monumental entrance on the western side clearly dates the whole of the larger enclosure to the time of Shoshenq III.[8]

Nevertheless Montet continues to defend the idea that Ramesses built an earlier wall and entrance which was incorporated into Shoshenq's work. He cites as evidence pieces belonging to a monumental entrance from the time of Ramesses II in the material used by Shoshenq III for his entrance. However, these elements were no longer in situ when they were excavated by Montet, and therefore their use to prove an earlier date is very doubtful.

Montet also cites, as evidence for an earlier date, the discovery of two foundation sacrifices, skeletons of an infant and an adult in pottery containers under the wall. Montet first dated them as early as the Hyksos period,[9] but he subsequently lowered this to the time of the Ramessides. However, the fact that a similar jar with a skeleton was found in relation to the entrance made by Shoshenq indicates that the others probably belong to this later period also.

There is no need to go into an investigation of the various buildings at Tanis. Even though Montet believes that there were temples dating from the Ramesside period, there is no clear archaeological evidence to prove this. Montet himself admits this:

> Ces édifices ont remplacé des temples de Ramesès II qui n'existent plus qu' à l'état de pièces detachées. Pas une pierre n'est restée certainment à sa place.[10]

7. Montet, *Les Enigmes*, pp. 13–27.

8. Ibid., pp. 14 ff.

9. Montet, *RB*, *39* (1930), 19. This led Gardiner, *JEA*, *19* (1933), 124, and von Beckerath, *Tanis und Theben*, p. 33, to attribute a Hyksos settlement to Tanis. However, there is no evidence which would suggest such a date for these burials. See, however, von Beckerath's latest view in *Untersuchungen*, pp. 151–59.

10. Montet, *Les Enigmes*, p. 50.

He feels that these earlier temples were all completely demolished and reconstructed on the same spot. This is very unlikely. It is true that in the construction of a new capital, the kings of Egypt, particularly Ramesses II, used monuments and materials from other sites and earlier periods. However, whenever a king honored a deity at the same place, the practice was to restore and amplify the existing edifice. This principle is richly illustrated by the temples of Thebes. Consequently, an alternative to Montet's proposal of a complete rebuilding of the Ramesside temples was not sufficiently considered by him. It would, in fact, be far easier to explain the archaeological phenomena of Tanis by the proposal that the capital was moved to Tanis from another location by the Twenty-first Dynasty.

The chief arguments for the identification of Tanis with Avaris and Pi-Ramesses have centered around the inscriptions on the monuments.[11] For the Hyksos period there are some statues, originally from the Twelfth and Thirteenth Dynasties which were usurped by Apophis.[12] These, in turn, were usurped by the Ramessides and then by the later pharaohs of the Twenty-first and Twenty-second Dynasties. More Hyksos monuments were found in Tanis than in any other site, yet none of them were in situ. There was neither architectural phase nor stratigraphic level which could be associated with the Hyksos. The monuments by themselves do not constitute valid evidence for the location of Avaris.

Likewise from Tanis come the most impressive monuments of the Ramesside period of any place in the Delta. These monuments include beautiful stelae, the 400-year Stela for example, statues of kings and gods, obelisks, and parts of buildings, such as beautiful inscribed columns.[13] In the inscriptions on these monu-

---

11. Note particularly Gardiner's change of mind, *JEA, 19* (1933), 123. Most other scholars followed suit.

12. See J. Vandier, *Manuel d'archéologie égyptienne, 3* (Paris, 1958), 204–13.

13. For a description with bibliography see Montet, *Les Enigmes,* pp. 52–93.

ments there are references to all the principal deities of Pi-
Ramesses known from other literary sources.[14] On the columns,
for instance, are dedications to two of these deities, Ptah-of-
Ramesses and Pre'-of-Ramesses. Gardiner argues that any object
bearing such a dedication and "obviously in situ" could only be
found in the city of the god named on it.[15] The clear fact is, however, that the columns were "obviously" *not* in situ,[16] and the fact
that a column, identical to those found in Tanis, has come to light
in Bubastis makes them all the more suspect.[17] The excavators of
Tanis even tried to reconstruct some architectural unity from the
columns and other building remnants, but without success.[18]

Another important consideration is the complete lack of any
archaeological strata before the Twenty-first Dynasty. While the
Ramesside monuments are very impressive, there are no small
finds such as pottery, scarabs, or small stelae of private persons
dating to the Ramesside period or earlier.[19] Here is yet another
indication which agrees entirely with the conclusion about the
architecture: the town did not come into existence until the
Twenty-first Dynasty. All the granite building blocks and the
statuary inscribed by earlier pharaohs must have been brought to
Tanis by the rulers of the Twenty-first Dynasty in order to con-
struct and adorn their new capital.[20] This appears to be the best
interpretation of the archaeological data.

14. Montet, *RB, 39* (1930), 26 f.; *Les Enigmes*, pp. 86 ff.

15. *JEA, 19* (1933), 123 f.

16. Montet, *Les Enigmes*, pp. 33, 45 f.

17. This fact is admitted by Gardiner, *JEA, 19* (1933), 124. He concludes
from this: "Nothing could have been easier than for the Bubastite king to
transport this column from Tanis to his own capital." Could not the same be
said for the columns at Tanis?

18. Montet, *Les Enigmes*, pp. 33, 45.

19. Note particularly the absence of tombs and foundation deposits before the
Twenty-first Dynasty. Montet, *Les Enigmes*, pp. 106 ff., 133 ff. The attempt to
find evidence for earlier graves dating to the Ramesside period, the Middle
Kingdom, and even the Old Kingdom (Montet, *Les Enigmes*, pp. 114 f.) contains the same weakness as his dating of the walls and the buildings.

20. Hayes, *Scepter of Egypt, 2,* 329.

### Khataʿna-Qantir

The other possible site for the location of Avaris and Pi-Ramesses is the district of Khataʿna-Qantir.[21] This area is now mostly under cultivation, but there remain some tells in the area of Ezbet Rushdi es-Saghira and Tell ed-Dabʿa (Fig. 21).[22] The whole area stretches about three kilometers from north to south and about one and a half kilometers from east to west. Only a few small excavations have been conducted in this region, but the finds have been quite significant.

The earliest settlement was probably built in the Middle Kingdom by Amenemhet I when the town was established as a fortress and a center for foreign commerce.[23] It is known that Amenemhet I and his successors paid great attention to the defenses of the Eastern Delta.[24] A short distance north of Khataʿna a monumental doorway of red granite was found which states that its builder, Senwosret III, renewed the great edifice built by Amenemhet I.[25] A statue of the latter king and an offering table of Senwosret III have been found at Tell ed-Dabʿa nearby.[26] At Ezbet Rushdi a complete temple of the Middle Kingdom as well as some houses and a palace of this period were uncovered by Shahata Adam.[27] Along with these were discovered stelae and inscriptions by officials of the Twelfth Dynasty.

21. On the archaeological finds, see F. Ll. Griffith, *Seventh Memoir of the Egypt Exploration Fund* (London, 1890), pp. 56 f., Pl. XIX. Hamza, *Ann Serv, 30* (1930), 31–68. Hayes, *Glazed Tiles from a Palace of Ramesses II at Kantir* (New York, 1937). H. Gauthier, "Une Tombe de la XIXᵉ dynastie à Qantir (Delta)," *Ann Serv, 32* (1932), 127 f. Habachi, *Ann Serv, 52* (1954), 444–562. S. Adam, "Recent Discoveries in the Eastern Delta," *Ann Serv, 55* (1958), 316–24; ibid., *56* (1959), 207–26.

22. The map of the area is taken from Adam, *Ann Serv, 56* (1959), Pl. 1.

23. See H. Kees, *MDIK, 18* (1962), 1–13.

24. G. Posener, *Littérature et politique*, pp. 24 ff.

25. Habachi, *Ann Serv, 52* (1954), 448 ff.

26. Ibid., pp. 452 ff.

27. Adam, *Ann Serv, 56* (1959), 207–26.

A number of statues belonging to the last ruler of the Twelfth Dynasty, Queen Sobeknofru and a minor king of the Thirteenth Dynasty, Aamu-Sahornedjheriotef, a Semite, were also found in this region.[28] Likewise two pyramidions, one belonging to a rather important King Ay of the Thirteenth Dynasty, have come

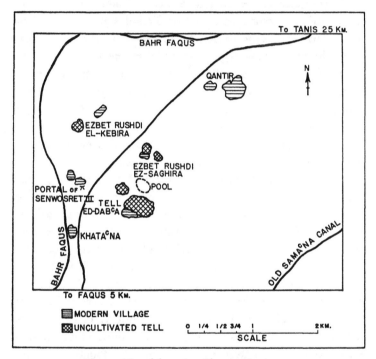

*Fig. 21*   Map of the region, Khata‹na-Qantir

to light and would suggest that some kings of the period were buried in the region.[29] This would certainly seem to indicate that Khata‹na-Qantir had great political significance in the Middle Kingdom and that its importance increased in the Second Intermediate Period.

28. Habachi, *Ann Serv, 52* (1954), 458 ff.
29. Ibid., pp. 471 ff.

Very little from this area has yet been found that can be dated to the Hyksos period. Even so, the excavations by Adam at Ezbet Rushdi have given evidence of continuous settlement from the Middle Kingdom to the Hyksos period.[30] In the early phase of settlement there was pottery typical of the Middle Kingdom, while the later phases contained Tell el-Yahudiyeh ware and scarabs of the Second Intermediate Period style. One of these scarabs has the name of Khyan preceded by the epithet *ḥḳ3 ḫ3swt*. From this same region came the fragment of a small stela of the Hyksos princess, Tany.[31] These finds, although rather meager, are more significant archaeologically than the statuary of Tanis since they definitely indicate a Hyksos settlement in this vicinity, and one which was in unbroken continuity with the former Middle Kingdom site. Nevertheless this evidence alone does not yet prove that this was their capital.

In contrast to the Hyksos period, the evidence from the Rameside times is very rich and much more conclusive. The most significant of the finds from Qantir are the numerous glazed tiles and clay molds from which they were made.[32] The scenes represented on the tiles are characteristic of the throne room of a palace, and Hayes has been able to reconstruct various elements, such as the royal dais, the window of audience, and ornamental entrances. There can be no doubt that a great palace of Ramesses II of exceptional beauty was situated at Qantir. L. Habachi, working in the same area, was able to reconstruct twenty-four complete doorways of the Ramesside period.[33] He also found a well just east of Qantir with the name of Ramesses II inscribed on the

---

30. Adam, *Ann Serv*, *56* (1959), 207–26. See Rowley, *From Joseph to Joshua*, p. 28 n., where he cites an objection to Qantir, namely, that there are no Hyksos remains. These, however, have now been found a short distance to the south-west.

31. See W. K. Simpson, "The Hyksos Princess Tany," *Chr d'Eg*, *34* (1959), 233. The provenance of the object is given as Tell ed-Dabʿa.

32. See Hamza, *Ann Serv*, *30* (1930), 46–62. Hayes, *Glazed Tiles*.

33. Habachi, *Ann Serv*, *52* (1954), 490.

blocks.[34] All these architectural elements found at Qantir are certainly in situ. There is no other important building phase of a later period in the whole area. This fact gives to the finds at Qantir an entirely different significance from those at Tanis.

The statuary and stelae of the region are also of considerable importance. In 1954, Adam excavated the base of a colossus of Ramesses II with only a part of the feet remaining.[35] Other pieces were also buried nearby, but the whole could not be reconstructed. Nevertheless, judging from the scale of other colossi of this king, Adam estimated the original height at about 10 meters. This would make it the second largest statue of this king—the largest is the colossus in the Ramesseum of Thebes.

Habachi has made a special study of the stelae from Qantir, those excavated on the spot and the ones bought in the antiquities market.[36] Most of the stelae are small and belonged to various civil, military, and religious officials. It is possible to reconstruct the facts that in this region there were palaces with extensive bureaucracy, storehouses and workshops, military installations, and temples. The latter included temples of Amun, Ptah, Reˁ, and Ma3et, the principal gods of Pi-Ramesses, as well as Sobek and Seth. Ramesses II was also acknowledged as a god.

Of considerable interest is a private stela, coming from Qantir, of a certain military official, Usermare-Nakhtu by name.[37] According to the text of the stela he was given a tract of land west of Pi-Ramesses for his service in Asia. The upper part of the stela shows the king slaying Asiatics before the god Seth. This god's human form and peculiar attire are strikingly similar to that

34. Ibid., pp. 479 ff.

35. Adam, *Ann Serv*, 55 (1958), 316–24.

36. Habachi, *Ann Serv*, 52 (1954), 501–59. A large number of these stelae bought on the open market were thought to come from Horbeit. This led scholars to think that there were important Ramesside installations at this site. See, for instance, Kees, *Ancient Egypt*, p. 201. However, Habachi has shown quite clearly that these stelae originally all came from Qantir.

37. Ibid., pp. 507 f., Pl. XXIX.

found on the 400-year Stela. It is obvious that Seth in this form
was worshiped in the area of Qantir, and these two monuments
must, in fact, belong together. While the 400-year Stela was not
in situ, there can be little doubt that the other stela originated
in the region of Qantir. Furthermore, Hamza, while excavating
at Qantir, found five ostraca which speak of a vineyard to the
west of Pi-Ramesses belonging to Usermare-Nakhtu, the same
name that is mentioned on the stela.[38]

From the archaeological evidence it is possible to conclude that
in the Ramesside period there were palaces, temples of the gods of
Pi-Ramesses, and military installations in the region of Qantir. In
contrast to Tanis, none of this material could have been brought
to Qantir in the Twenty-first Dynasty since there is no evidence
for a later occupation of the site. Furthermore, at Qantir there
is a significant archaeological context of small objects from this
same period [39] entirely lacking at Tanis, and the names of the
royal monuments represent an unbroken series for the whole of
the two Ramesside dynasties, after which royal monuments
cease.[40]

It is unlikely that two places in the Northeastern Delta were of
equal importance and honored the same gods. Kees tries to overcome the difficulty by making the royal domains stretch from
Tanis to Qantir, he even suggests that the kings spent most of
their time at the latter place.[41] This compromise has no archaeological foundation. If a choice between the two sites must be
made from the archaeological data alone, then Qantir is certainly
preferable. Everything found at Tanis from the Ramesside period
and earlier can be easily explained as having come from Qantir
at the start of the Twenty-first Dynasty. However, there is no
way of explaining how the data from Qantir came there except

38. Hamza, *Ann Serv*, *30* (1930), 43–45.

39. Ibid., 31–68. These include the tiles, mold, ostraca, etc. There is also
evidence of tombs. See Gauthier, *Ann Serv*, *32* (1932), 127 f.

40. Hayes, *Glazed Tiles*, p. 7. Habachi, *Ann Serv*, *52* (1954), 558 f.

41. Kees, *Ancient Egypt*, p. 201.

to say that it was the capital, Pi-Ramesses, in the Ramesside
Period.

## LITERARY EVIDENCE

Two kinds of literary evidence will be presented here:[42] the
first deals with descriptions of the general vicinity in which the
capitals were located; the second states the position of the capitals
in relation to the other geographic loci—town, rivers, nomes, etc.
The time-range covered by the literary evidence is very great,
stretching from sources contemporaneous with the Hyksos and the
Ramessides to documents of Greco-Roman and Byzantine times.
The late sources, however, are by no means unimportant, for the
information may be related to the classical geographers, an in-
dispensable link in our search for the geography of the Pharaonic
period.

A number of ancient sources describe the layout of the two
ancient capitals and the vicinity in which they were located.
In Josephus' version of Manetho, Avaris is described as being very
favorably situated, well fortified, and in a strategic military position. In the region of the capital the Hyksos carried on great military maneuvers. The Kamose stela confirms this and adds that
the area was rich in agriculture, particularly orchards and vine-
yards, and that the city had a suitable harbor for a large number
of seagoing ships.[43]

The many descriptions of Pi-Ramesses are similar to the Kamose description of Avaris. In the papyrus Anastasi III a certain
scribe Pibesa gives the following picture:

> It is a fair spot, there is not the like of it; resembling Thebes,
> it was Reͨ who founded it himself. The Residence is agree-
> able to live in, its fields are full of all good things; it is

42. The literary evidence has been conveniently collected and translated by
Gardiner, *JEA*, 5 (1918), 127–38, 179–200, 242–71.

43. M. Hammad, "Découverte d'une stéle du roi Kamose," *Chr d'Eg*, 30
(1955), 205 f.

furnished with abundant provisions every day; its backwaters
are full of fishes and its pools of birds; its meads are verdant
with herbage, the greenery is a cubit and a half in height,
. . . its granaries are full of wheat and spelt, they draw near
to the sky; . . . pomogranates, apples and olives; figs from

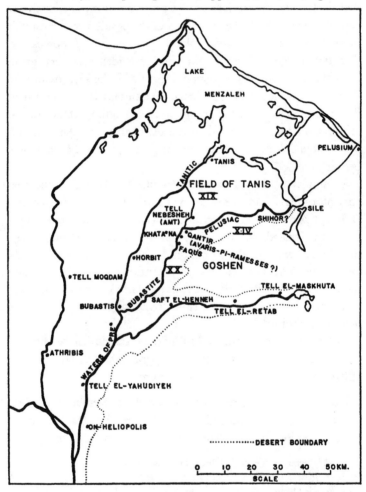

*Fig. 22* The Eastern Delta

the orchard; sweet wine of Kenkeme surpassing honey; red *wd*-fish from the lake of the Residence. . . . The Waters-of-Horus (Shi-Hor) yield salt and *Phr* natron. Its ships fare forth and return to port.[44]

In this same papyrus is a panegyric of Merneptah which speaks of Pi-Ramesses as "the marshalling place of thy cavalry, the rallying point of thy soldiers, the harbourage of thy ships' troops." Its location was "between Palestine and Egypt," "the forefront of every foreign land." As such, it was a strategic military base from which troops set out for Asia by way of the land route through Ṣile. The palaces of the city are referred to as "beauteous of balconies, dazzling with halls of lapis and turquoise."[45] It should not be surprising, therefore, that the biblical narratives of Genesis and Exodus speak of Goshen, or "the land of Rames-ses," in the vicinity of Avaris and Pi-Ramesses, as the best of the land of Egypt.[46]

Yet another text, Anastasi IV, emphasizes the great size of Pi-Ramesses. It states that "everyone hath left his town and settled within its territory," and goes on to give the limits of the region by stating, "Its western part is the house of Amun, its southern part the house of Setekh. Astarte is in its Orient, and Buto in its northern part."[47] An explanation of this passage will be given below.

Are these portrayals of the capitals at all applicable to Tanis? During a recent trip to Egypt, I had the opportunity of visiting Tanis and of confirming the descriptions of it given by Kees in his *Ancient Egypt*.[48] The region around Tanis and as far south as Tell el-Faraꞌun (Tell Nebesheh), a distance of fourteen kilo-meters, is largely "desolate waste" with only a few patches of

44. Gardiner, *JEA*, 5 (1918), 185 f.
45. Ibid., pp. 186 f.
46. Gen. 47:6, 11.
47. Gardiner, *JEA*, 5 (1918), 187.
48. Kees, *Ancient Egypt*, p. 196 f.

vegetation which are the result of modern efforts. There are very
few trees. The land is very low and often flooded from the sea
so that the terrain is primarily sandy salt flats that can support
no growth. The region can never have been an important agricultural area comparable to Pibesa's description.

The prime importance of Tanis was as a strategic naval base
on the Tanitic arm of the Nile from which it carried on sea
trade with Asia. Yet this role was late in developing and cannot
date to the Hyksos and Ramesside periods. In these times "Egyptian ports lay far up the arms of the Nile because of the shallow
mouths of the river and the flat unprotected coastline. . . . No
one wanted unloading places in an area of lagoons [Tanis] only
to be reached with difficulty from the landward side. Goods
from abroad were destined for the seat of government and state
warehouses." Kees also mentions the very difficult land approach
to Tanis since the region is often flooded. Consequently from the
military point of view "the neighboring plain of Tanis offered no
good testing-ground for the miraculous new weapon of the time,
the horse-drawn fighting chariot." [49] Tanis has no direct land
connection with the frontier fortress of Şile and would be a very
poor place from which to send out troops to Asia. In antiquity
there were no bridges, and crossing rivers involved the use of
ferries.

It is obvious from these observations that Tanis is entirely unsuitable as a location for Avaris and Pi-Ramesses, even when we
make allowance for some exaggeration in the sources. Moreover,
no scholar has ever explained how Tanis could be considered a
"most suitable location" for the capital of the Hyksos or the
Ramessides.

On the other hand, what is the case for Khataᶜna-Qantir? The
area is still part of the most fertile agricultural spots in Egypt.
The Egyptian scholar Aly Shafei has pointed out that the descrip-

49. Ibid.

tion given by Pibesa fits the region very well.[50] He mentions that
the "backwaters" and "pools" refer to the drains which ran along
the low regions beside the old Nile branch. One such drain is the
Bahr el-Baqar which even in fairly recent times provided good
fishing and duck hunting. The "lake of the Residence" referred
to in the text likewise still exists on the northern side of Tell
ed-Dabʿa. In fact, another name for this tell is Tell el-Birka
which means "mound of the lake." The reference to natron is
also of interest since this product came from this region as well
as from the Wady Natrun.

From the military point of view there was ample room for
army installations and maneuvering troops, and abundant provisions for campaigns. A confirmation of such installations and
storehouses may be seen in the so-called Horbeit stelae which
L. Habachi has shown were from this very region.[51] They give
the names of important military personnel as well as officials in
charge of the state warehouses. Furthermore, Qantir offers a
direct land route to the frontier fortress of Ṣile and was situated
on the eastern branch of the Nile which links it with Upper
Egypt and with all the important Middle Kingdom and Second
Intermediate Period sites of the Eastern Delta. This is confirmed
by the Middle Kingdom installations and inscriptions found in
the region which speak of the place as the "Mouth-of-the-Two-
Ways,"—the route to Ṣile and the route to Sinai.[52]

Moreover, in the Ramesside period there were palaces at Qantir
with "halls of lapis and turquoise" as the beautiful tiles found
there fully attest. No palace has yet been found at Tanis so that
Kees has been led to suggest that the kings spent more time at
Qantir than in Tanis itself. Moreover, Kees is compelled to cor-

50. A. B. Shafei, "Historical Notes on the Pelusiac Branch," *Bulletin de la
Société de Géographie d'Egypte, 21* (1943–46), 240 ff. I must thank Ahmed
Fakhry for calling this important article to my attention.

51. Habachi, *Ann Serv, 52* (1954), 514 ff.

52. Adam, *Ann Serv, 56* (1959), 216; see also Kees, *MDIK, 18* (1962), 3.

rect the ancient sources by suggesting that the writers of the
Anastasi papyri were also including Qantir in their descriptions
of Pi-Ramesses.[53] This correction of ancient sources is unnecessary
if one excludes Tanis from a consideration and simply identifies
Qantir with Pi-Ramesses. This is the only site which fits the requirements.

With regard to the four estates of Amun, Setekh, Astarte, and
Buto it is unclear as to their exact relation to Pi-Ramesses, particularly as the latter two are not especially deities of the capital.
I am inclined to think that these four estates are the cardinal limits
of the whole region, the "land of Ramesses," and the intention in
naming them is to indicate that the region is very large indeed.
Thus the southern limit was Avaris, perhaps Tell ed-Dabʿa itself,
while the northern limit was *Imt* (Tell Nebesheh), the holy
place of Buto. The estates of Amun to the west of the city would
comprise the land on the western side of the eastern Nile Branch.
That Astarte and other Semitic deities had estates in the eastern
part of the Fourteenth nome is very likely since a temple of Baal
Zaphon is known to have been in this region.[54] While this explanation of the text is only a conjecture it at least fits the geography of Qantir. On the other hand, it is difficult to offer any
explanation whatever for the vicinity of Tanis.

In turning to the second kind of literary evidence, one is faced
with several problems. Until the present time most of the points
of reference in the ancient sources have been uncertain. There
is also uncertainty about the identification and ancient courses of
various waterways. Because of this, any identification of Avaris
and Pi-Ramesses with a particular site fixes the location of a
whole series of interrelated geographical features in the Eastern
Delta. Consequently, the argument must rest upon the suitability
of a whole complex of identifications rather than the fixing of a
single location.

53. Kees, *Ancient Egypt*, p. 201.
54. Helck, *Beziehungen*, pp. 482 f.

There are two conditions for the location of Avaris given by Manetho:[55] first, that it was situated in the Sethroite, or Fourteenth, nome; second, that it was east of the Bubastite branch of the Nile. Pi-Ramesses may be similarly located by means of ancient authorities. It was associated with the "Waters of Preꜥ," which according to the Golenischeff Glossary is the most eastern branch of the Nile.[56] In a similar geographic list the "Waters of Avaris" occurs in place of the "Waters of Preꜥ."[57] Pi-Ramesses is also associated with Shihor, which is referred to as the river of the Fourteenth nome,[58] and is the Eastern boundary of Egypt, according to various biblical passages.[59] Consequently, the "Waters of Preꜥ," the "Waters of Avaris," and Shihor are all names for the Bubastite branch of the Nile, or a part of it. This branch, in turn, is the equivalent of the Pelusiac branch, and on this river both Avaris and Pi-Ramesses were situated.[60]

Montet has attempted to apply these two conditions to Tanis.[61] He points out that in one rendering of Josephus Avaris is spoken of as in the Saite nome. He then shows that this nome is not to be confused with Sais in the Western Delta but should be taken as an alternate rendering in the Greek authors of Tanitic, and in this he is entirely convincing. Yet, his equation of the Tanitic nome with the Sethroite nome in the other versions of Manetho is a non sequitur. The epitome of Manetho in Eusebius and Africanus mention the Saite (or Tanitic) nome in connection with an etiology of this name, but they keep it quite distinct from the Sethroite nome. The text of Josephus in which the name Sethroite was eliminated has suffered a corruption.

55. Waddell, *Manetho*, pp. 79–83.
56. Gardiner, *JEA*, *5* (1918), 198.
57. Gardiner, *JEA*, *10* (1924), 92.
58. Gardiner, *JEA*, *5* (1918), 251 f.
59. Josh. 13:3; Is. 23:3; Jer. 2:18; I Chron. 13:5.
60. Gardiner, *JEA*, *5* (1918), 251 f.
61. Montet, *RB*, *39* (1930), 9 ff. See also his *Géographie de l'Egypte ancienne* (Paris, 1957), pp. 192–99.

Moreover, it is fairly certain that the capital of the Sethroite nome was Şile.[62] The question is, can Tanis be put into the same nome? Scholars, including Gardiner, had long felt that Tanis ought to be considered as located in the Nineteenth nome, with *İmt* (Tell Nebesheh) as its chief city.[63] However, Montet persuaded Gardiner, among others, that the proximity of Tanis to Tell Nebesheh and its great distance from Şile should not be used as an argument to say that Tanis belongs to the Nineteenth nome with Tell Nebesheh, and not the Fourteenth nome with Şile.[64] This may be true, but the territory between Tanis and Şile offers no reasonable geographic unity, while that between Tanis and Tell Nebesheh does. Furthermore, Ptolemy, the classical geographer, makes the Bubastite River the dividing line between the Fourteenth and the Nineteenth nomes, and this would put Tanis and *İmt* in the same nome, the Nineteenth.[65] To make the Tanitic branch equivalent to the Bubastite branch is no solution. This would still put the Nineteenth nome east of the river, together with the Fourteenth nome. Montet's proposal cannot be reconciled with Ptolemy's account.

Montet also tries to associate the other names of the Bubastite branch with the Tanitic branch,[66] but not very successfully. He states that Shihor cannot be a river, since the name implies a "basin" or "pool," and therefore he identifies it with Lake Menzaleh. However, Gardiner has shown that Shihor was a part of the Nile, associated with the Fourteenth nome, and extending to the vicinity of Şile.[67] All this makes the identification with Lake Menzaleh unsuitable. In antiquity, the lake did not extend

---

62. Gardiner, *JEA*, 5 (1918), 242.

63. Ibid.

64. Montet, *RB*, 39 (1930), 7; Gardiner, *JEA*, 19 (1933), 125.

65. Gardiner, *JEA*, 5, (1918), 244 f.

66. Montet, *RB*, 39 (1930), 23 f. See, however, *Géographie*, p. 200, "On peut admettre que le Chi-Hor correspond à la branche pelusiaque qui passait à Defeneh et à El-Kantara et que des canaux le réunissaient à la branche tanitique."

67. Gardiner, *JEA*, 5 (1918), 251 f.

to Şile; the Pelusiac River went all the way to the Pelusiac mouth, and it did not empty into Lake Menzaleh, proof that Lake Menzaleh and Shihor are not the same. However, the river may have branched off to form a lake in the eastern part of the nome, extending south to the region of Şile, and this would account for the name.

Furthermore, the "Waters of Pre'" are also spoken of as watering the Arabian nome, the chief city of which was Phacusa.[68] This nome stretched between Phacusa and Saft el-Henna, bordering on the Fourteenth nome in the north and the Bubastite nome on the west. It is difficult to see how the Tanitic branch could be described as watering this nome. It must certainly mean the Pelusiac branch. Gardiner admits that the transference of the designation "Waters of Pre'" "to the Tanitic branch leaves the Pelusiac branch without a native Egyptian name." [69]

A number of arguments center on the geographic designation "Field of Tanis (Djaˁnet)." [70] This term is known from the Ramesside period and designates the region south and east of the later city of Tanis. Montet points out that "the Field of Tanis" is closely associated with the Fourteenth nome. However, the relationship is always described as the *phw* of the Fourteenth nome. This does not mean that it was in the nome. On the contrary it constituted the "hinterland" or "boundary" of the nome.[71] Taking the Pelusiac branch as the boundary of the Fourteenth nome, one can easily see how the "Field of Tanis" could be spoken of as the *phw* of this nome since it lay on the northeast side of the river. If Tanis and Şile were in the same nome, the expression *"phw* of the Fourteenth nome" would be unintelligible.[72]

68. Ibid., p. 258.

69. Gardiner, *JEA, 19* (1933), 125; see also his *Onomastica, 2,* 168* f.

70. Montet, *RB, 39* (1930), 12 f; *Géographie,* pp. 201 f.

71. See particularly Gardiner, *JEA, 5* (1918), 247 f.

72. Gardiner does not try to give any new explanation for this phrase in his retraction, *JEA, 19* (1933), 126. On the Fourteenth nome in the Middle Kingdom,

Another strong argument against the site of Tanis as the location of Pi-Ramesses is found in the Golenischeff Glossary of
the Twenty-first Dynasty,[73] where the names of both cities occur
with several names between. Gardiner could offer no explanation
for this. However, J. von Beckerath proposes that the Pi-Ramesses
here refers to another city by this name, situated in the Western
Delta.[74] Although this is possible, it does not seem very likely.

On the basis of the biblical evidence, there are further objec-
tions to Tanis. The "land of Goshen" (also called "the land of
Ramesses") was located in the vicinity of the capital in the time
of Joseph (= Avaris) and in the time of Moses (= Pi-Ramesses).[75] The Greek tradition of the Septuagint identifies the "land
of Goshen" (Gesem) with the Arabian nome which was certainly not in the vicinity of Tanis.[76]

It is clear from this examination that Tanis does not fit the

see H. G. Fischer, "Some Notes on the Easternmost Nomes of the Delta in the
Old and Middle Kingdoms," *JNES, 18* (1959), 135 ff. He discusses the nome's
Egyptian name, *ḫnt ʿзb*, which he takes to mean "Front of the East." However,
his attempt to locate this nome between Tanis and Şile does not take sufficient
account of two factors. First, there is no clear evidence that Tanis was in existence
in the Middle Kingdom. Secondly, he avoids the question of the Eastern branch
of the Nile and of the corresponding relation between the Nineteenth nome and
the Fourteenth nome. It is far more likely that the "Front of the East" designates
the area lying along the Pelusiac River between Şile and the region of Qantir,
at which point the river bends south. The "Eastern" nome would border on the
"Front of the East" and correspond to the Twentieth or Arabian nome.

73. Gardiner, *JEA, 5* (1918), 198; cf. *JEA, 19* (1933), 126. Gardiner's further
argument that complete silence about Tanis in the Ramesside Period proves that it
must have been the capital, Pi-Ramesses, is not so cogent as he thinks. It may
also prove that Tanis did not exist at all in this period.

74. von Beckerath, *Tanis und Theben,* p. 30 f.

75. Rowley's scepticism, *From Joseph to Joshua,* pp. 25 f., in equating the
period of Joseph to that of the Hyksos is quite unjustified. There is, of course, a
strong etiological factor throughout the story. The mention of Egyptian suscepti-
bilities with respect to shepherds is probably an etiological explanation for the
later animosity against the Hyksos rule and for the predominant Semitic population of the Arabian nome. The Hyksos were not nearly so un-Egyptian in their
behavior as Rowley assumes, and they certainly did not despise the god Re.

76. Gardiner, *JEA, 5* (1918), 261.

evidence since the resulting geographical picture leads only to confusion. Can a better case be made for Qantir?

An initial problem which besets the treatment of the site of Qantir is to locate the ancient course of the Pelusiac branch of the Nile. Most Egyptologists seem to follow the reconstruction proposed by J. Ball.[77] However, since he identified the classical Phacusa with Saft el-Henna he has the river flowing much too far to the east through the edge of the desert. Since Phacusa is undoubtedly the modern Faqus, a different route must be sought north of Bubastis. Another scholar, Ali Shafei,[78] working along the same principles that the Nile branches follow the ridges of the land and the natural drains follow the depressions, has traced the Pelusiac branch along the Bahr Faqus to the town of Faqus. From here it follows roughly in the line of the modern Samaᶜ na canal, which passes to the west of Tell ed-Dabᶜa and Qantir. In this region the Bahr Faqus and the Bahr el Baqar are natural drains and could never have been the old course of the Nile.[79] The ancient river flowed northward from Qantir and then, turning eastward, passed south of Tell Nebesheh and proceeded in a northeasterly course to the Pelusium mouth. Shihor was a lake region which branched off from the Pelusiac river extending southwards as far as the vicinity of Ṣile near the modern town of Kantara.

If this reconstruction is correct, then the region of Tell ed-Dabᶜa-Qantir, being east of the Pelusiac branch, would fulfill all the requirements of the ancient authorities with regard to the eastern branch of the Nile and the location of the Fourteenth nome. On the other hand it would be very difficult to account

77. J. Ball, *Egypt in the Classical Geographers* (Cairo, 1942). Cf. Prince Omar Toussoun, *Mémoire sur les anciennes branches du Nil: Mémoires présenté à l'Institut d'Egypte, 4* (Cairo, 1922).

78. A. Shafei, *Bulletin de la Soc. de Géog.*, 21 (1943–46), 233 ff.

79. Montet, *Géographie*, Pls. 1 & 2, makes the Eastern Branch follow the Bahr el Baqar and makes the Tanitic Branch follow the Bahr Faqus Drain, both of which cannot be correct according to Shafei's principle.

for the great importance of Khata‹na-Qantir from the Middle
Kingdom to the Ramesside period if it were not on the eastern
branch of the Nile.

Furthermore, the requirement about Goshen being near both
capitals would also be met. As mentioned above, the Septuagint
identifies the land of Goshen with the Arabian nome, of which
the chief city was Phacusa, the modern Faqus, which is only
three or four miles from Khata‹na-Qantir. Moreover, E. Naville
has shown that the name "Goshen" is actually preserved in the
name Pharcusa (Faqus).[80] He states that � ☖☗ is to be read
*gsmt* since �, which may be read *g* or *ꭍs*, is here a hieratic variant
for ☖, as is clearly indicated by a hieroglyphic rendering of
the name, and must be read as *g*. From *gsmt* (MK *gsm*) one
may easily derive both the Hebrew Goshen and the LXX Gesem.
A late form of this name dropped the "m" and appears with the
article *p3* in the classical sources as Phacusa.[81] Thus the requirements of the biblical narratives are also met by the location of
Qantir.

There is an interesting confirmation of this identification in
the narrative of Abbess Aetheria who travelled in the Bible lands
in A.D. 533–540. She states the following:

> But from the town of Arabia [Faqus] it is four miles to
> Ramesses. We, in order to arrive at Arabia, our stopping
> place, had to pass through the midst of Ramesses, which
> town of Ramesses is now fields, so much so that it does not

80. Naville, "The Geography of the Exodus," *JEA, 10* (1924), 28 f.

81. The position of Naville is opposed by Gardiner, *JEA, 5* (1918), 218 ff.,
who reads the name as *ꭍsmt* and connects it with ▭ ▩ ▭ *ꭍsmt*-land.
However, there is little reason for equating these two places, especially since they
are orthographically distinct as early as the Middle Kingdom. On the other hand,
I agree with Gardiner (also *JEA, 10* [1924], 95) that Phacusa is the modern
Faqus and that it must be kept distinct from Saft el-Henna. Thus *gsmt*, with its
chief city Phacusa, is in the northern part of the Twentieth nome, the so-called
Arabian nome, while Per-Soped (Saft el-Henna), the gateway to the *ꭍsmt*-land,
is in the southern part of the Twentieth nome.

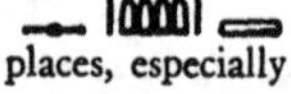

possess a single habitation. It is true that it is visible, since it both was huge in circuit and had many buildings; for its ruins, however tumbled-down they may be, appear endless even to this day.[82]

Tell ed-Dabᶜa is only four Roman miles from Faqus, and it is certain that the Abbess is referring to this site. In her time the ruins were still very impressive, although since then they have been a quarry for building materials and for obtaining lime from the limestone. If so much of the capital still remained as late as this, there is every reason to accept the fact that a correct tradition about its identity was preserved down to Greco-Roman times, and this would give far greater weight to the Greek sources.

When all the evidence is duly considered, both archaeological and literary, there is little doubt left that Khataᶜna-Qantir is to be preferred to Tanis as the location of Avaris and Pi-Ramesses. It remains now to consider the significance of this location, particularly Avaris.

### SIGNIFICANCE OF THE LOCATION

The clue to the historical understanding of the location of the Hyksos capital lies in the etymology of the name, "Avaris." In Egyptian, the name consists of two elements, $hwt$ $wᶜrt$. Concerning the first element, $hwt$, J. Černý states that it denotes "a planned rectangular settlement surrounded by a high brick wall, the plan of which is depicted by the hieroglyph 𓉗 itself, as opposed to the spontaneous agglomeration of inhabitants in ⊗, $niwt$, 'town' or 'village.'"[83] This agrees well with the description of Avaris in the Kamose stela as a walled settlement.

The second element, $wᶜrt$, is more problematical. Gardiner takes it as descriptive of the region on the border of Egypt and translates it as "desert strip."[84] In this he is followed by P.

---

82. Gardiner, *JEA, 5* (1918), 263. See also Naville, *JEA, 10* (1924), 27 f.
83. Černý, "The True Form of the Name Snofru," *RSO, 38* (1963), 89.
84. Gardiner, *JEA, 3* (1916), 100.

Labib.[85] Similarly Kees renders it as "dunes" and associates it
with the terrain in the vicinity of Tanis.[86] Both meanings, however, would contradict the descriptions of Avaris as rich in agriculture. A much more likely possibility is to understand the word
*wꜥrt* in its usual meaning of "department" or "administrative
district." The word was used in this sense in the Middle Kingdom
to designate the main divisions of the land created by the reform
of Senwosret III.[87] Our previous discussion of this administrative
reform showed that the Department (*wꜥrt*) of the North which
included the nome of Memphis and the whole of the Delta, had
as its center the important settlement around Khataꜥna. Such a
planned settlement (*ḥwt*), with all its administrative bureaus
and its military installations, fits exactly the designation "Headquarters of the Department," *ḥwt wꜥrt*—Avaris.

When Avaris is identified with this important settlement of
the Middle Kingdom, its location takes on a new significance.
It becomes clear that all the monuments in Tanis from the Middle
Kingdom and early Second Intermediate Period, including those
usurped by the Hyksos Apophis, come from the vicinity of
Khataꜥna. These statues, along with the ones actually found on
the site, bear witness to the great importance of Khataꜥna from
the Middle Kingdom through the Hyksos Period. The Hyksos,
by taking control of this strategic center, inherited the Middle
Kingdom structures of government which administered the
whole of Lower Egypt. They also had control of the vital access
routes to Asia. In Khataꜥna they could establish their most effective capital and grace their sacred buildings with the royal monuments of the previous periods.

It is quite possible that the shift of control of the Delta by
Asiatics is reflected in the *Admonitions:* [88] "Foreigners have be-

85. Labib, *Die Herrschaft der Hyksos*, pp. 20 f.
86. Kees, *Ancient Egypt*, p. 197.
87. See above, Chapter 7.
88. See above, Chapter 8.

come people (Egyptians) everywhere" (1:9); "The entire Delta will no longer be hidden; the confidence of the Northland is a beaten path. . . . The foreigners are now skilled in the work of the Delta" (4:6–8); "Lower Egypt weeps. The storehouse of the king is the common property of everyone and the entire palace is without its revenues" (10:3–4). Thus the Asiatics rose to power in the administration of the Northern Department and gradually took control. They brought freedom of movement and trade with Asia to the frontiers of the Delta and they shut off the South from valuable commodities, such as metals and lumber, completely crippling its power to resist. This only could have been done through effective control of Avaris, the key to trade, defense, and administration of the North. This fact has hitherto been completely obscured by the identification of Avaris with Tanis. The location of Avaris at Khataᶜna-Qantir, therefore, can only result in a new understanding of the Hyksos rise to power, and a new evaluation of their rule in Egypt.

# CHAPTER 10

# THE "DYNASTIES" OF THE HYKSOS

One of the most vexing and controversial problems related to the history of the Hyksos is the names and order of the Hyksos and the "dynasties" to which they belong.[1] At the present time the sources are too limited to give any complete answer. Nevertheless, in recent years new material makes possible at least a partial answer that definitely excludes certain earlier proposals. In spite of the new evidence, many scholars have retained the notion of two or more Hyksos "dynasties."

Our ancient literary sources are only of limited help. The Turin Canon, the only king-list which makes any mention of the Hyksos, is full of lacunae at this point.[2] It does, however, give the name of the last Hyksos as Khamudy, and it gives the total number of Hyksos kings as six, with the total length of their reign as 108 years. From about 700 B.C. comes a list of the successive high priests of Memphis which gives the name of the king during each priest's term of office.[3] Among the kings, there appear

1. On the Hyksos "dynasties," see particularly Stock, *Studien*, pp. 63–70; "Der Hyksos Chian in Bogazköy," *MDOG, 94* (1963), 77–80. H. E. Winlock, *The Rise and Fall of the Middle Kingdom in Thebes*, pp. 97 ff. T. Säve-Söderbergh, *JEA, 37* (1951), 65 ff. Hayes, *The Scepter of Egypt, 2*, 1–8; *CAH²*, 2, ch. 2, pp. 15–25. Helck, *Beziehungen*, pp. 93 ff., and the chronological chart at the end of the book. Albright, in *BANE*, pp. 335 f. Gardiner, *Egypt of the Pharaohs*, pp. 171 f., 442 f. von Beckerath, *Untersuchungen*, pp. 127–37.

2. Gardiner, *The Royal Canon of Turin* (Oxford, 1959); von Beckerath, *Untersuchungen*, pp. 20–26.

3. L. Borchardt, *Ein Stammbaum memphitischer Priester*, SPAW, Phil.-Hist. Klasse 24 (Berlin, 1932); von Beckerath, *Untersuchungen*, pp. 27 f.

to be three Hyksos, ꜥꜣkn, šꜣrk, and ipp (Apophis). Only the last
of these three is attested from other sources.[4]

Another literary source for the names of the Hyksos is Manetho
as preserved in Josephus and the various epitomes, Eusebius,
Africanus, and the Scholia of Plato.[5] These do not all agree on
the names, number, and order of the kings, or even to the dynasty to which they belong. The names may be listed as Salatis
or Saites, Bnon, Apachnan, Iannas or Staan, Archles or Aseth,
and Apophis. Both Josephus and Africanus give all six names
and assign them to the Fifteenth Dynasty. The total of six kings
seems to agree with the Turin Canon, although the length of the
dynasty in these two recensions of Manetho is impossible. Eusebius and the Scholia of Plato, on the other hand, allow only 103
years to the Hyksos dynasty, which they assign to the Seventeenth
Dynasty. A rule of a 103 years agrees fairly well with the 108
years of the Turin Canon. Putting the various elements together,
we may regard the principal dynasty of the Hyksos as consisting
of six kings who ruled for about 108 years, and for the sake of
convenience we may call them the Fifteenth Dynasty. Africanus
also ascribes the Sixteenth and part of the Seventeenth Dynasties
to the Hyksos. However, he does not give the names of the rulers
and only indicates that they were quite numerous. These are
generally regarded as secondary rulers of restricted areas, and
many of them were contemporaneous with each other.

As an independent source for this period, Manetho is of rather
doubtful value. This is particularly true with respect to the names
of the kings; only one of them, Apophis, is definitely attested
from the monuments and literary sources of the period. Some
justification for this skepticism may be seen in Manetho's mutila-
tion of the Eighteenth Dynasty names. One would assume that

4. Stock, *MDOG, 94* (1963), 78 f., attempts to identify šꜣrk with Salatis of
Manetho, but this is very unlikely both on linguistic and chronological grounds.
Likewise, ꜥꜣkn is taken by some to be ꜥꜣknnrꜥ Apophis, but this is very doubtful.

5. Waddell, *Manetho*, pp. 79–83; von Beckerath, *Untersuchungen*, pp. 11–20.

his sources should have been better for the Eighteenth Dynasty than for the Hyksos period, and yet even many of the names can hardly be recognized.[6]

A number of literary texts make reference to Apophis. One of these is the Rhind Mathematical Papyrus, which is dated to the thirty-third year of ʿAwoserreʿ Apophis.[7] With the discovery of the Kamose stela in 1954,[8] it was learned that ʿAwoserreʿ Apophis was a contemporary of Kamose; he must have been an elderly monarch at the time. The same king is also probably mentioned in a late story of the Ramesside period [9] together with Seqenenreʿ Taʿo, the father of Kamose.

The other sources for a reconstruction of the Hyksos "dynasties" consist of a large number of scarabs inscribed with various names, and a number of monuments, mostly small and occasionally including a short inscription.[10] Some previous attempts at a reconstruction, primarily on the basis of scarabs, have proved unsuccessful. For instance, the careful investigation by Stock,[11] based on the typological development of scarab styles, appeared to have settled the order in which the most important kings ruled. With the discovery of the Kamose stela, however, it was learned that ʿAwoserreʿ Apophis, the ruler whom Stock had placed at the beginning of the Fifteenth Dynasty, was, as a contemporary of Kamose, very close to the end of the line. Another scholar who attempted to draw far-reaching conclusions

6. It is, therefore, rather surprising to see Helck, *Beziehungen*, place such complete confidence in the names of Manetho.

7. E. Peet, *The Rhind Mathematical Papyrus* (Liverpool, 1923).

8. Habachi, "Preliminary Report on Kamose Stela . . . ," *Ann Serv, 53* (1956), 195 ff.; Hammad, "Découverte d'une stéle du roi Kamose," *Chr d'Eg, 30* (1955), 198–208.

9. *Papyrus Sallier I*, translated by B. Gunn and A. H. Gardiner, *JEA, 5* (1918), 40–45. Wilson, *ANET*, pp. 231 f.

10. A convenient collection of these monuments may be found in P. C. Labib, *Die Herrschaft der Hyksos*, pp. 23–34. For a bibliography on scarabs, see Stock, *Studien*, pp. 9–10. To these may be added the scarabs of the Metropolitan Museum, New York, in Hayes, *Scepter of Egypt, 2, 5.*

11. Stock, *Studien*.

on the basis of scarabs was R. Weill,[12] who used the scarabs as evidence that the Hyksos were contemporaneous with the Twelfth Dynasty pharaohs. No other scholar, however, follows Weill in this reconstruction of Egyptian history, and his results cast suspicion on his method.[13] He completely ignored certain basic criteria in the evaluation of scarabs, and his work on scarabs is of small value.[14]

While it is obvious that the scarabs and monuments can be used to prove too much, Helck seriously underestimates their value.[15] His concern with the importance of Manetho has certainly led to some erroneous conclusions.[16] The scarabs and monuments do preserve the names of important rulers of the period who are unknown from other sources. These objects also give us some control over the names preserved in the literary sources, particularly in Manetho.

Any reconstruction of the Hyksos dynasties must begin with Apophis. He is known from the literary sources mentioned above, and his place and importance are open to no doubt. His monuments may be listed as follows: [17]

1. A large number of scarabs, either with the name of Apophis or the prenomen ʿAwoserreʿ. Some have also associated the

12. R. Weill, *XII° dynastie, royauté de Haute-Egypte et domination Hyksos dane le nord*. See also his previous work, *La Fin du moyen empire égyptien* (Paris, 1918).

13. See particularly the review of Wilson, *JNES, 14* (1955), 131–33.

14. For instance, he does not seem to recognize the fact that scarabs with the names of Twelfth Dynasty kings were made in the Second Intermediate Period and later. This completely vitiates his arguments on style.

15. Helck almost completely ignores the scarabs and gives only brief consideration to a few of the monuments of Khyan and Apophis, *Beziehungen*, pp. 109, 166 n.

16. Ibid., p. 93, and the chart at the end of the book, denies that Khyan is to be equated with Manetho's Iannas, whom he places after Apophis. What he does with Khyan is a mystery, since he appears to acknowledge his importance on p. 190; Khyan is completely missing in his chart.

17. For these monuments and the literature see Labib, *Die Herrschaft der Hyksos*, pp. 27 f.

scarabs bearing the name ššy with this king since the š ⇒ was often confused with the p □ sign. However, this identification remains doubtful.

2. A scribe's palette from the Fayyum with a dedication to Apophis. It speaks of the Hyksos ruler as "beloved son of Reᶜ," "the living image of Reᶜ on earth," and "light on the day of war, greater is his name than any other king, renown even to foreign lands."

3. A block of granite from a building in Gebelein with the king's name inscribed on it.

4. An adze blade, recently acquired by the British Museum, is inscribed: "The good god, ʿAwoserreᶜ, beloved of Sobk, Lord of Sumenu." Sumenu, an important center of the worship of Sobk in Upper Egypt, was probably situated in the region of Gebelein.[18]

5. A fragment of a stone jar with the name of Apophis and his daughter found in the grave of Amenhotep I. There was no attempt to mutilate the cartouches of the Hyksos.

6. A piece of a building inscription from Bubastis containing only the son of Reᶜ name Apophis.

7. Two monuments containing the name of a certain princess Tany, together with that of Apophis. One was a reused offering stand of the Twelfth Dynasty, and the other was part of a stela found at Tell ed-Dabᶜa in the Delta.[19]

In addition to these objects are a few others which contain two different prenomina, nb-ḫpš-rᶜ and ᶜ3-ḳnn-rᶜ. One with nb-ḫpš-rᶜ is:

8. A sword of nḥmn in the grave of ᶜ3bd in Saqqara.
Those with ᶜ3ḳnn-rᶜ are:

18. T. G. H. James, "A Group of Inscribed Tools," *BMQ, 24* (1961), 40, Pl. XIII:6.

19. On these two objects, see particularly W. K. Simpson, *Chr d'Eg, 34* (1959), 233–39.

9. A fragment of a large jar found in Memphis.

10. Usurped statues found in Tanis though obviously not in situ. One was the statue of *mr-mš‹*, a Thirteenth Dynasty pharaoh; the other two were Middle Kingdom sphinxes.[20]

11. A dagger found at Thebes.

12. An offering table of black granite with an inscription: "Live Horus, Pacifier of the two lands, the good god, ‹Aqenenre‹; this is what he made for his father Seth, Lord of Avaris, when he placed all lands beneath his feet."

The three prenomina raise the problem of whether or not there were more than one king with the name Apophis. H. E. Winlock proposed that all three names belonged to the same person,[21] but this is strongly opposed by most scholars of Egyptian history. His critics point out that the ‹Awoserre‹ Apophis was closely associated with Khyan at the height of Hyksos power, so that a different Apophis must belong to the period of Hyksos decline.[22] The tendency, therefore, was to put ‹Awoserre‹ at the beginning of the Hyksos rule over Egypt as a whole, and to make ‹Aqenenre‹ the pharaoh of the decline.[23] The Kamose stela, however, has shown Winlock to be correct in making ‹Awoserre‹ contemporary with Kamose and has virtually eliminated the possibility of other Apophises following ‹Awoserre‹.[24] Nevertheless, Hayes continues to include three kings following ‹Awoserre‹, one of which is ‹Aqenenre‹.[25] He considers them to be restricted in their rule to the Delta, but he does not explain

20. For a discussion of the so-called Hyksos monuments of Tanis, see J. Vandier, *Manuel d'archéologie égyptienne* (3 vols. Paris, 1952–58), *3*, 204–13.

21. Winlock, *The Rise and Fall of the Middle Kingdom*, pp. 145 f. So also Helck, *Beziehungen*, p. 166 n.

22. Säve-Söderbergh, *Bibl Or*, 6 (1949), 88; R. O. Faulkner, *JEA, 34* (1948), 124.

23. So Stock, *Studien*, pp. 68 f. He was followed in this by Säve-Söderbergh, *JEA, 37* (1951).

24. Von Beckerath (*Untersuchungen*, pp. 127 ff.) comes to the same conclusion.

25. For references see p. 152 n. Also Albright in *BANE*, pp. 335 f.

the inscription on the offering table in which ʿAqenenreʿ cele-
brates his accession to the throne as the ruler of the whole of
Egypt and countries beyond its borders. Even allowing for a
certain exaggeration in language, it can hardly reflect a ruler,
limited to a small area in the Eastern Delta, who was in retreat
before the new power of the Eighteenth Dynasty. Consequently,
it is entirely likely that ʿAqenenreʿ and Nebḥepešreʿ represent
early prenomina of the one king Apophis. This proposal should
not be considered strange. Kamose seems to have modified his
titulary,[26] and the same was true in the Eleventh Dynasty, particularly Menthotpe I.[27]

Sewoserenreʿ Khyan must be closely associated with Apophis
in time and importance. Besides his numerous scarabs, he left
two monuments in Egypt which indicate his connection with
Apophis. These are:[28] a block of granite in the region of Gebelein bearing his name; and a Middle Kingdom statue in Bubastis
which Khyan usurped and on which he placed his own name.

Monuments beyond Egypt bearing his name are widely dis-
persed: a small basalt lion, bought in Baghdad from an antiquities dealer; the lid of an alabaster jar, found in the palace of
Knossos in Crete; an obsidian vase fragment from Bogazköy;[29]
and scarabs found in Palestine.

Scarabs form the only extant evidence from the Hyksos period
for the other foreign rulers. Along with the name of the king,
they also give the royal epithets, *nfr nṯr,* "good god," or *s3-rʿ,*
"son of Reʿ." These scarabs yield so many names that they cannot all be considered as primary rulers of Egypt. If we consider

26. The change in the titulary was interpreted otherwise by H. Gauthier (in
*Griffith Studies,* pp. 3–8), who understood it as an indication of two pharaohs
named Kamose.

27. See Gardiner, "The First Menthotpe of the Eleventh Dynasty," *MDIK, 14*
(1956), 42–51.

28. For the monuments of Khyan, see Labib, *Die Herrschaft der Hyksos,* pp.
31 f.

29. See Stock, *MDOG, 94* (1963), 73–80.

that names compounded with *r* indicate prenomina, than these may belong with some of the "Son of Re" names. This is certain in the case of at least three rulers, *mr-wsr-r* Ja'qob-har, *swsr-n-r* Khyan, and *'3-wsr-r* Apophis. Even if there were one-half the number of names, there would still be too many kings for the period.

It may still be possible to discern the more important rulers from among these names. One criterion helpful in this respect is the distribution of their scarabs. There the three rulers, *m3'-ib-r*, *šy*, and Ja'qob-har, whose scarabs are found in Palestine in the north, throughout Egypt, and as far south as Kerma in Nubia.[30] Although these little objects cannot be taken as proof of political domination, they certainly signify commercial and diplomatic relations.[31] It is instructive that a similar distribution is attested for the scarabs of a chancellor, *Ḥ3r*,[32] who may have served as a powerful vizier for one or more of these kings. The widespread distribution cannot be explained on any other basis than the fact that the kings had more than local power and prestige.

Another group of scarabs of special interest are those containing the epithet *ḥk3 ḥ3swt*. These scarabs include the names *smqn*, *'nt-ḥr*, and Khyan. While Khyan used the other epithets of Egyptian royalty, *smqn* and *'nt-ḥr* are only known by the title *ḥk3 ḥ3swt*. These scarabs may belong to pre-Fifteenth Dynasty rulers of the Delta. I suspect that during the Hyksos domination of the whole of Egypt only the principal rulers, Khyan and Apophis for example, bore the titles *ḥk3 ḥ3swt*.[33]

On the basis of the evidence considered above, the following

30. See chart, in Säve-Söderbergh, *JEA*, *37* (1951), 65, Fig. 3.

31. See Säve-Söderbergh, "The Nubian Kingdom of the Second Intermediate Period," *Kush*, *4* (1956), 60. See also his earlier view in *Ägypten und Nubien*, pp. 128 f.

32. Säve-Söderbergh, *JEA*, *37* (1951), 65 f.

33. Apophis is called *ḥk3*, "ruler," while Kamose is only a *wr*, "chieftain" (or vassal?). This distinction is generally maintained also in the *Papyrus Sallier* I, where Sequenenre is called a *wr*, "prince," while Apophis is called *nswt*, "king." However, even a *wr*, "prince" or "chieftain," may use royal epithets.

reconstruction of the so-called "dynasties" of the Hyksos may be offered. If we accept the designation of the Fifteenth Dynasty as including the Hyksos who ruled the whole of Egypt until their final expulsion by Ahmose, then we must certainly include in it Khyan and Apophis. These two rulers probably occupied well over half of the latter part of the period. At the very end of the period comes a certain Khamudy, according to the Turin Canon. Nothing else is known concerning this last king. In the first half of the period may be placed *mꜣꜥ-ib-rꜥ*, *ššy*, and Jaꜥqob-har, although their order is entirely unknown. It is possible, as Hayes suggests,[34] that *mꜣꜥ-ib-rꜥ* is the prenomen of *ššy*, and these two names would therefore represent only one king. However, until a monument with both names together is found, we have no confirmation of this conjecture. Furthermore, it is not possible to identify with certainty the names appearing in Manetho, apart from Apophis, with any of these names.

The remaining names from the scarabs are generally assigned to the Sixteenth Dynasty, but the designation of "dynasty" certainly has no basis in fact. They may very well represent local princes, Egyptian and foreign. On this point there seems to be a certain measure of agreement. However, more about this will be said below.

The absolute chronology of the Hyksos period depends on the chronology of the Eighteenth Dynasty. If we accept the high chronology of Rowton,[35] the date of Ahmose, under whom the Hyksos were expelled, would be about 1577–1552 B.C. Allowing about ten years before the final expulsion, we arrive at 1567 B.C. If we accept the 108 years of the Turin Canon, then the main group of Hyksos ruled about 1675–1567 B.C. The lower chronology of Parker,[36] on the other hand, would reduce this date by 25 years.

34. Hayes, *Scepter of Egypt*, 2, 5.

35. Rowton, "Comparative Chronology at the Time of Dynasty XIX," *JNES, 19* (1960), 15 ff.

36. R. A. Parker, "The Lunar Dates of Thutmose III and Ramesses II," *JNES, 16* (1957), 39 ff.

I have already indicated above the reasons for acknowledging a Hyksos rule in Lower Egypt prior to the Fifteenth Dynasty. The beginning of this period on the basis of the 400-year Stela would be 1725 or 1710, depending on the high or low chronology of the Ramesside period.

# CHAPTER 11

# THE NATURE OF HYKSOS RULE

On the basis of the archaeological evidence, it is safe to conclude that there were strong commercial and cultural connections between Palestine-Syria and Egypt in the Second Intermediate Period. This culture of Syria-Palestine represents a continuous development from the Old Babylonian to the Egyptian conquest in the New Kingdom period. At the beginning of the Second Intermediate Period, the political forms in Syria-Palestine were characteristic of the Amurrite world, and it is entirely reasonable to assume that they continued throughout the whole Middle Bronze II. The earliest contact between Egypt and Syria-Palestine was in the Middle Kingdom, and there is reason to believe that the Middle Kingdom pharaohs used the type of international diplomacy current in the Amurrite world in their relations with the princes of Syria-Palestine.[1] Likewise the Hyksos, who according to Manetho were "foreign kings from Phoenicia," could be expected to reflect the political structure and international diplomacy which is now so fully documented from the Mari Age. The sources of information from the Hyksos period itself are few, but they are adequate to indicate a connection in political traditions between the Old Babylonian world and the Hyksos of Egypt.

In a recent study, J. M. Munn-Rankin has outlined the basic characteristics of diplomacy in Western Asia as reflected in the

1. See above, Chapter 5.

Mari archive.[2] She states that the whole region, which included Syria, Mesopotamia, Babylonia, and the lands east of the Tigris, was made up of a number of confederations of small states, each under the leadership of a principal city with its king.[3] This is reflected clearly in a well-known letter from Mari which states:

> There is no king who, of himself is the strongest. Ten or fifteen kings follow Hammurapi of Babylon, the same number follow Rim-Sin of Larsa, the same number follow Ibal-pi-El of Eshnunna, the same number follow Amut-pi-El of Qatanum, twenty kings follow Yarim-Lim of Yamhad.[4]

Some of the parties in the coalition were independent states, allied by parity treaties. Any one coalition had, at most, small vassal kingdoms which acknowledged the leading king as suzerain. While the vassal king had some jurisdiction over his own area, he was subject to the suzerain in foreign affairs. Likewise, he was required to supply troops in wartime and to pay tribute for "protection."

The terminology used in the correspondence between allied states to indicate their political relationship was presented in terms of kinship.[5] Thus kings of equal rank would refer to each other as "brother," while an overlord would be referred to as "father," and a vassal as "son." This general statement, however, needs some qualification. It was often the case that among "brothers" there was one who was superior to the others and who could be regarded as their "lord." It is also true that the "brothers" of allied states actually represented family relationships, as was the case with the sons of Šamši-Adad, Iasmah-Adad and Išme-Dagan,

2. J. M. Munn-Rankin, "Diplomacy in Western Asia in the Early Second Millennium B.C.," *Iraq, 18* (1956), 68–110. Also Poserer, *CAH²*, 2, ch. 21, pp. 24 ff.

3. Ibid., p. 74.

4. Quoted from Munn-Rankin, ibid., p. 74; first published in *Syria, 19* (1942), 117–18.

5. Ibid., p. 76.

as well as the brothers Abba-El of Aleppo and Yarim-Lim of Alalakh.[6] Furthermore, it was possible for an older king to address the younger ruler of an independent state as "son" without any definite political implications.[7]

Indications from the Hyksos period point to this same political structure and diplomatic intercourse. For instance, Manetho speaks of the Hyksos as "shepherds and brothers" from Phoenicia.[8] The term "shepherd" obviously refers to the Egyptian *ḥḳȝ ḫȝswt*, a term which was used since the Middle Kingdom to designate the Amurrite princes of Syria-Palestine.[9] The term "brother" in a political sense is also known from the Middle Kingdom Sinai inscriptions in which a few of them speak of a certain "brother of the prince (*ḥḳȝ*) of Retjenu." These "brothers," along with the princes, occur again in the New Kingdom in the lists of prisoners taken by Amenhotep II in Syria. One is left with the impression that the political structure of Syria-Palestine did not essentially change from the Old Babylonian period to the New Kingdom; the Hyksos rule was a part of this same political phenomenon. Thus, the ruler of Egypt in this period was probably an overlord of a number of vassals, some of whom were probably in Syria-Palestine. He may also have had alliances with other rulers in Syria and perhaps diplomatic relations even further afield. This political system also encouraged a revival of the old nobility in Egypt, with local princes in bonds of personal loyalty to the one ruler.

Confirmation of this reconstruction may be seen in the royal objects bearing the names of Khyan,[10] which would seem to indicate that he carried on diplomatic relations with Northern Syria and

6. Ibid., pp. 77 ff.

7. Ibid., p. 83.

8. Waddell, *Manetho,* 79–99. On 95 n., Waddell questions the term "brothers" and supposes that this is a corruption in the text. Leibovitch, *IEJ, 3* (1953), 101 f., takes it as a political term, and I have followed his view here.

9. See below, Chapter 13. See also von Beckerath, *Untersuchungen,* pp. 144–51.

10. On these monuments see above.

Crete. It is unlikely, however, that he made actual contact with either the existing power in Babylon or the ruler of the Hittites, as the provenance of two of these objects, the basalt lion and the obsidian vase fragment, would suggest. Stock has suggested that their origin is probably to be sought in Alalakh or Aleppo and that they were taken as booty in the raid of Hattušiliš I or Muršiliš I.[11] If it was Muršiliš, this would account very well for the distribution in both Babylon and Bogazköy. However, the uncertainty in matters of Hittite and Mesopotamian chronology make this suggestion rather hypothetical.[12]

From the time of ʿAwoserreʿ Apophis come important sources for our knowledge of the politics and diplomacy of the Hyksos period. Primary among these are the records of the war between Apophis and Kamose, found on the Carnarvon Tablet I [13] and the Kamose stela.[14] These documents are significant because they reflect the height, as well as the final stage, of Hyksos power. The texts are two halves of a single episode and therefore will be considered together.[15]

The texts mention three main powers in a treaty relationship with each other: the lands of Lower and Middle Egypt, under the Hyksos rule of Apophis; Upper Egypt, under Kamose; and Cush, under a native Nubian ruler. They represented a division of the territory previously under the control of the Middle King-

11. Stock, *MDOG*, *94* (1963), 76 f.

12. This explanation would only fit the so-called Middle chronology of Sidney Smith, in which the raid of Mursilis on Babylon would date about 1600 B.C. On the chronology of Alalakh, see A. Goetze, *JCS*, *11* (1957), 68 ff.

13. Translated by Gunn and Gardiner, *JEA*, *5* (1918), 45–47, and by J. A. Wilson, *ANET*, pp. 232 f.

14. M. Hammad, *Chr d'Eg*, *30* (1955), 198–208. L. Habachi, *Ann Serv*, *53* (1956), 195 ff. T. Säve-Söderbergh, *Kush*, *4* (1956), 54–61.

15. The Carnarvon Tablet (CT) was a schoolboy's copy of a stela, fragments of which have been found at Karnak and published by P. Lacau, "Une Stéle du roi 'Kamosis'," *Ann Serv*, *39* (1939), 245–71, Pls. 37–38. It is now clear that these two stelae stood together and that each contained approximately half of the full account.

dom. There were definite boundaries between them: Cusae between Hyksos territory and Upper Egypt; Elephantine between Upper Egypt and Cush. This division is reflected in the remark made by Kamose:

> (One) prince is in Avaris, another is in Cush, and (here) I sit associated with an Asiatic and a Nubian ($nhsy$). Each man has his slice of Egypt (CT 3).

and in the words of the nobles:

> Behold, it is Asiatic water as far as Cusae . . . we are at ease in our (part of) Egypt. Elephantine is strong, and the middle (of the land) is with us as far as Cusae . . . He holds the land of the Asiatics; we hold Egypt. Should someone come and act against us, then we shall act against him (CT 5–7).

Kamose does not want to recognize this division. He considers that all three areas belong to Egypt, and come under his rule, as the only legitimate Egyptian king. His nobles, on the other hand, acknowledge the borders and speak only of Upper Egypt as "Egypt," while the land held by the Hyksos is called "the land of the Asiatics." [16] Apophis, in his letter to the king of Cush in the Kamose stela, also uses "Egypt" in the more restrictive sense. This would suggest that there were treaties delineating the boundaries between the respective realms and that Kamose was in rebellion against them. This is the very accusation Apophis makes against Kamose when the latter begins his raid:

> Have you seen what Egypt has done to me? The ruler therein, Kamose-$kn$ granted life, is driving me from my lands, though I have not attacked him in the same way as all that he did to you. He has consigned the two lands to misery, even my land and thy land, and he has hacked them (KS 21–22).

16. Stock, *MDOG*, *94* (1963), 78, takes this phrase to mean Syria-Palestine, but this is not at all appropriate to the context.

Apophis implies in this passage that Kamose has acted in bad faith toward both of his neighbors, giving them a legitimate *casus belli* and the right to eliminate his realm.

There are further indications of a treaty between the Hyksos and Upper Egypt. The nobles, in their speech to Kamose (CT 5–7), emphasize that they have the right to pasture cattle in the Delta and hold land in agricultural estates. These generous rights must have been guaranteed by treaty agreements. The nobles insist that their privileges have not been violated; they are naturally reluctant to precipitate a break, for they would have a great deal to lose.

If there was any alliance between the Hyksos and the Seventeenth Dynasty rulers of Thebes, then Apophis was certainly the senior member. In the tale of Papyrus Sallier I,[17] Seqenenreꜥ is clearly a vassal of Apophis and has to pay tribute. Even though the story suffered from exaggeration as a result of adverse propaganda against the Hyksos by the later storyteller, the inscribed blocks at Gebelein would support the opinion that the South was fairly well controlled by the Hyksos at the height of their power.[18] Nevertheless, before the hostilities under Kamose, good relations seem to have existed between the two areas, for the South was able to regain some of its strength. When one considers that at the end of the Thirteenth Dynasty there was not enough timber in Thebes for coffins,[19] it is indeed surprising that Kamose could have fitted out a navy strong enough to threaten the Hyksos seriously. Upper Egypt was again in commercial contact with Syria

17. See Gunn and Gardiner, *JEA*, 5 (1918), 40–45. Wilson, *ANET*, pp. 231 f.

18. See above, pp. 156, 158. On their significance see Winlock, *The Rise and Fall of the Middle Kingdom*, p. 146; Säve-Söderbergh, *JEA*, 37 (1951), 63. This is also suggested by an inscription on an adze published by T. G. H. James (see p. 156) in which ꜥAawoserreꜥ Apophis is spoken of as "beloved of Sobk, Lord of Sumenu." James, in *BMQ*, 24 (1961), 40, points out that Sumenu is in the region of Gebelein and that "no king of Egypt would describe himself as beloved of a god of a particular place unless he had some control over that place."

19. Winlock, *The Rise and Fall of the Middle Kingdom*, p. 101.

and its products, even if, as Kamose complains (CT 4), tariffs
were imposed.

There may also be some archaeological confirmation of an alliance between the Thebans and the Hyksos. Mention has already
been made of the fragment of an alabaster vase with the name
of Apophis and his daughter on it, found in the grave of Amenhotep I. The fact that the royal names were in no way mutilated
seems to indicate that this was a royal gift by Apophis to the
Theban royal house. Likewise in the North were found monuments of the princess Tany associated with the name of Apophis.
If Tany is to be considered a Theban princess, as her name would
indicate, then it is entirely possible that these monuments represent the intermarriage of two royal families, the Hyksos and the
Seventeenth Dynasty.[20] This practice was common in the Amurrite period as a means of cementing alliances.

Kamose describes the relationship between himself and Apophis
as that between a vassal and an overlord. He defiantly boasts that
he will be able to throw off this yoke: "It will be a bad report in
your town when you are driven back at the side of your army,
your authority being too restricted to make me a vassal ($wr$),
yourself being the ruler ($hk3$)" (KS 1).[21] Alliances and diplomacy were not able to stem rising nationalism or the ambitious
princes of Thebes.

These texts also give some insight into the relations between
the Hyksos and Nubia.[22] In his letter to the King of Kush, Apophis greets the other king as "my son," an expression of kinship
typical of Amurrite diplomacy.[23] It might be interpreted to mean

20. This is suggested by W. K. Simpson, *Chr d'Eg, 34* (1959), 237.
21. The translation of the opening line of the Kamose stela is problematic.
For this translation with a discussion of the difficulties, see Säve-Söderbergh,
*Kush, 4* (1956), 54. Cf. Hammad, *Chr d'Eg, 30* (1955), 205.
22. On this, see Säve-Söderbergh, *Kush, 4* (1956), 54–61.
23. The phrase can also be translated "the son of the king of Kush," but this
is less likely. See Säve-Söderbergh, ibid., p. 56 n.

that Nubia was a vassal state of Avaris, but the sequel seems to indicate that it was quite independent. Here it is a case of an older king addressing a younger one.

Apophis begins the letter by reprimanding the younger king for not informing him of his succession to the throne, a serious breach of diplomatic courtesy for any two ruling families who are bound in alliance and commercial and diplomatic relations. This letter, therefore, clearly indicates that Nubia was not a part of a Hyksos empire. The evidence of cultural contact and the scarabs of certain Hyksos in Kerma may be explained entirely by commercial and diplomatic ties encouraged for the mutual prosperity of both areas.[24]

The Carnarvon Tablet and the Kamose stela indicate that there were lesser vassals under Apophis, in both Egypt and Asia. In referring to the Hyksos boundary, the nobles of Kamose state: "It is Asiatic water as far as Cusae, and they have pulled out their tongues that they might speak all together" (CT 5). The last part of the statement is ambiguous, but I take it to mean that "they," the nobles of Middle and Lower Egypt, have committed themselves to oaths of loyalty to the Hyksos ruler.[25]

One of these local princes of the Hyksos confederacy may have been Teti, the son of Pepi, referred to in the Carnarvon Tablet, apparently as the commander of a garrison near the border of Upper Egypt. Some scholars have taken this Teti to be the son of Apophis—possible but not so likely.[26] It is a fact that the Eighteenth Dynasty had a difficult time, after the defeat of the Hyksos, in suppressing the local princes throughout Egypt.[27] They must have gained their power during the Second Intermediate Period, and this would only have been possible if the Hyksos rule was

---

24. Ibid., pp. 60 f.
25. For a different interpretation see Wilson, *ANET*, p. 232 n.
26. Gardiner, *JEA*, *3* (1916), 110.
27. See Steindorff and Seele, *When Egypt Ruled the East*, p. 32.

similar in political structure to that of the Amurrite confederacies and if these local princes took oaths of loyalty to the Hyksos ruler.[28]

The Kamose stela also indicates Apophis' influence beyond Egypt. Kamose describes the booty which he captured from the Asiatics in the vicinity of Avaris: "300 *baw* ships of cedar, filled with gold and lapis-lazuli, silver and turquoise and copper axes without number as well as olive oil, incense, fat, honey . . . and all their precious woods" (KS 13–14). This was called "the good tribute (*inw*) of Retjenu," intended for Apophis, "chief of Retjenu." The last two expressions would seem to suggest that Apophis had a certain amount of power in Syria-Palestine; the nature of commodities enumerated points particularly to Syria and Lebanon. Did Apophis have important coastal cities, such as Byblos, in his control? It is entirely possible, although they were probably held by diplomatic and commercial alliances in the tradition of Amurrite politics of the Mari Age, not by military conquest.

28. The authority of these nomarchs or local princes had been strongly suppressed in the latter part of the Middle Kingdom. Yet these princes again possessed a certain power in the Second Intermediate Period. The obvious conclusion is that they cooperated with the Hyksos in their rise to power and worked against any Egyptian kings who represented a centralized authority. Indications of such defection to foreigners may be found in the *Admonitions* as indicated above.

# CHAPTER 12

# THE RELIGION OF THE HYKSOS

The sources for a discussion of this subject from the Hyksos period are meager: only a few names have theophoric elements; the scarabs of the period contain representations of deities, but they are not identified by inscription, and their iconography is often doubtful; there are only a few short dedicatory inscriptions containing the names of their deities; and there is a complete lack of temples, cult objects (except for one offering table), identified representations, or texts of a mythological or religious nature, apart from those mentioned above. Consequently, any treatment of the subject must remain somewhat hypothetical. Nevertheless, in spite of the tenuousness of the evidence, the subject of "Hyksos" religion calls for some consideration. It bears directly on the identity and character of "Hyksos" culture.

From the time of Apophis comes an offering table with the formula, "he made it as a monument for his father Seth, Lord of Avaris." [1] Although the object was not found in situ, there can be no doubt that it was actually placed in a temple of Seth in Avaris. This is confirmed by the story of Seqenenreᶜ and Apophis in the Papyrus Sallier I:

> Then king Apophis—life, prosperity, health!—made him Seth as Lord, and he would not serve any god who was in the land except Seth. And he built a temple of good and eternal work

1. Labib, *Die Herrschaft der Hyksos,* pp. 29 f., Pl. 5. See also von Beckerath, *Untersuchungen,* pp. 160–64.

beside the House of King Apophis—life, prosperity, health!
—and he appeared every day to have sacrifices made . . .
daily to Seth. And the officials of the king—life, prosperity,
health!—carried wreaths, just exactly as is done (in) the
temple of Re Har-akhti.[2]

Seth is known from inscriptions of the Ramesside period as primarily associated with Avaris. The continuity of his worship in
this place from Hyksos times can hardly be doubted;[3] this continuity is also the most logical interpretation of the 400-year Stela.[4]
Papyrus Sallier I, therefore, accurately preserves the tradition of
the worship of Seth by the Hyksos, but it goes too far in its
statement that the Hyksos worshiped Seth exclusively. In fact,
the text contradicts itself by emphasizing a very close association
with the worship of Reᶜ Har-akhti, chief deity of Heliopolis.
Moreover, there is the inscription of the scribe's palette, mentioned previously, in which Apophis is spoken of as the "beloved
Son of Reᶜ" and "the living image of Reᶜ on earth."[5] The Hyksos
also compounded their prenomina and epithets in Reᶜ, which may
signify merely the borrowing of Egyptian conventions. However,
it is almost certain indication that they were not hostile to the
worship of Reᶜ or to any of the Egyptian gods.

A text which has often been used as evidence of such hostility
to Egyptian worship is an inscription set up by Queen Hatshepsut
on the façade of her temple in Middle Egypt:

I have restored that which had been ruined. I raised up that
which had gone to pieces formerly, since the Asiatics were in
the midst of Avaris of the Northland, and vagabonds were
in the midst of them, overthrowing that which had been

2. *ANET*, p. 231. See also Gunn and Gardiner, *JEA*, 5 (1918), 40–45.

3. For a collection of the references with discussion, see R. Weill, "The Problem
of the Site of Avaris," *JEA*, 21 (1935), 14–17, Pl. ii.

4. See above, Chapter 8.

5. Labib, *Die Herrschaft der Hyksos*, p. 27.

made. They ruled without Reˁ, and he did not act by divine command down to [the reign of] my majesty.[6]

In this text the queen boasts about her great temple-building activities; it may be doubted whether the Hyksos actually destroyed Egyptian temples as she implies. They may have usurped monuments and stone from previous buildings for their own constructions, but this practice was common enough and does not necessarily imply any condemnation of Egyptian religion. The ruins which Hatshepsut restored were primarily those of Middle and Upper Egypt which had gone to ruin simply from neglect. The statement that the Hyksos ruled without Reˁ is not intended to reflect upon their religion; it refers to their legitimacy to rule, and in this respect even the queen's predecessors of the Eighteenth Dynasty are culpable—they failed to build temples of the gods.

There can be no doubt, at any rate, that the Hyksos worshiped Seth as "Lord of Avaris," the principal deity of the monarchy. The reason for their choice of Seth as the patron deity of their rule was largely political and has been discussed previously.[7] The following remarks will be primarily concerned with the nature of their worship of Seth and other deities—whether they be Egyptian or Asiatic.

It is generally assumed among scholars that when the Hyksos adopted the worship of Seth they identified this Egyptian god with their own principal Asiatic deity. This assumption finds support in the analogy of the Egyptian goddess Hathor who, in the foreign environment of Byblos and Sinai, was assimilated with a corresponding Asiatic deity. Syncretism in the Hyksos period is also suggested by the Asiatic character of the Seth cult when it emerged again in the Ramesside period. Some caution must be taken not to read back into the Hyksos period, 250 years earlier, all the characteristics of the Seth cult, particularly the

6. *ANET*, p. 231; see Gardiner, *JEA*, 32 (1946), 43–56, Pl. VI.
7. See above, Chapter 8.

iconography of the god found in the later period.[8] Nevertheless, it remains highly probable that the process of assimilation was begun in the Hyksos period itself.

The first problem is to identify the Asiatic deity assimilated with the god Seth. Material for this identification comes largely from the Nineteenth Dynasty. In the iconography of Seth, which is best known from the 400-year Stela of Ramesses II,[9] the god is represented in foreign attire, wearing a high conical cap with gazelle horns protruding from the front. A ribbon, attached to the top, falls down behind the god almost to the ground. He has bracelets, armlets, and bands ornamented with round disks criss-crossing his chest. In addition, he wears a short kilt with tassels. There are many examples of this type of representation of the god both in Egypt and in Syria-Palestine,[10] although in every case the representation is by Egyptian craftsmen. Although the various elements of Seth's costume are foreign, some of them are of recent date, while others have a very long history in Syria-Palestine.

The important point to observe is that the Egyptians represent not only Seth but also Baal by this iconography.[11] From Ras Shamra comes a stela portraying Seth, who is then identified as

8. For a discussion on the iconography of Seth in the 400-year stela, see Montet, *Kêmi*, 4 (1933), 200–10. Montet, however, sees certain similarities in costume with the Sea-Peoples and wants to use this as evidence that the Sea-Peoples were in contact with Egypt in the Middle Kingdom. It is much easier to account for the similarities in costume by assuming continual modification in the representation of a deity whose attire was foreign. There is no evidence that Seth was represented in exactly this way in the Hyksos period. However, the idea for this type of portrayal must have come from the earlier period, and the similarity to the iconography of the storm god on Syrian cylinder seals makes the connection all the more possible.

9. Montet, *Kêmi*, 4 (1933).

10. For a bibliography of these see ibid. Also J. Leibovitch, *IEJ*, 3 (1953), 102 ff. Not included in these discussions are the seal of Seth and Ramesses in A. Rowe, *Catalogue*, pp. 252 f., Pl. XXVIII, S. 61. Habachi, *Ann Serv*, 52 (1954), Pl. XXIX.

11. See Albright, *From the Stone Age to Christianity* (New York, 1957), p. 224. He seriously overstates the case, since the identifications are not that sim-

Baal Saphon—the name of the god being written with a Seth Animal determinative.[12] A confirmation of this iconographic identification may be seen in the treaty between Ramesses II and the Hittites.[13] The Egyptian text uses Seth in place of the ideogram for Storm god in the Hittite text, whether of Hatti or of Syria.[14]

In the mythology of the New Kingdom are indications of a strong Asiatic influence. One very fragmentary text makes mention of Astarte and Yam (the Sea) [15] in a manner reminiscent of the contest between Baal and Yam of Ugaritic mythology.[16] The place of Baal, however, seems to have been taken by Seth, although the details of the struggle are completely lost. However, Gardiner cites a reference in the Hearst Medical Papyrus which refers to Seth's victory over Yam.[17] His place in the Egyptian pantheon, with his Egyptian consort Nephthys, is augmented by two Asiatic goddesses as consorts, Anat and Astarte.[18] Anat is spoken of as the "milch cow of Seth," [19] and Seth is called the "bull of Retjenu"—an epithet further applied to Ramesses II as

---

ple. He states: "Even in iconography the Ramesside representations of Seth-Baal are practically indistinguishable, except in artistic technique, from those of the Canaanite Baal which have been found in considerable numbers during recent excavations in Palestine and Syria." I fail to see the sense of this statement; we have no certain representations of Baal by Canaanites from this period.

12. Schaeffer, "Les Fouilles de . . . Ras Shamra, Deuxième Campagne," *Syria, 12* (1931), 10–11.

13. *ANET*, pp. 199–203.

14. J. Zandee, in his study, "Seth als Sturmgott," *ZÄS, 90* (1963), 144–56, has collected a number of references from the coffin texts which characterize Seth as a stormgod with many attributes similar to Baal. These are (1) god of thunder and rain, (2) god of heaven, (3) "bull of the northern heavens," (4) god of the earth, (5) god of vegetation. Since this material comes largely from the time of the Middle Kingdom, it is very important for a study of the early assimilation of Seth and Baal. However, as yet the coffin texts are unavailable in translation.

15. *ANET*, pp. 17 f.

16. Ibid., pp. 129–31, the so-called III AB Baal cycle.

17. Gardiner, *JEA, 19* (1933), 98. See also Helck, *Beziehungen*, p. 491.

18. *ANET*, p. 15 (*Papyrus Chester Beatty* I).

19. Helck, *Beziehungen*, p. 494.

the living image of Seth.[20] In the Ugaritic texts Anat is portrayed as the wife or sister of Baal and is, likewise, characterized as a cow in her association with the bull, Baal.[21] Although the consort of Astarte is not indicated in the Ugaritic texts, her relationship to Baal is nevertheless close, since she is referred to in one place as Astarte-name-of-Baal.[22] She is also the virtual twin of Anat in her role as a goddess of war, love, and fertility.

On the basis of iconography and mythology, it seems reasonable to conclude that, in the time of the Ramessides, Seth was identified primarily with Baal of Syria-Palestine and secondarily with the stormgods of the Hittites and the Hurrians. Can the identification of Seth with Baal be extended back to the Hyksos period? This may be supported by a number of considerations. There is every reason to believe that the worship of Seth at Avaris continued unbroken from the Hyksos to the Ramesside period. The 400-year Stela pushes this continuity back to the very beginning of the Hyksos period, if not before. Although the Hyksos were expelled, a large part of the foreign population probably remained and carried on the worship of Seth very much as before.[23] From the mid-Eighteenth Dynasty are references to a number of Asiatic deities, included in the inscriptions among the gods of Egypt.[24] Such a domestication of foreign deities can only mean that their cults were practiced for some time.

20. An epithet used on the obelisks of Ramesses II found at Tanis, see Montet, *Le Drame d'Avaris*, pp. 140 f.

21. On the character of Anat, see M. J. Dahood, "Ancient Semitic Deities in Syria and Palestine," in S. Moscati, ed., *Le Antiche Divinita Semitiche* (Rome, 1958), pp. 80 f. See also M. H. Pope, "Anat," in H. W. Haussig, ed., *Wörterbuch der Mythologie* (Stuttgart, 1963), *1*, fasc. 2, 240 ff.

22. Keret text, 127–56. On the character of Astarte see Pope, "Astarte," in Haussig, ed, *Wörterbuch*, pp. 250 ff.

23. From the time of Hatshepsut comes a reference to ʿprw in the Eastern Delta region. See T. Säve-Söderbergh, "The ʿprw as Vintagers in Egypt," *Orient Su, 1* (1952), 1–14.

24. For a convenient collection of the material on foreign gods in Egypt, see Helck, *Beziehungen*, pp. 482–514. See also *ANET*, pp. 249 f.

It may be objected that the Semitic character of Egyptian religion in the Eastern Delta during the New Kingdom can be accounted for entirely by the prisoners captured by the Eighteenth Dynasty pharaohs. It is unlikely, however, that they had the freedom to establish cults and temples to any great degree. These prisoners, after all, were divided up as booty among the various temples, particularly Amun of Thebes. The captive princes and their families were kept as hostages and trained in Egyptian customs; the heir of a Syrian king was thoroughly Egyptianized when he came to the throne. Proof that prisoners had little to do with the establishment of cults in Egypt may be seen in the fact that although a large number of Hurrians were taken as captives by the Eighteenth Dynasty pharaohs, no Hurrian gods were worshiped in Egypt. The cult of Tešub is not known, whereas his Semitic counterpart, Baal, had at least two important temples in Egypt besides being worshiped as Seth.[25] If the Hyksos did worship Seth as Tešub for over a century, as Helck suggests,[26] then it is remarkable that we find no trace of it; and in its place are only Semitic cults and mythology.

It is highly unlikely that the Asiatics of the Hyksos period restricted themselves to the worship of Seth alone. On the scarabs of the period there are representations of numerous deities containing both Egyptian and Asiatic characteristics. While the identifications are not always certain, one has the impression of a pantheon of deities and a degree of syncretism between the Egyptian gods and their Asiatic counterparts. It is perhaps possible to suggest what a few of these syncretisms might have been if we assume, on the basis of the previous demonstration, that Seth was assimilated to Baal and that the Hyksos religion was, therefore, Semitic. There are indications from the Ramesside period that Reꜥ was, in fact, identified with El. In one version of "the

25. Helck, *Beziehungen,* pp. 482 f.
26. Ibid., p. 109.

contest of Horus and Seth" [27] from this period, Re‹ is described as "the Bull Residing in Heliopolis"; it is he who presides over the council of the gods, and he is described as having the Semitic goddesses Anat and Astarte as his daughters. In another mytho-logical text of the Nineteenth Dynasty, "the Deliverance of Man-kind from Destruction," [28] Re‹ is described as an old god who is losing control as ruler of gods and men. In these texts there is no reference to his role as the Sun, but instead they correspond entirely with the position and characteristics of El in the Ugaritic texts.[29]

Another deity one would expect to find alongside Baal and El is Anat.[30] The name of this goddess is attested in the Thirteenth Dynasty in the list of Asiatic slaves in the Brooklyn Papyrus pub-lished by Hayes,[31] as well as in the name of the Hyksos Anat-har. Anat seems to be represented on scarabs of the Hyksos period as a nude deity with cow ears, horns, and Hathor curls. The assimi-lation with Hathor, the Egyptian deity, is likewise suggested by the two mythological texts mentioned above. In the "contest of Horus and Seth," Hathor is spoken of as cajoling the old god Re‹ by uncovering her private parts before his face, a motif entirely characteristic of Anat, the supreme goddess of love and war in Syria.[32] In the "Deliverance of Mankind from Destruction," [33] Hathor, in the form of Sekhmet, carries out a great slaughter in much the same way as did Anat in the Baal cycle.[34] Nevertheless, the syncretism between the two deities was not complete. Anat continued to be known as a goddess in Egypt under her Semitic

27. *ANET*, pp. 14–16.
28. Ibid., pp. 10–11.
29. On the characteristics of El, see M. H. Pope, *El in the Ugaritic Texts* (Leiden, 1955).
30. On this goddess in Egyptian sources, see Helck, *Beziehungen,* pp. 494 f.
31. Ibid., p. 81.
32. *ANET*, p. 15. Cf. with Anat's more threatening persuasion of El, in V AB of the Baal cycle, ibid., p. 137.
33. Ibid., pp. 10–11.
34. See V AB, ibid., p. 136.

name. As such, she is spoken of as the mother of Ramesses II and very likely had a temple in the vicinity of the capital.[35] She was also known as the consort, or "milch cow," of Seth.[36]

Another goddess whose cult is firmly attested in Egypt by the mid-Eighteenth Dynasty is Astarte.[37] She plays an important part in the mythological text, "Astarte and the Sea," [38] which dates from the New Kingdom. This goddess had associations with love and war and was very similar to Anat; they were a closely linked pair and even considered as one.

The Semitic god Horon also became prominent in Egypt in the New Kingdom.[39] He was assimilated (by assonance of their names) with Horus and was, therefore, represented as a falcon. This identification may explain why a falcon-headed god is very common on scarabs of the Hyksos period from Palestine. That Horon was worshiped in Palestine as early as the Thirteenth Dynasty is attested by the name of the god occurring as a theophoric element in two names from the Execration texts.[40]

The worship of Rešef is well attested from the time of Amenhotep II on, and there are indications that it was known in Egypt earlier.[41] In contrast to some of the other Asiatic deities, he does not seem to have been assimilated to any Egyptian deity.[42] In iconography [43] he occasionally shares some of the features of Seth-Baal, such as the gazelle horns and the tassels on the short skirt.

35. Note the monuments of Anat found at Tanis, Montet, *RB, 39* (1930), 21, Pl. IV; *Le Drame d'Avaris*, Pl. XIII.

36. Helck, *Beziehungen*, p. 494.

37. Ibid., pp. 490 f.

38. *ANET*, pp. 17 f.

39. Helck, *Beziehungen*, pp. 489 f.

40. Ibid., pp. 55, 61.

41. Ibid., pp. 485 ff. See also W. K. Simpson, "Reshep in Egypt," *Orientalia,* 29 (1960), 63–74. One of the occurrences of Resef in Egyptian sources is in an inscription by a certain *I°ḥ-msw*, and this name would suggest an early Eighteenth Dynasty date.

42. Simpson, *Orientalia, 29* (1960), 72 f.

43. See *ANEP*, nos. 473, 474, 476, and a complete list of representations in Helck, *Beziehungen*, pp. 486 f.

Rešef, however, is usually distinguished from Seth by his more Asiatic facial features, particularly the Asiatic beard (instead of Seth's small Egyptian beard) and two straight streamers from the headdress (in place of Seth's one long wavy streamer, ending in a flower).[44] Rešef was added to the Egyptian pantheon as a warlike deity, bringing death to the enemies of the king.

It is not possible to say for certain how many of these gods were worshiped by the Hyksos and in precisely what form. Yet it is probable that the Hyksos brought into Egypt a pantheon and a mythology similar to that known from the Ugaritic texts. During the century and a half of their residence in Egypt, Hyksos cults and mythology were so firmly established that it was no longer possible for the Eighteenth Dynasty to eradicate them or even distinguish them as foreign cults. This admittedly hypothetical reconstruction seems to be the best explanation of the evidence. There is, however, no evidence whatever to suggest that the foreign aspect of Hyksos religion was anything other than Semitic. Any proposal that the Hyksos religion was Hurrian rests entirely on the prior claim that the Hyksos themselves were Hurrian. The question of ethnic origins will be discussed below, but the religion of the Hyksos, insofar as our evidence may be accepted as valid, can only support a continuity of culture with the West-Semitic world.

44. In a representation of Mikal (*ANEP*, no. 487) dating from Thutmose III, both the short streamers and the long wavy streamer are present. It has been suggested by W. Rollig, "Mikal," in *Wörterbuch, 1*, fasc. 2, 298 f., that Mikal is a form of Resef. Cf. the earlier view by R. P. H. Vincent, "Le Baal canaanéen de Beisan et sa paredre," *RB, 37* (1928), 512–43.

# CHAPTER 13

# THE ORIGINS OF THE HYKSOS

The question of the ethnic identity of the Hyksos remains the most controversial aspect of the Hyksos problem. The choices have narrowed down to (1) the Hurrians, (2) a West-Semitic group, and (3) some combination of the two. A choice among these possibilities is very important for an understanding of the Middle Bronze Age of Syria and Palestine, the rise of the Hyksos to power in Egypt, and the contributions of the period of foreign domination to subsequent Egyptian civilization.

Let us consider first the onomastic evidence.[1] A few rulers of the Hyksos period have indisputably West-Semitic names; *ʿḳb-ḥr* and *ʿnt-ḥr*. They are considered by some, however, as merely vassal rulers.[2] Another name which may be explained as Semitic is Khyan, found among the ancestors of Šamši-Adad, at Ugarit, in the Canaanite inscription of Samʾal, in the Old Testament, and in Nabatean.[3] Albright explains the ending in *n* as a hypocoristic ending in *anu, ana*.[4] There is little doubt that the name is West-Semitic. Another name of the Hyksos period with a similar ending is *Smḳn*, explained by A. Gustavs as Hurrian,[5] but it may

1. See most recently B. Landsberger, *JCS, 8* (1954), 59 n. Albright, in *BANE*, pp. 335, 354 n. Helck, *Beziehungen*, pp. 102 f.
2. So Helck, *Beziehungen*, pp. 93 f.; but see above, Chapter 10.
3. See Landsberger, *JCS, 8* (1954), 33. Albright in *BANE*, p. 354 n. R. Dussaud, "L'Origine de l'alphabet et son evolution première d'après les découvertes de Byblos," *Syria, 25* (1946–48), 37.
4. Albright in *BANE*, p. 354 n.
5. A. Gustavs, "Subaräische Namen in einer ägyptischen Liste syrischer Sklaven und ein subaräischer (?) Hyksos-Name," *ZÄS, 64* (1929), 57 f. The Hurrian

very well also be West-Semitic.[6] The name Salitis from Manetho
has been understood as a Semitic title, "Sultan," [7] and as a Hurrian or Indo-Aryan name to be compared with Zayaluti of Aleppo
in the sources from Alalakh VII.[8] However, speculation on this
name is of no value, since the names in Manetho are often completely corrupted. Other names of the Hyksos, such as Apophis,
are Egyptian.

Helck, who argues strongly for a Hurrian identity of the Hyksos, brings forth additional names of this period which he regards
as Hurrian.[9] He mentions the princess Tany (*ti-na*), the sister of
Apophis, and compares her name with Taena of Nuzu. W. K.
Simpson, however, suggests that the name is to be associated with
the Theban kings called Ta-o, and that she may have actually
come from Thebes.[10] Helck regards the princess *ḥ-r-ta*, daughter
of Apophis, as Hurrian, comparing her name with Haluti of
Nuzu. Yet W. A. Ward points out that the Egyptian name is too
broken to make it the basis of an argument.[11] Two other names
from a stela of the Seventeenth Dynasty, *bu-ta* and *iḳr.t*, the explained by Helck as Hurrian, but Ward shows that they are both
good Egyptian names. The name of the mother of Ahmose of
El-Kab, *a-bi-na*, is compared by Helck with Abianna of Nuzu
and Abenni of Alalakh. However, this name is of the form Ahi-
yana, common at Ugarit. It is a good West-Semitic name—a possibility one must also face at Alalakh and Nuzu.[12] Likewise, the

---

name which he uses for comparison, however, ends in *šenni*, not *eni* as he states.
Cf. also Landsberger, *JCS, 8* (1954), 60 n.

6. Albright in *BANE*, p. 354 n., and Landsberger, *JCS, 8* (1954).

7. Hayes, *The Scepter of Egypt, 2,* 4.

8. Albright in *BANE*, p. 354 n.; also Helck, *Beziehungen*, p. 102.

9. Helck, *Beziehungen*, pp. 102 ff.

10. Simpson, *Chr d'Eg, 34* (1959), 223–39.

11. Ward, *Orientalia, 33* (1964), 137.

12. Harald Ingholt has suggested comparing this name with the feminine
personal name, Abina, found at Palmyra. It occurs as אבנא in PS 23 and as אבינא
in PS 371. See H. Ingholt, *Studien over Palmyrensk Skulptur* (Copenhagen, 1928),

name of a certain prince of Amenhotep I, *Sa-pa-ar*, is considered by Helck to be Hurrian, but it may be compared with a Semitic name from Hayes' list of slaves of the Middle Kingdom.[13] Finally, Helck argues that one of the slaves given to Ahmose of El-Kab, *Ištar-ummi*, is a Hurrian, but this name is clearly West-Semitic.[14] Of the two other foreigners in the same list, *T'amutj* is also West-Semitic, being compared with biblical Amos,[15] and *P3 '3m* is an Egyptian designation for one belonging to the Amurrites.[16] To these names may be added others of this period, such as, *'3bd, Nḥmn*, and *'pr*, which are also West-Semitic.[17]

The conclusion from the onomastic evidence is that not a single name of this period in Egypt can be identified, with certainty, as Hurrian. On the other hand, an explanation as West-Semitic is either certain or quite probable for almost all the foreign names.[18]

One argument in support of a Hurrian element among the Hyksos has to do with the introduction of the horse and chariot into Egypt.[19] This is part of a much wider and more complex problem, the development of chariot warfare. Strong philological evidence indicates that the Mitannians had some competence in the use of the light chariot in warfare and in the training of

---

pp. 47, 131. For the meaning, "our father," see M. Lidzbarski, "Epigraphisches aus Syrien, II," *Nachr Göttingen*, Phil.-hist. Klasse (Berlin, 1924), p. 48.

13. Albright, *JAOS*, 74 (1954), 229, no. 21.

14. The name is written, *Iš-t3-r-iw-mi* (Urk. IV, 11). At Ugarit the personal names Attar-ab and Attar-um have been found (Dahood, in *Le Antiche divinita semitiche*, p. 87), and from Larsa in the time of Hammurapi there is the name *Ištar-ummi-e-ni-iš-tim* (*TCL* X, p. 107, line 28).

15. See Wilson in *ANET*, p. 233b n.

16. On the meaning "the Amurrite" see below. This may be compared with the name *P3 Ḥ3rw*, "the Hurrian," which first occurs and becomes very common in the late Eighteenth and Nineteenth Dynasties. See Gardiner, *Onomastica, I*, 185*.

17. Albright in *BANE*, p. 354 n. Also Helck, *Beziehungen*, p. 107 n.

18. This is the conclusion of Albright in *BANE*, p. 335. See also von Beckerath, *Untersuchungen*, p. 119 n., and his criticism of Helck.

19. E. A. Speiser, "Ethnic Movements in the Near East in the Second Millennium B.C.," *AASOR, 13* (1933), 49 ff.; also Helck, *Beziehungen*, p. 103 f. Cf. von Beckerath, *Untersuchungen*, p. 117.

horses to pull them.[20] This skill, however, must be associated with the Indo-Aryan warrior class, the *maryannu,* and not with the early Hurrians. There is no indication that the Hurrians of the Old Babylonian period had any advanced ability in this respect. In fact, horsemanship in the Alalakh VII texts is associated entirely with the Amurrites.[21] Furthermore, although chariots were certainly used in the Old Babylonian period, their exact function in warfare is not altogether clear.[22]

The Egyptian evidence, moreover, is entirely indecisive. From the Hyksos period there is reference, in the accounts of Kamose's war with Apophis, to *ḥtr,* "horses," [23] and *t3 nt-ḥtry,* "chariotry." [24] The terminology is Egyptian, and the accounts do not indicate that the horses and chariots were used in battle. The style of warfare described in these texts is primarily naval, and the idea that the Hyksos overwhelmed Egypt with chariotry is highly dubious. The earliest record of Egyptians encountering chariots in battle is in their Asian campaigns.[25] The development of Egyptian chariotry probably resulted from the necessity of war in Asia, and not before then. The horse was probably known in Egypt since

20. A. Goetze, *Iraq, 25* (1963), 124 ff.

21. I. J. Gelb, *JCS, 15* (1961), 41b. See also C. J. Gadd, "Tablets from Chager Bazar and Tall Brak, 1937–38," *Iraq, 7* (1940), 31. In the Chager Bazar tablets, horses and chariots and five grooms with a trainer are mentioned, but their names are not given.

22. On the evidence for the early use of chariotry in Mesopotamia see Yadin, *The Art of Warfare in Biblical Lands,* pp. 36 ff., 74 f.

23. Gardiner, *JEA, 3* (1916), 107.

24. KS, line 13. See L. Habachi, *Ann Serv, 53* (1956), 201, and M. Hammad, *Chr d'Eg, 30* (1955), 207. See also A. R. Schulman, "The Egyptian Chariotry: A Reexamination," *JARCE, 2* (1963), 84 ff.

25. See the biography of Ahmose of El-Kab, K. Sethe, *Urk, 4,* 1 ff., also *ANET,* pp. 233 f. This text mentions pharaoh riding a chariot at the siege of Avaris and the capture of a chariot in the land of Naharin in the time of Thutmose I. The terminology used for chariot, *wrt,* or *wryt,* may be Hurrian (see Speiser, *AASOR, 13* [1933], 49 f.), but since the biography was written after campaigning in Northern Syria, the use of such terminology is not surprising and proves nothing about the Hyksos' use of chariots in a "Mitannian" fashion.

the time of the Middle Kingdom.[26] Consequently, the use of the horse and chariot in the Hyksos period in Egypt may have been no different from the use of the horse and chariot in the Old Babylonian period in Syria-Palestine. It is hardly possible to postulate an Indo-Aryan, or *maryannu,* element among the Hyksos. This group is unknown in Northern Syria as late as Alalakh VII. The question of chariots, therefore, ought to be dropped from the discussion of Hyksos origins.

One major reason for associating the Hurrians with the Hyksos is the seeming coincidence of the Hurrian movement and the Hyksos rise to power.[27] This coincidence, however, rests on very high chronology. With the revision of Mesopotamian chronology, the connection is very difficult, if not impossible to support.[28] This has not been taken seriously enough by most scholars, many of whom, including Albright, persist in associating the terre pisée fortifications of Syria-Palestine with the Hurrians.[29] This association remains entirely unsubstantiated, and I have given reasons above for associating the development with the Amurrite civilization of Syria-Palestine.

The fact that there was a Hurrian–Indo-Aryan penetration into Palestine in the second millennium cannot be denied. Some attempt, therefore, may be made to suggest when this migration took place. The evidence is primarily based on onomastic material from Egypt in the New Kingdom. The following considerations are important.

26. The skeleton of a horse was found at Buhen in a Middle Kingdom context. See Emery, *Kush, 8* (1960), 8.

27. Speiser, *AASOR, 13* (1933), 49. See also Engberg, *The Hyksos Reconsidered,* pp. 31 f.

28. A. Alt, *Die Herkunft der Hyksos,* pp. 72–98. See review by J. Koenig, *RAss, 50* (1956), 193 f.; also Landsberger, *JCS, 8* (1954), 60 n.; J. R. Kupper, "Northern Mesopotamia and Syria," *CAH*², 2, ch. 1, pp. 37 ff.; von Beckerath, *Untersuchungen,* pp. 113 f.

29. See Albright, *The Archaeology of Palestine* (Baltimore, 1961), pp. 86 f., and in *BANE,* p. 336. These statements can hardly be reconciled with his low chronology.

One of the names of Palestine in the Ramesside period is the "land of Hurru." [30] The name obviously derives from an important element of the population living there. It is difficult to decide exactly how far back this designation goes, but it was applied possibly to Syria-Palestine first in the Amarna Age. In the annals of Thutmose III, different designations are used for Palestine and Syria, Djahi and Retjenu respectively. Furthermore, in the booty of Megiddo, the "works of Hurru" are distinguished from the "works of Djahi." When the term, "land of Hurru" occurs in Egyptian for the first time in the account of the battle of Megiddo by Thutmose III, it designates the homeland of certain contingents from the far north together with those of Naharin, Mitanni, and Kedy (Kizzuwatna). [31] This also agrees with the geography of the cuneiform sources for this period. [32] The application of the name "land of Hurru" to Syria-Palestine, therefore, cannot be dated much before the Amarna Age.

In the annals of Thutmose III and Amenhotep II, Hurrians and *maryannu* are mentioned for the first time. Many are listed as prisoners, although their homeland is not given. It is clear from other sources that in this period Hurrians and *maryannu* warriors were establishing themselves in Syria-Palestine. [33] It also seems

30. On the "land of Hurru" and "Hurrian" see Gardiner, *Onomastica, I,* 180 ff. See also Helck, *Beziehungen,* p. 275. Both treatments are prejudiced by the view that the Hurrians were in Palestine and Egypt in the Second Intermediate Period. Gardiner has since rejected his earlier view (see *Egypt of the Pharaohs,* p. 157).

31. See *ANET,* p. 235b. Helck, *Beziehungen,* p. 275, states, "Die Ägypter kannten also zunächst nur eine hurritische Bevölkerung, aber kein Land hu-ru." This statement is directly contradicted by the earliest references to the Hurrians in the annals of Thutmose III which speak of the "land of the Hurrians."

32. See A. Goetze, *Kleinasian* (München, 1957), pp. 62 f. Cf. I. J. Gelb, *Hurrians and Subarians* (Chicago, 1944), pp. 70 ff., where Gelb seems to equate Mitanni, Hurri, and Naharin; but the reference from the annals of Thutmose III cited above does not seem to support this.

33. See Albright, "A Prince of Taᶜanach in the Fifteenth Century B.C.," *BASOR, 94* (1944), 12–27. R. Bottéro, "Les inventaires de Qatna," *RAss, 43* (1949), 1–40. C. Epstein, "A New Appraisal of Some Lines from a Long Known Papyrus," *JEA, 49* (1963), 49–56.

likely that this penetration was at its height in the latter part of the fifteenth century B.C., when there was a marked increase in Hurrian prisoners taken by Amenhotep II.

There is every indication that the Hurrian movement penetrated Syria-Palestine only in conjunction with the *maryannu* and, therefore, after the establishment of the Mitanni power. This did not take place until some time after the fall of Alalakh VII; no *maryannu* class is discernible there.[34] Once the Mitanni power was established, after ca. 1600 B.C., and the early pharaohs of the Eighteenth Dynasty had seriously crippled resistance by the Amurrite kingdoms, then the Hurrians and Indo-Aryans moved into the region. The beginning of this development cannot antedate Thutmose III, and it probably belongs entirely to the late fifteenth century B.C. There is no evidence to suggest that the migration took place any earlier.

Until now the discussion has been largely negative. Yet it is possible to suggest a positive answer to the question of origins. First there is the terminology used in referring to the foreigners.[35] Manetho calls the foreign rulers "Hyksos," which he explains as meaning "shepherd kings." [36] This term, however, is to be correctly explained as made up of the Egyptian words $ḥḳ3$ $ḫ3swt$, "ruler of foreign lands." [37] The latter phrase is found on a few scarabs of the Second Intermediate Period bearing the names of foreign rulers. The term is also probably to be restored in the Turin Canon for the six principal rulers of the Hyksos period. It clearly refers only to the rulers, and it is not an ethnic designation for the foreigners. Manetho has often been wrongly blamed for giving this term a false ethnic sense. Only Josephus applies the term to the people as a whole, and his recension of Manetho is highly suspect.[38] The so-called epitomes of Manetho use the term

---

34. Gelb, "The Early History of the West Semitic Peoples," *JCS*, *15* (1961), 39.
35. See K. Galling, "Hyksosherrschaft und Hyksoskultur," *ZDPV*, *62* (1939), 97 ff. Hayes, *Scepter of Egypt*, 2, 1. Gardiner, *Egypt of the Pharaohs*, pp. 156 ff.
36. Waddell, *Manetho*, p. 83.
37. See *Wb*, 171, nos. 28–29, also *Belegstellen*, for references.
38. See above, Chapter 8.

correctly, speaking only of the rulers. Moreover, when the term *ḥḳ3 ḫ3swt* is used in the Middle Kingdom, in the *Story of Sinuhe*,[39] it refers to the rulers of Syria-Palestine. In the New Kingdom the term occurs in the Amada stela of Amenhotep II alongside the "princes of Retjenu."[40] Some scholars have attempted to see a distinction between the two terms,[41] but this is unwarranted. Apophis in the Kamose stela is called a "chief of Retjenu,"[42] and Retjenu is often spoken of as made up of foreign countries, *ḫ3swt*.[43] The epitomes of Manetho, likewise, couple the "brothers [of the princes]" together with the Hyksos as the foreign rulers of Egypt and speak of them all as coming from Phoenicia (Retjenu).[44]

The term used in Egyptian literature to designate the foreign population of Egypt in the Hyksos Period is *ꜥ3mw*.[45] The exact designation of the term is difficult to establish. It is not the generic adjective derived from the name of a territory, and therefore the rendering "Asiatics" is misleading. That translation should be reserved for *sṯtyw*, the generic of *sṯt*, "Asia." Nor is *ꜥ3mw* simply an occupational term; it is restricted to the population of the Levant and refers to both sedentary and nomadic peoples.[46] Etymologically it may have arisen as a designation for those who use the boomerang.[47] If this is so, it certainly outgrew this restricted usage quite early.

The term *ꜥ3mw* makes its first appearance in the late Sixth Dynasty, where it refers to a sedentary group of Asiatics, but the location of their settlements is difficult to determine.[48] In the

39. *Sinuhe*, B 98. It also occurs in the singular, *ḥḳ3 ḫ3st*, in the tomb painting of Khnumhotep II (Newberry, *Beni Hasan*, 1 [London, 1893], Pl. 30).
40. See *ANET*, p. 247.
41. So Wilson, *ANET*, p. 247 n.
42. KS, line 4.
43. See Barkal stela, *ANET*, p. 238a.
44. Waddell, *Manetho*, pp. 91–99.
45. Gauthier, *Dict géog*, 1, 138 f.
46. Thus the frequent translation "Semitic bedouin" is not entirely correct.
47. Gauthier, *Dict géog*, 1, 133.
48. See the biography of Weni, *Urk*, 1, 101–05; translated in *ANET*, pp.

First Intermediate Period, ꜥꜣmw are described in the *Instructions for Merikare* as the seminomadic population of Palestine,[49] and this fits very well the archaeological picture of MB I. In the Middle Kingdom the term is again consistently used to designate the ethnic population of Syria-Palestine, and the ꜥꜣmw are also linked together with ḥḳꜣ ḫꜣswt.[50] Most important are the ethnic epithets, ꜥꜣm and ꜥꜣm.t, used to distinguish the Asiatic slaves from Egyptian slaves in the late Middle Kingdom. In every case, foreign names of ꜥꜣmw are always of the West-Semitic type. The conclusion can hardly be avoided that ꜥꜣmw designates the Amurrite population of Syria-Palestine in the Middle Bronze Age.[51]

Furthermore, the fact that the foreign population of Egypt and its leaders in the Hyksos period is called by the same terminology strongly suggests that the Egyptians recognized a direct ethnic and cultural continuity in these foreigners with those of Syria-Palestine in the Middle Kingdom. This agrees with the archaeological conclusions concerning the Middle Bronze Age. The same usage of ꜥꜣmw continues for the early part of the Eighteenth Dynasty. Toward the end of the Eighteenth Dynasty, ꜥꜣmw is largely replaced by Ḫꜣrw as the most important ethnic component of Syria-Palestine. It is clear, therefore, that if there had been a large Hurrian element among the foreigners in Egypt in the Hyksos period one would have expected the use of the term Ḫꜣrw in place of or alongside ꜥꜣmw.

To this evidence of terminology may be added the indications from the New Kingdom of a strong Amurrite Canaanite cultural

---

277 f. On this text see most recently H. Goedicke, "The Alleged Military Campaign in Southern Palestine in the Reign of Pepi I (VI Dynasty)," *RSO, 38* (1963), 187–97.

49. *ANET*, p. 416b ꜥꜣm(w) is rendered by "Asiatic(s)."

50. The Execration texts combine the ḥḳꜣw of cities in coastal Syria-Palestine with the ꜥꜣmw of the area. See also *Sinuhe*, 98, 175 f.

51. So Alt, "Herkunft der Hyksos," pp. 90 f., who takes the Hyksos situation as a further development of the situation reflected in the Execration texts. See also Koenig, *RAss, 50* (1956), 196.

element in the Delta as a result of the Hyksos period. This is
evident in the number and importance of Semitic deities in
Egyptian religion from the Eighteenth Dynasty on. The cults
of these foreign deities were located in the Eastern Delta and as
far south as Memphis. The reasons for tracing this influence back
to the Hyksos Period have been given above. Another indication
of Amurrite culture in the Delta is the Semitic place-names,
such as, _T3rw_ (Sille), _Tku_ (Succoth), and _Mktr_ (Migdol).[52]
The first of these is definitely attested from the time of Thutmose
III, when it has considerable importance as a fortress town and
the last main station on the way to Asia.

Finally, a reiteration of the conclusions of our study of the
archaeological remains of the Hyksos Period in Egypt and the
MB II in Syria-Palestine: MB II represents a high level of cultural achievement in every respect; the creators of this culture
were the Amurrites. It had the strongest ties with Egypt throughout the Hyksos Period; there is every indication that the foreign
culture of Egypt in the Second Intermediate Period was in continuity with the Amurrite civilization of the Levant. The long
period of acculturation of coastal Syria and Palestine to Egyptian
arts and crafts fully prepared the "foreign rulers" and their
supporters for taking control of Egypt. This was achieved, not
by a sudden coup d'état from without, but in cooperation with a
fifth-column Amurrite group already established in the Delta.
The strong Amurrite princes of Syria-Palestine became heir to
the Egyptian throne in a time of the latter's dynastic weakness.

52. Albright, _JEA_, _10_ (1923), 6–8.

# CHAPTER 14

# CONCLUSION

The preceding discussions attempted a reconstruction of the history of the Second Intermediate Period in Egypt, the Hyksos domination in particular. In spite of the frequent reference, until now, to the "Hyksos," it would be best, nevertheless, to eliminate the use of this term from the following historical summary, since it inevitably carries with it what I consider a false ethnic connotation and arbitrarily isolates the foreigners of Egypt from their original and general Near Eastern context. It would seem preferable to speak only of an Amurrite occupation and domination of Egypt during the Second Intermediate Period.

On the basis of the archaeological investigation, the foreigners of Egypt are seen as a geographical extension of the corresponding culture of Phoenicia-Palestine in the MB II period, a culture with a highly advanced urban society. This civilization of the Levant has its roots in the Amurrite world of both Syria and Mesopotamia in the Old Babylonian period, and has a direct heir in the so-called Canaanite world of the Late Bronze Age. The MB II period began during the Middle Kingdom, and by the end of the Twelfth Dynasty the whole of Phoenicia-Palestine was under the influence of Egypt, with diplomatic ties and active cooperation between the rulers of the various city-states and the rulers of Egypt. During the early Thirteenth Dynasty, the foreigners had much freer access into Egypt. Many of them rose to places of high honor in the administration of the country. Many supporters of the pharaoh in Egypt viewed with great concern the weakness in dynastic rule, and they saw the increasing strength of the Asiatic city-states and their association with subversive elements in Egypt itself as a serious threat to the whole established order. These forebodings are expressed in the Execration texts and the *Admonitions of Ipuwer.*

The way in which an actual Ammurite dynasty was established in Egypt still remains largely unclear. Nevertheless, we must consider the following in any attempt to reconstruct the events.

There is every indication of a strong connection between the Amurrite rulers of the so-called Fifteenth Dynasty and the kings mentioned in the Execration texts; there was a strong link between the foreigners in Egypt during the Second Intermediate Period and the Amurrites in Egypt in the Thirteenth Dynasty. Nothing, archaeological or literary, extant from the Second Intermediate Period, suggests any difference in these two groups of foreigners. On the other hand, the Execration texts and the *Admonitions* seem to anticipate so accurately the fate which befell Egypt that, for methodological reasons, one must begin any discussion of the rise of foreign rulers to power in Egypt with these sources.

Any recourse to Manetho for light on this problem should be treated with great caution. The various extant recensions of this historian are not all of equal value. The one used by Josephus is the least reliable, being highly exaggerated, propagandistic, and the most inaccurate in the use of terminology. The epitomes, on the other hand, seem to preserve important elements which may reflect ancient chronicles.

There was active cooperation between the Asiatics and the Egyptians within Egypt itself in the Amurrite coup d'état. Disloyalty by important noble families may be understood in light of the strong centralization of administration by the pharaohs of the late Twelfth Dynasty. In the period of dynastic weakness, these families reasserted themselves. With the breakup of the land into the three departments of the previous Middle Kingdom administration, an Egyptian, Neḥesy, had control of the North, probably with Asiatic cooperation. It was merely a step for Amurrite princes themselves to take over the control of Lower Egypt and, in time, the whole of Egypt. No great military conquest was needed to accomplish this, and it is doubtful that any occurred. All that was required for the land to become an Amurrite dynasty was the recognition, by a sufficient number of the Egyptian nobility, of a strong foreign king in the strategic city of Avaris and submission to him as vassals (to their own economic advantage).

The continuity in government of the so-called Fifteenth Dynasty with the late Middle Kingdom is, likewise, suggested by the identification of Avaris, *Ḥwt wʿrt,* with the principal center of the Northern Department. Even though the foreigners very likely established an Asiatic "colony" at Tell el-Yahudiyeh, they maintained the administrative center of Lower Egypt, which was established in the Twelfth Dynasty, and continued the worship of the Egyptian deities of the region along with their own, in an eclectic manner typical of the Amurrite society of Phoenicia-Palestine. They sought to follow the cultural and artistic forms of the "classical" Twelfth Dynasty in many other aspects as well.

The nature of the foreign dynasties has been largely clarified by sources from the time of Kamose, particularly his stela. It now seems fairly clear that only one foreign dynasty ruled the whole of Egypt for little more than a century. The last important king was ʿAwoserreʿ Apophis, and foreign domination of Egypt ended in his time, or very soon afterward. Moreover, it seems very likely that there was only one Apophis; he used three prenomina in the course of his long reign. The only other name that can be included, with some certainty, into this dynasty is that of Khyan, while the names in Manetho (apart from Apophis) are entirely unreliable.

The way in which the Amurrite kings of Egypt ruled is also indicated most clearly from the Carnarvon Tablet I and the

Kamose stela. It is clear that Egypt was regarded as a conglomeration of vassal states, with Upper Egypt, centering in Thebes, as a separate, although dependent, entity. The political structure and diplomatic procedure appear to have been quite similar to what we know from the Amurrite world and find reflected in the Mari correspondence. Strong foreign connections were established with Nubia in the South and the eastern Mediterranean in the North. However, there is no basis for positing anything like an Asiatic empire. The power of the Fifteenth Dynasty was probably restricted to Egypt alone, although Phoenicia-Palestine carried on active commercial intercourse with Egypt throughout the period. Furthermore, there is no evidence for any great expulsion of peoples from Egypt into Asia. The defeat of the foreign dynasty was the result of a civil war, and the foreign population which was probably not very numerous simply continued to live in the Eastern Delta.

The continuity of a foreign population in the Eastern Delta region from the Second Intermediate Period to the Ramesside period had important historical repercussions. The clearest indication is religion. When the Ramessides established Pi-Ramesses in the vicinity of Avaris, they raised to a position of great honor the gods of the "foreign rulers," particularly the "semiticized" Seth. The influence of this foreign element in religion brought Asia into the worldview of the Egyptians as a land which rightly belonged to pharaoh and his gods. Consequently, in the wars of the Eighteenth and Nineteenth Dynasties, the gods which supported the Egyptian kings were both Egyptian and Canaanite-Amurrite. The association of these latter deities with the pharaoh must have originated in the period of foreign domination. It is, perhaps, in this fundamental ideological change more than in any particular material or technological advances that the real legacy of the Amurrite occupation is to be found.

The conclusions of this study are not intended as a novel set of suggestions in an area of history filled with uncertainties.

Instead, all these factors viewed together call for a new direction in the discussion of the Hyksos. In archaeology there must be an end to speaking of "Hyksos" fortifications and a new appreciation of the Amurrite civilization of Palestine in the Middle Bronze Age. Hyksos origins must be related to this great Amurrite civilization and not to some hypothetical Hurrian–Indo-Aryan invasion—unless some clear new evidence strongly suggests otherwise. There is little value in retaining this and other old notions about the Hyksos when the new evidence continues to suggest otherwise. This study has been a reevaluation of the Hyksos problem, and others will follow as new evidence comes to light. Such is the ongoing task of historical research.

# BIBLIOGRAPHY

Adam, S., "Recent Discoveries in the Eastern Delta," *Ann Serv*, *55* (1958), 301–24.

——, "Report on the Excavations of the Department of Antiquities at Ezbet Rushdi," *Ann Serv*, *56* (1959), 207–26.

Albright, W. F., "The Town of Selle (Zaru) in the Amarnah Tablets," *JEA*, *10* (1923), 6–8.

——, *The Excavations of Tell Beit Mirsim*, Part I: "The Pottery of the First Three Campaigns," *AASOR*, *12* (1932); Part IA; "The Bronze Age Pottery of the Fourth Campaign," *AASOR*, *13* (1933); Part II: "The Bronze Age," *AASOR*, *17* (1936–37).

——, "Soundings at Ader, a Bronze Age City of Moab," *BASOR*, *53* (1934), 13–18.

——, "Palestine in the Earliest Historical Period," *JPOS*, *15* (1935), 193–234.

——, "The Chronology of a South Palestinian City, Tell el-Ajjul," *AJSL*, *55* (1938), 337–59.

——, "A Prince of Ta‹anach in the Fifteenth Century b.c.," *BASOR*, *94* (1944), 12–27.

——, "The Early Alphabetic Inscriptions from the Sinai and their Decipherment," *BASOR*, *110* (1948), 6–22.

——, "Northwest Semitic Names in a List of Egyptian Slaves from the Eighteenth Century b.c.," *JAOS*, *74* (1954), 222–33.

——, "Stratigraphic Confirmation of the Low Mesopotamian Chronology," *BASOR*, *144* (1956), 6–30.

——, *From the Stone Age to Christianity*, 2nd, ed., Garden City, N.Y., Doubleday, 1957.

——, "Dunand's New Byblian Volumn: A Lycian at the Byblian Court," *BASOR*, *155* (1959), 31–34.

——, "The Role of the Canaanites in the History of Civilization," in *BANE*, 328–62.

——, *The Archaeology of Palestine*, Baltimore, Penguin Books, 1961.

——, "Abram the Hebrew: A New Archaeological Interpretation," *BASOR*, *163* (1961), 36–54.

——, "The Chronology of Middle Bronze I (Early Bronze-Middle Bronze)," *BASOR*, *168* (1962), 36–42.

——, "The Eighteenth-Century Princes of Byblos and the Chronology of Middle Bronze," *BASOR*, *176* (1964), 38–46.

——, "Further Light on the History of the Middle-Bronze Byblos," *BASOR*, *179* (1965), 38–43.

ALT, A., "Herren und Herrensitze Palästinas im Anfung des zweiten Jahrtausends vor Chr.," *ZDPV*, *64* (1941), 21–39.

——, "Die Herkunft der Hyksos in neuer Sicht," Berichte über die Verhandlungen der Sächsischen Akad. der Wissenschaften zu Leipzig. Phil.-hist. Klasse, 101, Heft 6 (1954). Reissued in *Kleine Schriften zur Geschichte des Volkes Israel* (München, C. H. Beck, 1959), *3*, 72–98.

AMIET, P., "Notes sur le répertoire iconographique de Mari à l'époque du palais," *Syria*, *37* (1960), 215–32.

AMIRAN, R. B. K., "Tell el-Yahudiyeh Ware in Syria," *IEJ*, *7* (1957), 93–97.

——, "The Pottery of the Middle Bronze Age I in Palestine," *IEJ*, *10* (1960), 204–25.

——, et al, *The Ancient Pottery of Eretz Yisrael* (in Hebrew), Jerusalem, The Bialik Institute and the Israel Exploration Society, 1963.

——, and A. Eitan, "A Canaanite-Hyksos City at Tell Nagila," *Archaeology*, *18* (1965), 113–23.

BAKIR, ABD EL-MOHSEN, "Slavery in Pharaonic Egypt," *Ann Serv*, *45* (1947), 135–43.

——, "Slavery in Pharaonic Egypt," *Ann Serv Suppl*, *18* (1952).

BALL, J., *Egypt in the Classical Geographers*, Cairo, 1942.

BARROIS, A. G., *Manuel d'archéologie biblique*, 2, Paris, A. Picard, 1953.

——, "Pillar," *The Interpreter's Dictionary of the Bible* (Nashville, Abingdon, 1962), *3*, pp. 815 ff.

BEN-DOR, I., "Palestinian Alabaster Vases," *QDAP*, *11* (1944), 93-112.

——, "A Middle Bronze Age Temple at Nahariyeh," *QDAP, 14* (1950), 1–41.

BISSON DE LA ROQUE, ET AL, *Le trésor de Tod,* IFAOC, Documents et Fouilles, 11, Cairo, 1953.

BORCHARDT, L., " Ein Rechnengsbuch des königlichen Hofes aus dem Ende des mittleren Reiches," *ZÄS, 28* (1890), 65–103.

——, *Das Grabdenkmal des Königs Sahure II, Die Wandbilder,* Leipzig, J. C Hinrichs, 1910.

——, *Ein Stammbaum memphitischer Priester,* SPAW, Phil.-hist. Klasse 24, Berlin, 1932.

BOTTÉRO, J., "Les inventaires de Qatna," *RAss, 43* (1949), 1–40.

——, *Le problème des Ḫabiru,* 4e Recontre Assyriogique Internationale, Paris, Cahiers de la Société Asiatique 12, 1954.

BREASTED, J. H., "When Did the Hittites Enter Palestine?," *AJSL, 21* (1904), 153–58.

BRUNNER, H., review of Z. Mayani, *Les Hyksos et le monde de la Bible, AfO, 18* (1958), 434.

BUCHANAN, B., "On the Seal Impressions on Some Old Babylonian Tablets," *JCS, 11* (1957), 45–52.

——, "Further Observations on the Syrian Glyptic Style," *JCS, 11* (1957), 74–76.

BULL, R. J., "A Re-examination of the Shechem Temple," *BA, 23* (1960), 110–19.

ČERNÝ, J., "Semites in Egyptian Mining Expeditions to Sinai," *Archiv Orientalni, 7* (1935), 384–89.

——, "La Fin de la Seconde dynastie ou la période sethienne," *Ann Serv, 44* (1944), 293-98.

——, "The True Form of the Name of King Snofru," *RSO, 38* (1963), 89–92.

CHILDE, V. G., *New Light on the Most Ancient East,* New York, Grove Press, 1957.

CLEVELAND, R., "Soundings at Khirbet Ader," *AASOR, 34–35* (1954–56), 79–98.

COUROYER, B., "La Résidence ramasside du Delta et la Ramses biblique," *RB, 53* (1946), 75–98.

DAHOOD, M. J., "Ancient Semitic Deities in Syria and Palestine," in

S. Moscati, ed., *Le Antiche divinità semitiche*, Roma, Università, 1958.

Davies, G. H., "High Place," in *The Interpreter's Dictionary of the Bible* (Nashville, Abingdon, 1962), 2, 602 ff.

de Vaux, R., "Excavations at Tell el-Farᶜah and the Site of Ancient Tirzah," *PEQ* (1956), 125–40.

——, "La Troisième campagne de fouilles à Tell el-Farᶜah, près Naplouse," *RB*, *58* (1951), 393–430, 566–90.

Dothan, M., "The Excavations at Nahariyeh, 1954–55," *IEJ*, *6* (1956), 14–25.

——, "Some Aspects of Religious Life in Palestine during the Hyksos Rule," *Antiquity and Survival*, *2* (1957), 121–30.

Du Mesnil, du Buisson, *Les Ruines d'el-Mishrifé*, Paris, University of Paris, 1927.

Dunand, M., *Fouilles de Byblos*, 2 parts, Paris, P. Guethner, 1939–58.

Dussaud, R., "Observations sur la ceramique du IIe millenaire avant notre ère," *Syria*, *9* (1928), 131–50.

——, review of R. M. Engberg, *The Hyksos Reconsidered*, *Syria*, *21* (1940), 343 f.

——, "L'Origine de l'alphabet et son evolution première d'après les découvertes de Bvblos," *Syria*, *25* (1946–48), 36–52.

Edgerton, W. F., "Egyptian Phonetic Writing, from its Invention to the Close of the Nineteenth Dvnasty," *JAOS*, *60* (1940), 473–506.

Emery, W. B., "A Preliminary Report on the Excavations of the Egyptian Exploration Society at Buhen, 1957–60," *Kush*, *7* (1959), 7–14; ibid., *8* (1960), 7–10; ibid., *9* (1961), 81–86.

Engberg, R. M., *The Hyksos Reconsidered*, SAOC, *18*, Chicago, University of Chicago Press, 1939.

——, P. L. O. Guy and, *Megiddo Tombs*, OIP *33*, Chicago, University of Chicago Press, 1938.

Epstein, C., "A New Appraisal of Some Lines from a Long-Known Papyrus," *JEA*, *49* (1963), 49–56.

Faulkner, R. O., "The God Setekh in the Pyramid Texts," *Ancient Egypt* (1925), 5–10.

——, review of H. E. Winlock, *The Rise and Fall of the Middle Kingdom*, *JEA*, *34* (1948), 124.

Fischer, H. G., "Some Notes on the Easternmost Nomes of the

Delta in the Old and Middle Kingdoms," *JNES, 18* (1959), 129–42.

FOUGEROUSSE, J. L., "Etudes sur les constructions de Tanis," *Kêmi, 5* (1935), 19–48.

FRANKFORT, H., "Egypt and Syria in the First Intermediate Period," *JEA, 12* (1926), 80–99.

——, *Cylinder Seals*, London, Macmillan, 1939.

——, *Art and Architecture of the Ancient Orient*, Baltimore, Penguin Books, 1955.

FRASER, G., *A Catalogue of Scarabs*, London, B. Quaritch, 1900.

FUGMANN, E., *Hama: L'architecture des périodes pré-hellénistique*, Copenhagen, Copenhagen Nationalmuseet, 1958.

FUNK, R. W., "The 1957 Campaign at Beth-Zur," *BASOR, 150* (1958), 8–20.

GADD, C. J., "Tablets from Chagar Bazar and Tall Brak, 1937–38," *Iraq, 7* (1940), 22–66.

GALLING, K., "Hyksosherrschaft und Hyksoskultur," *ZDPV, 62* (1939), 89–115.

GARDINER, A. H., *Admonitions of an Egyptian Sage*, Leipzig, J. C. Hinrichs, 1909.

——, *Notes on the Story of Sinuhe*, Paris, H. Champion, 1916.

——, "The Defeat of the Hyksos by Kamose: The Carnarvon Tablet No. 1," *JEA, 3* (1916), 95–110.

——, and B. Gunn, "New Rendering of Egyptian Texts II, The Expulsion of the Hyksos," *JEA, 5* (1918), 36–56.

——, "The Supposed Egyptian Equivalent of the Name of Goshen," *JEA, 5* (1918), 218–23.

——, "The Delta Residence of the Ramessides," *JEA, 5* (1918), 127–38, 179–200, 242–71.

——, "The Geography of the Exodus: An Answer to Professor Naville and Others," *JEA, 10* (1924), 87–98.

——, "Tanis and Pi-Ramesse: A Retraction," *JEA, 19* (1933), 122–28.

——, "The Astarte Papyrus," in *Griffith Studies*, pp. 74–85.

——, "Davies's Copy of the Great Speos Artemidos Inscription," *JEA 32* (1946), 43–58.

——, *Ancient Egyptian Onomastica*, 3 vols. London, Oxford University Press, 1947.

———, *Egyptian Grammar,* 2nd ed. Oxford, University Press, 1950.

———, T. E. Peet, and J. Černý, *The Inscriptions of Sinai,* 2 parts London, Egypt Exploration Society, 1952–55.

———, "The First Menthotpe of the Eleventh Dynasty," *MDIK, 14* (1956), 42–51.

———, *The Royal Canon of Turin,* Oxford, Printed for the Griffith Institute at the University by V. Ridler, 1959.

———, *Egypt of the Pharaohs,* Oxford, Clarendon Press, 1961.

———, "Once Again the Proto-Sinaitic Inscriptions," *JEA, 48,* (1962), 45–48.

GAUTHIER, H., "Une tombe de la XIXe dynastie à Qantir (Delta)," *Ann Serv, 32* (1932), 115–28.

———, "Les deux rois Kamose," in *Griffith Studies,* pp. 3–8.

GELB, I. J., *Hurrians and Subarians,* SAOC, 22, Chicago, 1944.

———, "The Early History of the West Semitic Peoples," *JCS, 15* (1961), 24–47.

GLUECK, N., *Explorations in Eastern Palestine,* part 1, *AASOR, 14* (1933–34); part 3, *AASOR, 18–19* (1937–39).

———, "Archaeological Research in Palestine, Transjordan, and Syria," *AJA, 42* (1938), 172 f.

———, "The Seventh Season of Archaeological Exploration in the Negev," *BASOR, 152* (1958), 18–38.

GOEDICKE, H., "Zur Chronologie der sogenannten 'Ersten Zwischenzeit'," *ZDMG, 112* (1963), 239–54.

———, "The Alleged Military Campaign in Southern Palestine in the Reign of Pepi I (VI Dynasty)," *RSO, 38* (1963), 187–97.

GOETZE, A., "Is Ugaritic a Canaanite Dialect?" *Language, 17* (1941), 134–37.

———, *Kleinasien,* 2nd ed. München, C. H. Beck, 1957.

———, "On the Chronology of the Second Millennium B.C.," *JCS, 11* (1957), 53–61, 63–73.

———, "Remarks on Some Names in the Execration Texts," *BASOR, 151* (1958), 28–33.

———, "Warfare in Asia Minor," *Iraq, 25* (1963), 124–30.

GREENBERG, M., *The Ḫab/piru,* New Haven, American Oriental Society, 1955.

GRIFFITH, F. LL., *The Antiquities of Tell el-Yahudiyeh*, London, Egypt Exploration Fund, 1890.

——, *Hieratic Papyri from Kahun and Gurob*, 2 vols. London, B. Quaritch, 1898.

GRIFFITHS, J. G., *The Conflict of Horus and Seth*, Liverpool, Liverpool University Press, 1960.

GURNEY, O. R., *The Hittites*, Baltimore, Penguin Books, 1961.

GUSTAVS, A., "Subaräische Namen in einer ägyptischen Liste syrischer Sklaven und ein subaräischer (?) Hyksos-Name," *ZÄS*, *64* (1929), 54–58.

HABACHI, L., "Khataᵃna-Qantir: Importance," *Ann Serv*, *52* (1954), 443–559.

——, "Preliminary Report on Kamose Stela . . . ," *Ann Serv*, *53* (1956), 195–202.

HAMMAD, M., "Découverte d'une stéle du roi Kamose," *Chr d'Ég*, *30* (1955), 198–208.

HAMZA, M., "Excavations of the Department of Antiquities at Qantir (Fakus District)," *Ann Serv*, *30* (1930), 31–68.

HANFMANN, G. M. A., "The Bronze Age in the Near East," *AJA*, *55* (1951), 355–65; ibid., *56* (1952), 27–38.

HAWKES, C., "Gold Ear-rings of the Bronze Age, East and West," *Folklore*, *72* (1961), 438–74.

HAYES, W. C., *Glazed Tiles from the Palace of Ramesses II at Kantir*, Metropolitan Museum of Art, New York, Papers No. 3, 1937.

——, "Notes on the Government of Egypt in the Late Middle Kingdom," *JNES*, *12* (1953), 31–39.

——, *The Scepter of Egypt*, 2 vols. New York, Harper, in cooperation with the Metropolitan Museum of Art, 1953–59.

——, *A Papyrus of the Late Middle Kingdom in the Brooklyn Museum* (*Papyrus Brooklyn 35.1446*), Brooklyn, Brooklyn Museum, 1955.

——, "The Middle Kingdom," *CAH*², *1*, ch. 20.

——, "Egypt: From the Death of Ammenemes III to Seqenenre II," *CAH*², *2*, ch. 2.

——, M. B. Rowton, and F. H. Stubbings, "Chronology: Egypt; Western Asia; Aegean Bronze Age," *CAH*², *1*, ch. 6.

HELCK, H. W., *Untersuchungen zu Manetho und den ägyptischen Königslisten*, Berlin, Akademie-Verlag, 1956.

——, *Die Beziehungen Agyptens zu Vorderasien im 3. und 2. Jahrtausend V. Chr.*, Ägyptologische Abhandlungen, 5, Wiesbaden, O. Harrassowitz, 1962.

HERRMANN, S., *Untersuchungen zur Überlieferungsgestalt mittelägyptischen Literaturwerke*, Berlin, Akademie-Verlag, 1957.

HUGHES, G. R., "Serra East," *Kush, 11* (1963), 124 ff.

ILIFFE, J. H., "Pottery from Ras el-Ain," *QDAP, 5* (1936), 113–26.

INGHOLT, H., *Studien over Palmyrensk Skulptur*, Copenhagen, C. A. Reitzel, 1928.

JAMES, T. G. H., "A Group of Inscribed Egyptian Tools," *BMQ, 24* (1961), 36–43.

——, "Egypt: From the Expulsion of the Hyksos to Amenophis I," *CAH²*, 2, ch. 8.

JUNKER, H. J. B., "Der nubische Ursprung der sogen. Tell el-Jahudiyeh-Vasen," *Sitzungsberichte der Akademie der Wissenschaften in Wien*, Phil.-hist. Klasse, 198:3, Abhandlung, Vienna, 1921.

——, "Phrnfr," *ZÄS, 75* (1939), 63–84.

KANTOR, H. J., "The Aegean and the Orient in the Second Millennium B.C.," *AJA, 51* (1947), 1–103.

——, "The Chronology of Egypt and its correlation with that of Other Parts of the Near East in the Periods before the Late Bronze Age," in R. W. Ehrich, ed., *Relative Chronologies in Old World Archaeology*, Chicago, University of Chicago Press, 1953.

——, "Syro-Palestinian Ivories," *JNES, 15* (1956), 153–74.

KARAGEORGHIS, V., "Horse Burials on the Island of Cyprus," *Archaeology, 18* (1965), 282–90.

KEES, H., "Tanis: Ein kritischer Überblick zur Geschichte der Stadt," *Nachr. Göttingen*, 1944, 145–82.

——, *Ancient Egypt, A Cultural Topography*, Chicago, University of Chicago Press, 1961.

——, "Ein Handelsplatz des MR im Nordostdelta," *MDIK, 18* (1962), 1–13.

KELSO, J. L., "The Fourth Campaign at Bethel," *BASOR, 164* (1961), 5–18.

KENYON, K. M., "Excavations at Jericho," *PEQ* (1952), 62–82; ibid. (1954), 45–63; ibid. (1955), 108–17; ibid. (1956), 67–82.

——, "Some Notes on the Early and Middle Bronze Age Strata of Megiddo," *Eretz-Israel, 5* (1958), 51\*–60\*.

——, *Archaeology in the Holy Land,* New York, Praeger, 1960.

——, *Excavations at Jericho: The Tombs Excavated in 1952–54, 1,* London, British School of Archaeology in Jerusalem, 1960.

KOENIG, J., "Aperçus nouveaux sur les Hyksos," *RAss, 50* (1956), 191–99.

KUPPER, J. R., "Notes lexicographiques," *RAss, 45* (1951), 120–30.

——, "Northern Mesopotamia and Syria," *CAH* ², 2, ch. 1.

LABIB, P., *Die Herrschaft der Hyksos in Ägypten und ihr Sturz,* Glückstadt-Hamburg-New York, J. J. Augustin, 1936.

LACAU, P., "Une Stéle du roi 'Kamosis'," *Ann Serv, 39* (1939), 245–71.

LAMBDIN, T. O., review of Z. Mayani, *Les Hyksos et le monde de la Bible, JBL, 77* (1958), 272–74.

LANDSBERGER, B., "Assyrische Königsliste und 'Dunkles Zeitalter'," *JCS, 8* (1954), 31–45, 47–73, 106–33.

LECLANT, J., AND J. YOYOTTE, "Les Obelisques de Tanis," *Kêmi, 14* (1957), 43–80.

LEEMANS, W. F., *Foreign Trade in the Old Babylonian Period,* Leiden, E. J. Brill, 1960.

——, *The Old Babylonian Merchant,* Leiden, E. J. Brill, 1950.

LEIBOVITCH, J., "Le Problème des Hyksos et celui de l'exode," *IEJ, 3* (1953), 99–112.

——, "Deux nouvelles inscriptions protosinaïtiques," *Le Muséon, 74* (1961), 461–66.

——, "The Date of the Proto-Sinaitic Inscriptions," *Le Muséon, 76* (1963), 201–03.

LEWY, J., "Old Assyrian Institutions," *HUCA, 27* (1956), 1–80.

LIDZBARSKI, M., "Epigraphisches aus Syrien, II," *Nachr Göttingen,* Phil.-hist. Klasse, Berlin, 1924.

LOUD, G., *Megiddo, II: Seasons of 1935–39,* 2 parts, OIP 62, Chicago, University of Chicago Press, 1948.

LUCAS, A., *Ancient Egyptian Materials and Industries,* 4th ed. London, E. Arnold, 1962.

MACIVER, D. RANDALL, AND C. L. WOOLLEY, *Buhen*, Philadelphia, University Museum, 1911.

MAXWELL-HYSLOP, R., "Daggers and Swords in Western Asia," *Iraq, 8* (1944), 1–65.

——, "Western Asiatic Shaft-Hole Axes," *Iraq, 11* (1947), 90–130.

MAYANI, Z., *Les Hyksos et le monde de la Bible*, Paris, Payot, 1956.

MEYER, E., *Geschichte des Altertums*, 2nd ed. Stuttgart and Berlin, J. G. Cotta, 1909, *1*, Part 2.

MONTET, P., *Byblos et l'Egypte; quatre campagnes de fouilles à Gebeil*, 1921–24, 2 vols., Paris, P. Geuthner, 1928–29.

——, "Notes et documents pour servir à l'histoire des relations entre l'ancienne Egypte et la Syrie," *Kêmi, 1* (1928), 83–93.

——, "Tanis, Avaris et Pi-Ramses," *RB, 39* (1930), 1–28.

——, "La Stéle de l'an 400 rétrouvée," *Kêmi, 4* (1933), 191–215.

——, *Le Drame d'Avaris: Essai sur la penetration des Semites en Egypte*, Paris, P. Geuthner, 1941.

——, *Les Enigmes de Tanis*, Paris, Payot, 1952.

——, "Notes et documents . . . , IV. Byblos et le Keftioy," *Kêmi, 13* (1954), 71–73.

——, "La Stéle du roi Kamose," *CRAIBL*, 1956, 112–20.

——, *Géographie de l'Egypte ancienne*, 2 vols. Paris, Impr. nationale, 1957.

——, "Notes et documents . . . , XI. Herichef a Byblos," *Kêmi, 16* (1962), 89–90.

MORAN, W. L., "Mari Notes on the Execration Texts," *Orientalia, 26* (1957), 339–45.

MÜLLER, W. Max, *Asien und Europen nach altägyptischen Denkmalern*, Leipzig, 1893.

MUNN-RANKIN, J. M., "Diplomacy in Western Asia in the Early Second Millennium B.C.," *Iraq, 18* (1956), 68–110.

MURRAY, M. A., "Some Canaanite Scarabs," *PEQ* (1949), 92–97.

NAGEL, W., and E. Strommenger, "Alalaḫ and Siegelkunst," *JCS, 12* (1958), 109–23.

NAVILLE, E., *Goshen and the Shrine of Saft el-Henneh*, London, 1887.

NAVILLE, E., *The Mound of the Jew and the City of Onias*, London, 1890.

——, "The Geography of the Exodus," *JEA, 10* (1924), 18–39.

NEWBERRY, P. E., *Beni Hasan*, 4 vols. London, 1893–1900.

——, *El-Bersheh, 1*, London, Egyptian Exploration Fund, 1898.

——, *Scarabs*, London, A. Constable, 1906.

NOTH, M., "Die syrisch-palästinische Bevölkerung des zweiten Jahrtausend v. Chr. im Lichte neuer Quellen," *ZDPV, 65* (1942), 9–67.

O'CALLAGHAN, R. T., *Aram Naharaim: A Contribution to the History of Upper Mesopotamia in the Second Millennium* B.C., Rome, Pontificium Inst. Biblicum, 1948.

OPPENHIEM, A. L., "Sea-faring Merchants of Ur," *JAOS, 74* (1954), 6–17.

ORY, J., "Excavations at Ras el-Ain II," *QDAP, 6* (1938), 99–120.

——, "A Middle Bronze Age Tomb at El-Jisr," *QDAP, 12* (1946) 31–42.

OTTO, H., "Die Keramik der mittleren Bronzezeit in Palästina," *ZDPV, 61* (1938), 147–277, Pls. 2–24.

PARKER, B., "Cylinder Seals from Palestine," *Iraq, 11* (1949) 1–42.

PARKER, R. A., "The Lunar Dates of Thutmose III and Ramesses II," *JNES, 16* (1957), 39–43.

PARR, P. J., "Excavations at Khirbet Iskander," *ADAJ, 4–5* (1960), 128–33.

PARROT, A., *MAM, 2, Le Palais*, 3 parts Paris, Geuthner, 1958–59.

PEET, E., *The Rhind Mathematical Papyrus*, Liverpool, Liverpool University Press, 1923.

PETRIE, W. M. FLINDERS, *Illahun, Kahun, Gurob*, London, D. Nutt, 1891.

——, *Hyksos and Israelite Cities*, London, Egyptian Research Account, 1906.

——, *Kahun, Gurob, and Hawara*, London, Kegan Paul, 1890.

——, *Scarabs and Cylinders with Names*, London, Egyptian Research Account, 1917.

——, *Beth Pelet, 1*, London, British School of Archaeology in Egypt, 1930.

——, *Ancient Gaza*, 4 vols. London, British School of Archaeology in Egypt, 1931–34.

PEZARD, M., *Qadesh, Mission archéologique à Tell Nebi Mend, 1921–1922*, Paris, Bibliotheque archéologique et historique, 1931.

POPE, M. H., *El in the Ugaritic Text*, Leiden, E. J. Brill, 1955.

——, "Anat," in H. W. Haussig, ed., *Wörterbuch der Mythologie, I*, fasc. 2 (Stuttgart, Ernst Klett, 1963), 235–41.

——, "Astarte," in H. W. Haussig, ed., *Wörterbuch der Mythologie, I*, fasc. 2 (Stuttgart, Ernst Klett, 1963), 250–52.

PORADA, E., "Syrian Seal Impressions on Tablets Dated in the Time of Hammurabi and Samsu-iluna," *JNES, 16* (1957), 192–97.

PORTER, B., and R. L. B. Moss, *Topigraphical Bibliography of Ancient Egyptian Hieroglyphic Texts, Reliefs, and Paintings*, 7 vols. Oxford, Clarendon Press, 1927–51.

POSENER, G., *Princes et pays d'Asie et de Nubie*, Brussels, Fondation Egyptologique Reine Elisabeth, 1940.

——, *Littérature et politique dans l'Egypte de la XIIe dynastie*, Paris, Champion, 1956.

——, "Les Asiatiques en Egypte sous les XIIe et XIIIe dynasties," *Syria, 34* (1957), 145–63.

——, "*Nḥsyw et Mḏзyw*," *ZÄS, 83* (1957), 38–43.

——, "Pour une localisation du pays Koush au Moyan Empire," *Kush, 6* (1958), 39–68.

——, J. Bottéro, and K. M. Kenyon, "Syria and Palestine c. 2160–1780 B.C.," *CAH* ², *I*, ch. 21.

PRAUSNITZ, M. W., "Abydos and Combed Ware," *PEQ* (1954), 91–96.

REISNER, G. A., *Excavations at Kerma I–V*, 2 vols. Cambridge, Mass., Peabody Museum of Harvard University, 1923.

——, and W. S. Smith, *A History of the Giza Necropolis*, 2 Cambridge, Mass., Harvard University Press, 1955.

——, "The Egyptian Forts from Halfa to Semna," *Kush, 8* (1960), 11–24.

RICKE, H., "Der 'Hohe Sand In Heliopolis'," *ZÄS, 71* (1935), 107–11.

ROEDER, G., "Sothis und Satis," *ZÄS, 45* (1908), 22–30.

ROLLIG, W., "Mikal," in H. W. Haussig, ed., *Wörterbuch der Mythologie, 1*, fasc. 2 (Stuttgart, Ernst Klett, 1963), 298–99.

ROTHENBERG, B., ET AL, *God's Wilderness, Discoveries in the Sinai*, London, Thames and Hudson, 1961.

ROWE, A., *A Catalogue of Egyptian Scarabs, . . . in the Palestine Archaeological Museum*, Cairo, Impr. de l'Institut français d'archéologie orientale, 1936.

————, "Three New Stelae from the South-Eastern Desert," *Ann Serv, 39* (1939), 187–94.

ROWLEY, H. H., *From Joseph to Joshua: Biblical Traditions in the Light of Archaeology*, London, Oxford University Press, 1950.

ROWTON, M. B. "Comparative Chronology at the Time of Dynasty XIX," *JNES, 19* (1960), 15–22.

SANDARS, N. K., "The First Agean Swords and their Ancestry," *AJA, 65* (1961), 17–29.

SÄVE-SÖDERBERGH, T., *Ägypten und Nubien: Ein zur altägyptischer Aussenpolitik*, Lund, Ohlssons, 1941.

————, review of H. E. Winlock, *The Rise and Fall of the Middle Kingdom in Thebes, Bibl Or, 6* (1949), 88.

————, "The Hyksos in Egypt," *JEA, 37* (1951), 53–71.

————, "The ʿprw as Vintagers in Egypt," *Orient Su, 1* (1952), 1–14.

————, "The Nubian Kingdom of the Second Intermediate Period," *Kush 4* (1956), 54–61.

SCHAEFFER, C. F. A., "Les Fouilles de Minet-et-Beida et de Ras Shamra, Deuxième Campagne (Printemps 1930)," *Syria, 12* (1931), 1–14.

————, *Stratigraphie comparée et chronologie de l'Asie occidentale (IIIe et IIe millenaires)*, Oxford, Oxford University Press, 1948.

————, *Ugaritica II*, Paris, P. Geuthner, 1949.

————, *Ugaritica IV*, Paris, P. Geuthner, 1962.

————, and J. Nougayrol, *Le palais royal d'Ugarit*, Paris, Impr. nationale, 1955.

SCHARFF, A., and A. Moortgat, *Ägypten und Vorderasien im Altertum*, Munchen, F. Bruckmann, 1950.

SCHULMAN, A. R., "The Egyptian Chariotry: A Reexamination," *JARCE*, 2 (1963), 75–98.

SETHE, K., "Der Denkstein mit dem Datum des Jahres 400 der Ära von Tanis," *ZÄS*, 65 (1930), 85–89.

————, *Die Ächtung feindlicher Fürsten, Völker, und Dinge auf altägyptischen Tongefässscherben des mittleren Reiches*, Berlin Akad. Abhandlungen, 1926, No. 5.

SHAFEI, ALY BEY, "Historical Notes on the Pelusiac Branch," *Bulletin de la Société de Géographie d'Egypte*, 21 (1943–46), 231–85.

SIMPSON, W. K., "The Hyksos Princess Tany," *Chr d'Eg, 34* (1959), 233–39.

————, "Reshep in Egypt," *Orientalia*, 29 (1960), 63–74.

————, "Studies in the Twelfth Egyptian Dynasty: I. The Residence of Itj-towy," *JARCE*, 2 (1963), 53–59.

SMITH, SIDNEY, *Alalakh and Chronology*, London, Luzac and Company, 1940.

SMITH, W. S., *The Art and Architecture of Ancient Egypt*, Baltimore, Penguin Books, 1958.

————, "The Old Kingdom in Egypt," *CAH* [2], *1*, ch. 14.

————, *Interconnections in the Ancient Near East: A Study of the Relationships between the Arts of Egypt, the Aegean, and Western Asia*, New Haven, Yale University Press, 1965.

SOLLBERGER, E., "Byblos sous les rois d'Ur," *AfO, 19* (1960), 120–22.

SPEISER, E. A., "Ethnic Movements in the Near East in the Second Millennium B.C.," *AASOR, 13* (1933), 13–54.

SPIEGEL, J., *Sociale und weltanschauliche Reformbewegungen in alten Ägypten*, Heidelberg, F. H. Kerle, 1950.

STEINDORFF, G., and K. C. Seele, *When Egypt Ruled the East*, Chicago, University of Chicago Press, 1957.

STOCK, H., *Studien zur Geschichte und Archäologie der 13. bis 17. Dynastie Ägyptens*, Ägyptologische Forschungen 12, Glückstadt-Hamburg-New York, J. J. Augustin, 1942.

————, *Die erste Zwischenzeit Ägyptens*, Analecta Orientalia 31, Rome, Pontificium Inst. Biblicum, 1938.

STOCK, H., "Der Hyksos Chian in Bogazkoy," *MDOG, 94* (1963), 73–80.

STUBBINGS, F. H., "The Rise of Mycenaean Civilization," *CAH* ², 2, ch. 14.

TOOMBS, L. E., and G. E. Wright, "The Third Campaign at Tell Balatah," *BASOR, 161* (1961), 11–54.

——, and G. E. Wright, "The Fourth Campaign at Balatah," *BASOR, 169* (1963), 1–60.

TOUSSOUN, O., *Memoire sur les anciennes branches du Nil*, Cairo, 1922 Mémoires présenté à l'Institute d'Egypte, 4.

TUFNELL, O., " 'Hyksos' Scarabs from Canaan," *Anatolian Studies, 6* (1956), 67–73.

——, *Lachish IV: The Bronze Age*, Oxford, Oxford University Press, 1957.

——, "The Courtyard Cemetery of Tell el-Ajjul, Palestine," *BIA, 3* (1962), 1–37.

VANDIER, J., *Manuel d'archéologie égyptienne*, 3 vols. Paris, Picard, 1952–58.

VAN SETERS, J., "A Date for the 'Admonitions' in the Second Intermediate Period," *JEA, 50* (1964), 13–23.

VERCOUTTER, J., *L'Egypte et le monde égéen préhellénique* Cairo, Impr. de l'Institut français d'archéologie orientale, 1956.

——, "Deux mois de fouilles à Mirgissa en Nubie Soudanaise," *BSFE, 37–38* (1963), 23–30.

——, "Fouilles à Mirgissa," *REg, 15* (1963), 69–75.

VINCENT, R. P. H., "Le Baal canaanéen de Beisan et sa paredre," *RB, 37* (1928), 512–43.

VON BECKERATH, J., *Tanis und Theben*, Ägyptologische Forschungen, 16, Glückstadt-Hamburg-New York, J. J. Augustin, 1951.

——, *Untersuchungen zur politischen Geschichte der zweiten Zwischenzeit in Ägypten*, Glückstadt, J. J. Augustin, 1965.

VON BISSING, W. F., "Das angebliche Weltreich der Hyksos," *AfO, 11* (1937), 325–35.

WADDELL, W. G., *Manetho*, Loeb Classical Library, Cambridge, Mass., Harvard University Press, 1940.

WAINWRIGHT, G. A., "The Occurrence of Tin and Copper near Byblos," *JEA, 20* (1934), 29–32

WARD, W. A., "Comparative Studies in Egyptian and Ugaritic," *JNES, 20* (1961), 31–40

———, "Egypt and the East Mediterranean in the Early Second Millennium B.C.," *Orientalia, 30* (1961), 22–45, 120–55.

———, "Egypt and the East Mediterranean from Predynastic Times to the End of the Old Kingdom," *JESHO, 6* (1963), 1–57.

———, review of Helck, *Die Beziehungen Ägyptens . . .* , *Orientalia, 33* (1964), 135–40.

WEILL, R., *La Fin du moyen empire égyptien*, 2 vols. Paris, 1918.

———, "The Problem of the Site of Avaris," *JEA, 21* (1935), 10–25.

———, *XIIe Dynastie, royauté de Haute-Egypte et domination Hyksos dans le nord*, IFAOC, Bibliotheque d'Etude, 26, Cairo, 1953.

WHEELER, N. F., "Dairy of the Excavations of Mirgissa Fort," *Kush, 9* (1961), 87–179.

WILSON, J. A., "The Egyptian Middle Kingdom at Megiddo," *AJSL, 58* (1941), 225–36.

———, review of Weill, *XIIe Dynastie, royauté . . .* , *JNES, 14* (1955), 131–33.

———, *The Culture of Egypt* (first published as *The Burden of Egypt*), Chicago, University of Chicago Press, 1961.

WINLOCK, H. E., *Excavations at Deir el-Bahri, 1911–31*, New York, Macmillan, 1942.

———, *The Rise and Fall of the Middle Kingdom in Thebes*, New York, Macmillan, 1947.

WOLF, W., "Der Stand der Hyksosfrage," *ZDMG, 83* (1929), 67–79.

WOOLLEY, C. L., *A Forgotten Kingdom*, Baltimore, Penguin Books, 1953.

———, *Alalakh: An Account of the Excavations at Tell Atchana in the Hatay, 1937–49*, Oxford, Oxford University Press, 1955.

WRIGHT, G. E., "The First Campaign at Tell Balatah (Shechem)," *BASOR, 144* (1956), 9–20.

———, "The Second Campaign at Tell Balatah," *BASOR, 148* (1957), 11–28.

———, ed., *The Bible and the Ancient Near East*, Garden City, N.Y., Doubleday, 1961.

———, "The Archaeology of Palestine," *BANE*, 73–112.

WRIGHT, G. E., *Shechem: The Biography of a Biblical City,* New York, McGraw-Hill, 1965.

YADIN, Y., "Hyksos Fortifications and the Battering-Ram," *BASOR, 137* (1955), 23–32.

——, "Excavations at Hazor, 1955–58," *IEJ,* 6 (1956), 120–25; ibid., 7 (1957), 118–23; ibid., 8 (1958), 1–14; ibid., 9 (1959), 74–81.

——, *The Art of Warfare in Biblical Lands in the Light of Archaeological Study,* New York, McGraw-Hill, 1963.

——, *Hazor,* 4 vols. Jerusalem, Hebrew University, 1958–63.

Zandee, J., "Seth als Sturmgott," *ZÄS, 90* (1963), 144–56.

# INDEX

ʿAamu, 87–96. *See also* Asiatics; Egypt
Aamu-Sahornedjheriotef, 133
Abba-El, 164
Abbess Aetheria, 148–49
Abishemu II, 102–03
Achzib, Phoenicia, 42
Adam, Shahata, 132, 134, 135
Ader, Transjordan, 12
*Admonitions of Ipuwer,* 5, 103–20, 125, 150–51, 170, 192
Africanus, 123–24, 143, 153. *See also* Manetho
Ahmose, 59, 160
Ahmose of El-Kab, 183
Akkad dynasty (Mesopotamia), 14
Alabaster, 60
Alalakh, Syria, 24–26, 32, 33, 40–41, 46, 52, 67–68, 165, 182, 184–85
Albright, W. F., 9–12, 15, 18, 20 n., 22 n., 36, 39, 52, 69 n., 78, 79 n., 81 n., 102 n., 120 n., 174 n., 181, 185
Aleppo, Syria, 68, 77, 82, 165
Alt, A., 2, 123
Amada Stela, 188
Amenemhet I, 7, 18 n., 77, 92–93, 117, 132, 156, 168. *See also* Senwosret I
Amenemhet II, 73
Amenemhet III, 74, 87–91, 94, 125
Amenemhet IV, 74, 78, 87
Ameny-Soshenen, 88 n.
Amun, 139, 142; temple of, 135, 177
Amurrites, 2, 3 n., 20–21, 25, 69 n., 126, 184, 189–95. *See also* Mesopotamia; Middle Bronze Age; Palestine; Syria
Anastasi papyri, 137, 139, 142

Anat, 175–76, 178. *See also* Astarte; Seth
Anat-har. *See* Anat
*Anra* scarabs, 64. *See also* Scarabs
Apachnan, 153
Apophis (ʿAwoserreʿ Apophis), 54 n., 59, 130, 150, 153–59, 171–72, 182, 193; name on Saqqara dagger, 57, 66; war with Kamose, 165–68, 184. *See also* Kamose Stela
ʿAqenenreʿ Apophis, 157–58. *See also* Apophis
Archles, 153
Arsaphes (ḥršf), 101
Aseth. *See* Archles
Ashcalon, Palestine, 29, 37
Asiatics: terminology for, 107–08, 186–90. *See also* Amurrites; Palestine; Syria
Assyrians, 121, 123
Astarte, 139, 142, 175–76, 178–79. *See also* Seth
"Astarte and the Sea," 179
Avaris, 92 n., 166, 169, 170, 194; founding, 98, 121–22; Seth at, 100–02, 171–72, 176; Hyksos capital, 114, 120, 124, 193; location, 127–51
ʿAwoserreʿ Apophis. *See* Apophis
Axes, 55–56. *See also* Weapons
Ay, 133

Baal, 44, 142, 174–78
Baal Zaphon. *See* Baal
Babylon, Mesopotamia, 82, 165
Bahr el-Baqar, 141, 147
Bahr Faqus, 147
Bakir, Abd el Mohsen, 110